Big Capital in an Unequal World

DISLOCATIONS

General Editors: August Carbonella, *Memorial University of Newfoundland,* Don Kalb, *University of Bergen & Utrecht University,* Linda Green, *University of Arizona*

The immense dislocations and suffering caused by neoliberal globalization, the retreat of the welfare state in the last decades of the twentieth century and the heightened military imperialism at the turn of the twenty-first century have raised urgent questions about the temporal and spatial dimensions of power. Through stimulating critical perspectives and new and cross-disciplinary frameworks that reflect recent innovations in the social and human sciences, this series provides a forum for politically engaged, ethnographically informed and theoretically incisive responses.

Recent volumes:

For a full volume listing, please see the series page on our website:
https://www.berghahnbooks.com/series/dislocations

Big Capital in an Unequal World

The Micropolitics of Wealth in Pakistan

Rosita Armytage

berghahn
NEW YORK · OXFORD
www.berghahnbooks.com

First published in 2020 by
Berghahn Books
www.berghahnbooks.com

© 2020, 2023 Rosita Armytage
First paperback edition published in 2023

Library of Congress Cataloging-in-Publication Data
A C.I.P. cataloging record is available from the Library of Congress
Library of Congress Cataloging in Publication Control Number: 2019042136

British Library Cataloguing in Publication Data
A catalogue record for this book is available from the British Library

ISBN 978-1-78920-616-6 hardback
ISBN 978-1-80073-633-7 paperback
ISBN 978-1-78920-617-3 ebook

https://doi.org/10.3167/9781789206166

CONTENTS

ACKNOWLEDGEMENTS

To all the men and women in Pakistan who taught me about power and the hundreds of tiny ways it is accrued and exercised every day. This book is dedicated to these powerful men and women, the clever, funny, insightful journalists, writers, artists and scholars they let into their inner circle, and the lawyers and regulators who monitored and investigated them.

My debt to those who welcomed me into their homes and parties, who sat and talked over coffee, tea and whisky, who interrogated and refined my thinking, provided introductions; invited me to their weddings, homes, parties, offices and factories; and shared their insights, meals and their friendship, is immense. To the many people who welcomed me into their worlds, and who I have not named to protect their privacy, know that I am deeply grateful. Many of the people who informed this analysis became dear friends, and to those people in particular, thank you for your insight, support and friendship. You know who you are.

Outside of my informant group, many people in Pakistan facilitated, guided and informed my research. Great thanks to Dr Ali Khan at the Lahore University of Management Science (LUMS) for supporting my research in Pakistan, and introducing me to his colleagues at LUMS. Hissan Ur Rehman made so much of my research in Lahore possible by enlisting his network; personally accompanying me to a number of interviews; answering my many questions about family, marriage and social expectations; and sharing his candour and friendship. Nusrat Javed, Amir Mateen and Babar Ayaz provided invaluable insights on Pakistan's politics and history, welcomed me into their homes and answered my many questions. Their enormous repository of knowledge greatly enriched this analysis. I am also particularly thankful to Aamir for his friendship, enormous generosity and incisive insights on business and social class.

Simbal Khan shared insights on elite families, shifting class boundaries and politics, and helped me feel at home in Pakistan. Ali Saigol generously shared his insights into the Pakistani business elite and

Pakistan's changing class structure. I am also grateful to the friends outside of my research, Sarah, Maha, Naima, Mahvish, Simbal, Caroline, Cyril, Asad, Mighty, Tom, Emrys and Johann for keeping me sane, and making life in Pakistan so much fun. Huge thanks to Norbert, Dione, Patricia and the munchkins, for making me feel so at home in Karachi.

In the process of writing this book I have been enormously blessed by the input of generous fellow researchers who contributed their insights and expertise. At the ANU I benefited from the feedback of a great many very talented anthropologists. Patrick Guinness was the best mentor one could hope to have. He engaged with and challenged my work throughout my fieldwork, generously providing his time and feedback, and immeasurably improving my research by requesting ever greater analytical rigour and clarity. Huge thanks also to Caroline Schuster who pushed me to engage with current thinking, provided incisive critique and suggestions, and has provided ongoing support for my work.

The feedback of my writing group at ANU, led by Caroline Schuster, with fellow writers Stephanie Betz, Shiori Shakutu, Faisal Shah, Joyce Mormita Das, Kathleen Varvaro and Mandip Rai helped enormously. So too did Channa Razaque who provided insights and feedback, and challenged my theoretical framework, and Kirsty Wissing who reviewed and expertly edited several chapters. Hussain Nadim provided excellent feedback on several chapters, enthusiastically debated the central concepts of my work, and recommended sources that proved to be hidden gems. Umair Javed provided extremely helpful comments on my research framework and issues of class in Pakistan. Thanks also to my dear friends in Canberra: Sana, Joyce, Farhana, Lina, Bec, Kirsty and Miah for Fridays at Fellows Bar, Bengali and Lebanese home-cooking, and many other forms of respite.

In the process of transforming my research into a book, the advice, critique and support of Sameen A. Mohsin Ali at the Lahore University of Management Sciences (LUMS), Stephen Lyon at the Aga Khan University, Andrew Sanchez at the University of Cambridge, Nicolas Martin at the University of Zurich, Caroline Schuster at the Australian National University and Matthew Hull at the University of Michigan have been absolutely invaluable – thank you.

Finally, my father, Livingston, has encouraged and challenged my thinking throughout this process, and provided valuable insights which strengthened and clarified my arguments. My mother, Lisa, gave me continuous and unflinching encouragement and support.

Finally, I am forever grateful to my partner in crime and legality, Markus Bell, for literally hundreds of discussions on the central concepts examined in this book, multiple chapter reviews and edits, and advice and support on every level throughout the years of conceptualising, researching, writing and editing.

Along with the men and women whom this work is about, this book is also dedicated to four of my most important people – Markus, Livingston, Lisa and Rafael.

ABBREVIATIONS

BOI   Board of Investment
CCP   Competition Commission of Pakistan
CDA   Capital Development Authority
CM   Chief Minister
DHA   Defence Housing Authority
FBD   Father's Brother's Daughter
FBR   Federal Bureau of Revenue
FEBC   Foreign Exchange Bearer Certificate
ISI   Inter-Services Intelligence agency
KP   Khyber Pakhtunkhwa
KSE   Karachi Stock Exchange
LAS   Lahore American School
LUMS   Lahore University of Management Sciences
NAB   National Accountability Bureau
NWFP   North West Frontier Province
OGRA   Oil and Gas Regulatory Authority
PML-Q   Pakistan Muslim League-Quaid
PIDC   Pakistan Industrial Development Corporation
PIFC   Pakistan Industrial Finance Corporation
POW   Prisoners of War
SECP   Securities and Exchange Commission of Pakistan
SRO   Statutory Regulatory Orders

NOTE ON ANONYMITY

The names used in this book are all pseudonyms to ensure the anonymity of my research participants, except when explicitly specified otherwise. Where necessary to ensure anonymity, specific identifiable information has been changed. In one or two instances, the experiences of two or more people have been merged to protect privacy. Where information has been drawn from already published secondary sources, the real names of prominent historical figures, contemporary politicians or businessmen have been used.

INTRODUCTION

Making Money in an Unequal and Unstable World

In a car ride from Islamabad to Lahore, my new acquaintance, Murtaza, asked me, 'So, how do you categorise class, and how do you measure who belongs to which class?'

I laughed and told him that was part of the great debate on class and tried to avoid getting into a very technical discussion by saying I was still coming to terms with the various class divisions in Pakistan.

He looked at me shrewdly and said,

> I can tell you how to define class and who belongs to it. You can use the categories we use in my cigarette company. The first category is the lower class. You can identify these people because they arrive at the store that sells the cigarettes by foot or bicycle, and they purchase the 'Explorer' brand. It is our cheapest cigarette, and uses the lowest quality tobacco and the harshest chemicals. Most of the cigarettes we sell are in this category. The second category is the lower middle class. They arrive at the store by motorcycle, and they purchase 'Steel' brand cigarettes, which are slightly more expensive. The third category is the upper-middle class; they arrive in a car, but probably a cheap car, and they buy 'Titanium' brand cigarettes, which are again more expensive. The fourth category is the elites. They buy 'Diamond' cigarettes. We sell much fewer of these, because they are much more expensive. They use our highest quality tobacco, and they have a much better taste. The people who buy these cigarettes arrive at the store in nice cars – foreign cars.

'So, do you also smoke Diamonds?' I asked, thinking I might be able to get him to acknowledge that he was also among the elite, something that no one I spoke with in Pakistan ever seemed to want to do. But he looked at me, and said, 'No, of course not. I smoke

Marlboros. And not the locally manufactured *Marlboros*. I specially import them because they taste so much better'.

My research began as an investigation into the aspirations of Pakistan's middle class, a small but growing group of increasingly affluent professionals and small business owners with whom I was already familiar through my previous work at a non-profit organisation in Islamabad. The conversation above occurred a few days after I had arrived back in Pakistan to begin my research. I had arranged a lift from Islamabad to Lahore in the car of Murtaza, who I had been introduced to by a mutual friend. Murtaza was a businessman engaged in large scale manufacturing and trade. From the leather-seated luxury of his BMW, during the four-hour drive to Lahore we started the normal round of chit-chat in which new acquaintances engage when confined to a small space. Murtaza asked me what I was doing in Pakistan, and I briefly introduced myself as a researcher studying social class in Pakistan. By the end of the drive, our discussion had entirely reconfigured my research on economic power and class.

As the above allegory demonstrates, not only did Murtaza have a clear sense of how to target his product to each tier of the market in order to extract maximum profit, he had a pragmatic understanding of the economic disparity that defines life in Pakistan – and across much of the world. The wealthiest Pakistanis purchase the highest quality products and services available on the global private market, thereby sidestepping the poorly performing public sector and its provision of electricity, schooling, medical care, safety and security. But what struck me most from Murtaza's market analysis of his cigarette consumers was that in purchasing his cigarettes from overseas, rather than smoking either his own or the domestically-produced version of an international brand, Murtaza positioned himself not only above his fellow consumer, but *outside of*, and *above*, the class structure he observed altogether.

In researching the elite, I had expected to uncover the political economy of Pakistan's power structure, and the complex set of institutions and structures that determined the allocation of wealth and political influence. I expected to uncover a road map to the institutions through which power and resources flow and are distributed – corporate, bureaucratic, military and political. But as the months of my fieldwork went on, the formal functioning of these institutions receded into the background of the deal-making and negotiations in which my informants engaged. The deals made in corporate offices, the battles fought in court and the punishments meted out to business groups by regulatory organisations for non-compliance, were largely ceremonial, pre-determined long before the formal negotiations took place, the regulation formalised, or the penalty applied. Underneath formal negotiations and the deals and contestations engaged in by corporate structures and legal and regulatory bodies, existed a complex network of familial and social structures through which economic and political competition, deals, alliances and agreements were pre-negotiated in living rooms and private social forums.

My informants, like the broader global elite of which they are a part, both determined the political and economic structures of their country – shaping its rules, regulations and institutional structures – and lived outside of the confines of these rules and frameworks, navigating and circumventing those which they found to be disadvantageous. Further, their role in shaping these laws, regulations and institutions, and the daily activities and negotiations through which they circumvented them, actively manufactured the social and economic inequality which enabled them to reap enormous profits hugely disproportionate to those accessible to the general public.

Inequality and the Global 1%

Unprecedented capital mobility has defined the financial markets of much of the world since the 1980s, linking developing countries within an interconnected global system. A number of scholars have argued that the world is increasingly dominated by 'hypercapitalism', defined by instantaneous transfers of money and information that leads to the substitution of genuine human relationships for market transactions (Rifkin 2000, 112, Graham 2000, Inda 2001, Friedman 2004), and by the homogenisation of the world at large (Scott 1998), as well as the increasing similarities in lifestyle and background of the transnational elite (Sklair 2016). This global integration has created new opportunities for wealth creation, destroyed other pre-existing sources of monopoly business, and created new avenues for the capture of wealth, privilege and political influence.

In tandem with this global integration, concern about wealth inequality, and particularly the excesses of the world's wealthiest – termed 'the 1%' – has risen over the past decade. Movements like 'Occupy Wall Street' in the United States reflected the growing unease and anger of ordinary citizens towards the lavish lives and excessive consumption of the rich, and what appeared to be their ability to thrive at a time of widespread economic hardship and loss. Not only did the world's wealthiest appear to be insulated from the economic shocks that had plunged many ordinary citizens into debt and hardship, but many felt that they had generated these problems in the first place, and further, that their wealth and privilege seemed to be growing *as a result* of the suffering of the broader population (see Keister 2014). The first of these perceptions, that the wealth of the world's richest was growing, was supported by economic data: in the US, the Congressional Budget Office documented that the share of total income going to top earners in the United States had risen continuously since the 1980s and was higher by 2007 than it had been at any point since the Great Depression (Keister 2014). Worldwide, the richest 1% – those who have US $1 million or more in assets – own 45 per cent of the world's wealth. 'Ultra high net worth individuals', those with more than $30 million in assets, own almost 12 per cent of the total global wealth, yet represent only 0.003 per cent of the world population (Credit Suisse 2018).

Today, large swathes of the 'developing world' or 'global south' are engaged in a process of rapid economic development, growth and modernisation. Inequality, and the gross concentration of wealth in the hands of a few, is the defining feature of the current age. Across the world we see the elite, the global 'super rich', adept at navigating – and exploiting – the laws and regulations of their countries. In Asia, rapid economic growth has lifted many people out of poverty. The effects of globalisation are transforming formerly agrarian village-based societies into centres of global commerce and trade, increasingly governed by impersonal global marketplaces, standardised economic regulations and instantaneous cash transfers. Despite these dramatic economic and social transformations in parts of Asia, the region's richest 1% has acquired a much larger proportion of these gains than the general population.

The consumer-based class analysis of my friend, Murtaza, was illuminating in examining his view of the social structure of which he was a part, but what it did not explain was how he and others like him had come to occupy the highest position in the social class structure, how membership within this class had changed over the past eighty years, or the strategies elite families had utilised to cope with and adapt to the enormous challenges Pakistan has faced, politically, economically, and in terms of security, during this time. Nor did his analysis reveal the vast network of interlinking family ties, friendships, acquaintances and business associates upon which his power was dependent.

Are we really transitioning to an increasingly homogenous world governed by a transnational elite, standardised institutions and norms of business, economic transactions, and even governance? Led by this group of transnational, globally educated elites, is developing Asia pursuing a linear path of standardised development, and evolving towards the West?

Chakrabarty (2009, 1991) critiqued Western scholarship for portraying capitalistic modernity as an unstoppable force that would inevitably (albeit slowly) transform the government and social structures of the 'developing' world into those resembling the 'developed' West. He argued that traditional Marxist class analysis was inappropriate for understanding power and inequality in India (and by extension South Asia). Instead of examining the structural inequalities that characterised Indian society, Chakrabarty identified Indian culture, and the colonial legacy, as the root cause of India's poverty, inequality and economic underdevelopment, arguing that in India, 'hierarchy and the violence that sustains it remain the dominant organising principles in everyday life'. The dismissal of class as an analytic framework was particularly apparent within influential South Asian scholarship that strongly associated class with a Western-centric view of the world which was unsuited to the realities of South Asia.

Capitalist development and class relations have taken a different form in South Asia, but they nonetheless remain relevant and critical in understanding the region's political–economic dynamics. Rather than viewing capitalist development as operating along 'an inexorable, unidirectional trajectory of historical change' as much Western scholarship has implied, the power of capitalism lies not in its ability to create a universal form of capitalist production, but its ability to negotiate, and thrive within, 'the world of difference' (Sanyal 2014, 8).[1]

Until recently, class and class relations had been out of fashion as a means for examining and explaining social, political and economic inequality. Starting from the 1980s and the decline of the industrial working class in the West, class began to be used much less frequently as a key unit of analysis in explaining other aspects of social interaction and organisation, including relations of kinship, family, gender, ethnicity and race. There was a growing sense both within academic scholarship, and public commentary more broadly, that class categories had been transcended (Kalb 2015). Others argued that earlier class divisions had been subsumed into an ever-expanding 'middle' class, suspended between a small group of the poor, and a tiny group of super-rich. In the context of this large and amorphous middle class, many felt that analyses of class relations were no longer relevant to understanding processes of power, development and social inequality (Touraine 1988). Some scholars went so far as to argue that, 'class is dead' (Pakulski and Waters 1996).

The enormous public interest in Thomas Piketty's (2014) analysis of global wealth inequality demonstrated the renewed public appetite for examining the relationship of class to wealth inequality. His research highlighted the crucial role that inheritance from parents to children plays in achieving and amassing high levels of wealth and the accumulative advantage and disadvantage this generates; once more placing family and kinship relations at the centre of discussions of wealth inequality.

Traditionally, the scholarship on elites has been divided between those that follow a Marxist understanding, defining groups in relation to their role in the means of production, and the social dominance or subordination this relationship determines, and those who follow a Weberian definition of 'status' groups which conceptualise elites as defined by the power and resources they possess. Despite these differences, both camps have conceptualised elites as a group possessing power, resources and authority over others (Khan 2012), and as occupying the apex of the social hierarchy (Abbink 2012). Detailed descriptions of who the elite are have also varied widely. Sociologists have tended to reduce class to a set of indicators based on income, ownership, debt and consumption (see, for instance, Savage et al 2013, and Goldthorpe and Jackson 2007). Other scholars have focused on class consciousness, defined as the joint interests and commonality a group possesses as a result of their shared relationship to production, their shared opposition to others (Thompson 2002), and the way that people self-identify (Amoranto et al 2010). Across disciplines elites are widely mischaracterised as a monolith (see Craig and Porter 2006, Hart 2001, Khan 2010), as the bearers of injustice (Khan 2012, Hart 2001) and as a faceless, self-serving, venal and corrupt group who actively seek to undermine all reforms they view as opposed to their own interests.[2] At their most simple, elites are 'those who are able to realise their will, even if others resist it' (Mills 1956, 10). While most academics and commentators agree on that point, beyond that, the definition of what the elite is, and of whom it is comprised remains nebulous, and often contradictory.

This is in large part because the private lives of the elite are notoriously under-researched. A number of popular books have recently attempted to document elites' private lives. The results have varied, but tend towards the salacious, extravagant and outrageous. The reader is encouraged to be outraged by the conspicuous consumption they document, the casual nature of the privilege depicted and, at times, the callousness of their elite subjects towards the hardships faced by those with whom they share a city and a country. These depictions often obscure more than they reveal.

Mention of the global elite makes many of us uneasy. The reasons for this discomfort range from the many social ills with which they have come to be associated, from capturing public and private space in urban centres like London, Sydney, Dubai, to driving up housing prices, and creating urban ghost towns of expensive – and empty – apartments and displacing local communities. Other accounts describe elites skewing the delivery of public services through their purchase of these services on the private market. Even more sinister are accounts of the rich interfering in and warping both domestic and foreign politics. Many people simply feel a general distaste for the ostentatiousness of wealthy lifestyles – flashy cars, expensive watches and too many yachts. They appear to exist outside of the structures that regulate the behaviours, relationships, investments and collaborations of the rest of society. They count among their friends the nation's most powerful politicians, influential bureaucrats and wealthiest business people. The news is peppered with accounts of the world's wealthiest being caught out for massive manipulations of the legal, economic and normative structures which structure most of our lives. What about the privilege of their lives caused them to feel safe from possible reprisals?

We cannot seek to understand inequality, or social stratification and mobility without first understanding the lives of the top one percent of wealth owners[3] – and the histories, relationships, negotiations and conflicts that have caused this group of the social strata to amass enormous wealth and privilege while broad swathes of the general population continue to suffer.

Internally, elites are linked to one another through the circumscribed circulation of relationships and interactions (Abbink 2012), shared rites of passage and demarcated social spaces. The elite hold an extensive network among the most powerful – a network of the nation's most powerful and influential with whom they feel comfortable, from whom they can seek advice and from whom they have learnt the complex set of dispositions seen to convey prestige, authority, credibility and poise. In the UK, for example, an overwhelmingly large proportion of the political and economic ruling elite are Oxford University graduates. Many of these global leaders hold the same Politics, Philosophy and Economics (PPE) degree, such as Bill Clinton, Benazir Bhutto, Aung San Suu Kyi and the Australian prime ministers Malcolm Fraser and Bob Hawke. In the US, the student body at Harvard University is one third legacy admissions, the tip of an iceberg of inherited privilege whereby the children of the wealthy benefit from the staff and facilities of prestigious schooling, and rigorous tutoring and test preparations. Globally, the educational backgrounds of the nation's politicians and financiers are remarkably similar. Beyond formal education, the children of the wealthy inherit their parents' networks amongst the business, political and bureaucratic leaders of the world, inculcating elite five-year olds with the historically and culturally specific norms and networks of the nation's established political, economic and social elite. From within the social worlds generated in elite educational institutions, social clubs and parties, appropriate marriage partners are pre-vetted, and inter-elite family alliances consolidated. Education, social forums and marriage are the critical and interlinked foundations of elite class reproduction. They also hold a critical role in networking not only a domestic class of elites, but a global one.

The Right Sort of People

Murtaza's analysis of his consumer base shifted my research towards understanding the nature of modern capitalism, power and class, the grand issues that have transfixed anthropologists, economists and sociologists for the last two centuries. To be elite is to exist *in relation* to other social groups: to have more, while others have less. I decided to research the Pakistani business elite, those belonging to families who generate at least US 100 million dollars in revenue per year – the economic and political '1%'. The families included in my research owned the nation's major industrial and business assets, but they were also often part of extended families with a major role in national or provincial politics, or who had close family ties to the senior-most ranks of Pakistan's very powerful military establishment.

Consequently, though my informants were all businessmen (and in a few instances, women), many were also prominent politicians, or the sons or nephews of prominent politicians. Many were also the sons or daughters of now retired Brigadiers and Generals.[4] And though many claimed to be a-political, all had fostered close relationships with senior members of the bureaucracy.

Though I set the boundaries of my study on the business elite, those belonging to families who generate at least US 100 million dollars in revenue per year, this economic definition of the elite was problematic for a number of reasons – including the difficulty of accurately assessing income in a country where tax minimisation, and under or over-reporting wealth, is common – but also because it failed to include so much of what my own informants understood to constitute class and 'the elite'. Clearly, being elite is much more than the possession of wealth, capital and resources (though these are also a prerequisite for membership). My elite informants were deeply occupied with being, and associating with, the 'right sort of people'. To complicate matters further, the category remains highly nebulous even within the class itself. The privileged Pakistanis with whom I interacted defined 'the elite' and their own placement within or outside of it in quite varied ways.

My closest informant, Abid, the owner of a large and extremely economically successful agricultural firm, placed himself within Pakistan's economic '1%' but firmly outside of the Pakistani 'elite'. To Abid, 'the elite' were the members of families whose wealth had existed over multiple generations, and whose histories of wealth accumulation were interlinked with either the British regime, or the first decade of Pakistan's inception (the timing of which, as I explore in Chapter Two, also implied an existing level of integration with highly privileged groups in pre-Partition India). Though his own family possessed high levels of intergenerational privilege, his family privilege was intertwined not with the British Raj, but with the esteem granted to local religious leaders, as his grandfather had been a religious scholar and was consequently a highly respected member of his community. Abid's perceived exclusion from 'the elite' was further compounded by his ethnic identity as a Pakhtun, and his sense that 'the elite' from which he was excluded was largely Punjabi, highly educated (usually in institutions with Western origins), English-speaking and irreligious. Abid accurately placed himself in the highest economic strata of the country, but had accurately ascertained that his inability to permeate the hallowed social clubs of the 'Established Elite' reflected their view that with his regional accent, imperfect English, religiosity and highly visible affluence – he was not 'the right sort of person'. Like most of the wealthiest men I interacted with in Pakistan, he believed that being rich and being elite were not synonymous. This sentiment was echoed by many of those within the families of the long-standing Established Elite (a group I define in detail in the pages to follow). Walid, a member of one of

Pakistan's most longstanding elite families provided the following definition, 'Elites are the chosen people. They are the ones God has chosen to lead and to provide guidance to the people'. He went on to lament,

> The elite has changed now. Now there are these *nouveau riche* businessmen coming in and they don't have any sense of social responsibility. Elites are there to serve as role models for the people. These *nouveau riche* do not do that at all.

This assessment of the new rich was not quite accurate. Abid and many of the new rich I came to know had a strong sense of social responsibility towards their local communities, and the large number of dependents who worked in their factories and lived on their family lands. Abid's dependents relied upon his family to address a broad range of problems ranging from funding care for a family illness, to having the roads by their house re-paved. Yet, though Abid demonstrated his social responsibility in myriad ways, what he did not have was a very specific form of distinction[5] that made him socially acceptable to the Established Elite. As Walid's quote implies, beyond business skill, political acumen and intra-elite networking, the power of elites – regardless of when their wealth was acquired – is at least partially located in their ability to acquire and demonstrate distinction[6] and other forms of symbolic capital. The economic logic of wealth accumulation my informants engaged in was often subordinated to other powerful logics: capital was often 'not valued in itself, but rather as a means of gaining status' (De Lomnitz 1987).

Until recently, 'Established Elite' families have primarily drawn their claims for distinction from hereditary sources. These claims depend largely upon family lineages intertwined with colonial power, (see Bhabha 1984, Johnson 2013, Paugam et al 2016 for their work in other contexts). Historically, intra-elite alliance-making has been limited to families possessing multi-generational elite histories. The status of these families rested primarily on their colonial-era legacy and inheritance, and the particular forms of distinction associated with these histories: the acquired dispositions, mannerisms and styles of living used to construct and evaluate the social world, and to perform a certain role within that world. These attributes were for the most part inherited, but they could also be learned, particularly when acquired very early through schooling. And these forms of distinction were used by the elite to police the boundaries of their power and privilege and to limit new entrants into their schools, social clubs, homes and families – the places where the most powerful members of society engaged, formed networks and ultimately, made critical decisions about the national allocation of economic and political resources.

The interlinking of these forms of distinction with notions of 'being elite' was so pervasive that many of the wealthiest and most successful businessmen I came to know whose wealth was more recently acquired rejected the label 'elite', often citing the supposedly humble origins of their fathers or grandfathers. When pressed, many of these men referred to themselves as 'upper-middle class', feeling that the term 'elite' implied a level of inherited privilege that would underplay or negate their own hard work in establishing the business empires that now placed them in the economic '1%'. These groups tended to associate their position of economic, social and political influence not with inherited privilege, but with a host of positive moral characteristics including integrity, hard work and determination.

Along with hard work, however, the fortunes of these families were often tied to the rise of other powerful institutions in Pakistan. As largely middle class institutions like the military and the bureaucracy expanded and consolidated their power through political rule in the decades following Pakistan's creation, they also provided patronage and opportunities for rapid upward social mobility for a small group of new families. The families who transitioned into the ranks of the economic 1% through their affiliations with the regime of General Zia ul Haq from the 1980s onwards[7] (and earlier by many accounts) became widely known amongst the elite classes as 'new money', or as *'Navay Raje'* in Punjabi meaning literally, 'new lords' and *nau daulatiye* in Urdu (explored in detail in Chapter Three). Many maintained close ties with the military regime, either through personal kinship ties as the close family of senior (now retired) personnel in the Zia regime, or through the maintenance of mutually beneficial business partnerships established with members of the military during the military regimes of General Zia, or later, General Musharraf.

The Configuration of Power in Pakistan

In most countries, the accumulation of wealth is at least in part closely intertwined with the activities and policies of government. In countries like Pakistan, the central government distributes economic privileges to shore up the political factions by which it is supported.

Whether military or civilian, the desire of each government to keep itself in power has encouraged patterns of production, accumulation and consumption that tie the support of powerful local leaders, business people and their patronage networks to the political regime in power.[8]

Pakistan provides a compelling case of elite power in the contemporary capitalist world as, like many non-Western, rapidly developing nations, it is both (a) run by an oligarchy of political and economic interests, and (b) is beset by high levels of political instability. Competition and conflict are defining activities within the oligarchy of ruling families, leading to a high degree of political instability as individual leaders and their families jostle for power. Despite the dramatic economic transformations that have taken place in the world over the past eighty years, and the massive shifts in political leadership and social structure these changes have engendered over the same period, the Pakistani elite class has routinely fortified and reconstituted the highly circumscribed power and privilege of its members in shared pursuit of profit and market dominance.

Pakistani society is vastly unequal, with great disparities in income, quality of life, government service provision and political representation. Despite consistent levels of economic growth, 65–80 per cent of Pakistanis earn their living through manual labour (Durr-e-Nayab 2011). The middle classes – those with at least one family member with tertiary education, and one family member employed in 'non-manual' work in sales, clerical or professional positions – are variously estimated to be from 18–34 per cent of the population. The upper middle classes (around 6 per cent of the population) can be categorised as those holding a college education from the nation's top schools and universities, or being educated abroad, and members of this group are most likely to be employed as professionals, legislators, senior officials, managers, or in military roles. The uppermost elite – those who comprise the focus of this study – hold similar employment categories but tend to occupy more prominent roles with much greater levels of income. The men in this class are almost certainly educated in foreign-universities. The women of this class, if not foreign educated themselves, will hold a university degree from one of Pakistan's top universities. This group is roughly estimated to comprise around 1 per cent of the population (Durr-e-Nayab 2011).[9]

The Pakistani elite has been very successful at protecting and increasing the wealth held by a small (and very slowly expanding) number of families. Yet, the rapid economic development that has reconfigured agricultural economies in other parts of South Asia into centres of finance, global trade and professional service has not emerged in Pakistan – and does not look likely to in the coming decades. Pakistan's elite-dominated economy demonstrates few signs of transitioning to a globalised high-finance economy, nor of replicating the economic growth patterns of India or China, its most stable and successful neighbours (Indrawati 2015). Neither are most of Pakistan's economic elite predominantly globally-focused players who flexibly move unhinged forms of capital around the world.[10] Instead, most of my informants derived the largest proportion of their profits from large-scale industrial projects, many in manufacturing. Others had made their fortunes in developing large-scale infrastructure projects. The enormous profits they have generated have emerged from the opportunities inherent in the classic industrialising society where workers' salaries and political representation are commensurately low. In achieving their high level of profits, many have focused on providing commodities to the domestic market, or on producing high demand export commodities for which they hold a monopoly or equivalent advantage in the world market. The disparities in wealth that have emerged in pursuing these forms of economic growth are astounding.

Power in Pakistan is configured across a small group of individuals and families and the powerful institutions they govern: the military, business sector and the major political parties. These individuals and institutions work in concert, and sometimes in conflict, to manage the dual goals of the elite class in Pakistan: maintaining capital accumulation, and ensuring the security critical to acquiring it.

The elite that forms the focus of this enquiry includes both those with inter-generational histories of family wealth, and those whose wealth is more recently acquired. Both established and more recent wealth holders in Pakistan have vastly disproportionate control and access to valued resources; broad advantages in the nation's economic, political and social spheres because of this ownership and the opportunities and benefits it provides; and are in a position to both influence and shape the lives of the broader population. The pursuit of wealth by those who possess the greatest amount of it, and the way that the intimate experience of people's everyday lives influence and are influenced by the broader political economy is at the heart of this book. This ethnography focuses on the micropolitics of the individuals and families positioned at the pinnacle of the economic, political and social structure – and the role of these micropolitics in generating and sustaining social and economic inequality.

The most useful starting point for understanding elite alliances and divisions, and their relationship to the state in Pakistan is the foundational work of Hamza Alavi (1972). Alavi's (1972) model emerged in response to what he saw as the inadequacy of Marxist conceptions of the state and of class relations for explaining the dynamics of power in non-European societies. In particular, he argued that post-colonial nations differed from European states in specific ways, and consequently, that Marxist analyses of 'the state' needed to be reconfigured in these contexts. Whereas Marx had argued that the state functioned as the instrument of a single ruling class, Alavi argued that post-colonial nations had a number of separate and distinct ruling classes that interacted with the state in different ways. Further, he argued that the post-colonial state was interdependent with these ruling classes in both receiving and providing reciprocal benefits.

Specifically, Alavi argued that post-colonial states need to be understood as comprising an 'overdeveloped' bureaucratic–military oligarchy. He argued that this oligarchy had emerged in response to the challenges the metropolitan colonial power faced in subordinating multiple indigenous social classes seeking both to assert their own positions of dominance and to resist the constraints placed upon them by colonial rule. He argued that unless the lower and middle classes were already highly organised and conscious of class relations at the moment of independence, the overdeveloped oligarchic structure of the colonial state would inevitably be inherited by the newly independent state. This resulted, Alavi claimed, in domestic elites dominating the population in much the same way as the colonial administrators they had replaced.

Alavi defined the multiple ruling classes of the post-colonial nation as being comprised of the indigenous bourgeoisie (the owners of industry and business which form the focus of this study), the metropolitan neo-colonial bourgeoisie (often in the form of transnational corporations) and of the landed classes. He argued that 'the bureaucratic–military state oligarchy' mediates between the competing and complementary interests of these three ruling classes and that this tension and competition occurs *via* the state: the three classes compete for state resources but do not *directly* negotiate or engage in conflict with one another. In this way the state mediates between elite groups while at the same time acting on behalf of them all to preserve the social order in which their interests are embedded. In these contexts, given that the state mediates between the competing interests of the three ruling classes, there is no great need for the separate ruling classes to heavily invest in fostering linkages between one another, because they can rely upon the state to protect their interests for them. They do not require *each other's* support to protect their separate and mutual interests.[11]

Despite being written over forty years ago, the categories Alavi used to define and differentiate members of the elite remain remarkably relevant. The indigenous bourgeoisie he identified corresponds to the business elite who comprise the central focus of this study. The landed elites, traditionally also the political class, also remains powerful, despite the growing primacy of the business elite. There also remains a metropolitan bourgeoisie, but its national identity has shifted entirely. Whereas, at the time of the Alavi's writing, Western nations were the major investors in Pakistan, the major foreign investor is now China – and its influence is highly visible across Pakistan's urban centres, as well as in certain rural sites.

A number of scholars have since argued that Alavi's analysis of the state and the ruling classes in post-colonial societies is now outdated (Akhtar 2008, Zaidi 2014). They argue that middle class groups representing both upper middle class professionals (particularly lawyers), and conservative religious movements, have undermined the power of traditional elites, usurping part of their power.[12] However, claims that the intermediate classes and religio-political movements have joined the elite alliance remain largely unsubstantiated. Religio-political movements undoubtedly rose to the forefront of national politics in the decades following Zulfikar Ali Bhutto's overthrow in 1977 (Nasr 2001, Haqqani 2005), but it is difficult to view these movements as signifying 'qualitative additions to the ruling coalition' (Akhtar 2008, 3). Rather, they appear more clearly as a force of *opposition* to the ruling coalition with possible future potential to challenge their dominance and privilege. Similarly, the evidence to suggest that the largely middle-class dominated institutions of the judiciary, the media and the parliament pose a genuine threat to the dominance of the elite ruling coalition is very limited. Middle class challenges to elite abuses of power, such as the 'lawyer's movement',[13] remain isolated instances of an elite challenge from within the upper-middle class.[14]

Thriving in Instability?

Over the fourteen months of my fieldwork, many of the businessmen I spoke with recounted their experiences of navigating risk, reducing family vulnerability and sustaining the position of their family at the top of Pakistan's economic hierarchy. They shared the various histories of upward social mobility that had propelled their own families into the elite economic and social class, and the multiple techniques they used to protect their advantages and position of dominance and to maintain the boundaries between the existing members of their class and new families seeking to gain entrance. In spite of weak governance, poor public service delivery, massive societal volatility and major challenges to safety and security that impede the quality of life of the broader population, these families had continued to flourish, politically as well as economically.

Like the broader global elite class to which they belong, Pakistan's elite holds disproportionately high levels of economic and political capital, and a great aptitude for navigating the restrictions of the domestic and international laws and regulations which seek to impede their ability to accumulate assets and maximise profits. The elites of this study engage in highly lucrative international trade and investment, as well as dominating the domestic market. Though often presented as an indivisible category, 'the elite' is comprised of different power blocs who employ various strategies of competition and collaboration depending on the changing historical and socio-economic circumstances in which they exist. The contestations and negotiations engaged in by elites to maintain their position of dominance not only provides insights into power and how it is acquired and maintained, it also provides surprising insights into both local economic processes and the lived realities of global capitalism.

For instance, many of the elite business families in this study entertain and successfully negotiate with Chinese, European and other investment delegations in their factories and through industry trade associations. Yet, most were part of corporatised structures, with family members holding the senior-most positions in the company's management, along with most, if not all, Company Board seats being reserved for family members. Most of these businesses were hierarchical structures with the family patriarch occupying the key leadership position. Beyond a family-dominated leadership, many employed a professional workforce for all middle and lower management roles, and a locally employed workforce of office and/ or factory workers. The involvement of multiple family members in many of these businesses, and strategies employed to spread and mitigate risk has fortified a system in which friendships, alliances, kinship, affection and animosities are instrumental in business intelligence, political decision-making and economic strategy. The will of the market is not the will of the market at all – but the shifting desires of the nation's most powerful.

However, an undeniable particularity of Pakistan that has enhanced the degree to which its elites can accumulate and expend political and economic power is the volatility of Pakistan's political system, the porousness of its legal and regulatory system, and its highly deregulated market, which gives largely free rein to the nation's most powerful families. This instability establishes the Pakistani elite as an exaggerated example of the behaviours, calculations and lifestyles of the global 'super-elite'.

Consequently, this book builds outward from the micro-politics within and among the most powerful families of a rapidly developing, often politically volatile nation, and across the nation's most powerful institutions, the military, business sector and government, to re-theorise the link between instability and economic accumulation. At the heart of this political assemblage is the sustained and complicit management of order and instability through a highly personalised means of conducting business and politics. While powerful international actors often decry Pakistan's political instability, weak regulatory structures and financial crises, this book shows how powerful families both benefit from and propagate instability through a 'culture of exemptions', as I explore in detail in Chapter Six.

What Do the Elite in Pakistan Reveal about Inequality and the Global 1%?

This book is an ethnography of the micro-politics of elite lives: the personal relationships, daily lives and family histories of Pakistan's most prominent and wealthiest business families. The intimate and social lives of Pakistan's business and political elite demonstrate how an elite group can shape and determine the economic and political structures of the nation through the daily interactions undertaken in their homes and private social forums – and how these private interactions affect the opportunities available to the broader population. As Pakistan's elite becomes increasingly adept at managing processes of regional trade and foreign investment, rather than dissolving the social ties and cultural practices engaged in by the nation's most powerful, these practices remain central to determining the allocation of national wealth – along with those who are excluded from partaking in it.

In many ways, Pakistan's elite closely resembles their class peers across the globe, in both developed and developing economies. However, as James Ferguson (2002) noted, the countries of developing Asia are not 'western nation-states in embryo'. Pakistan's elite-dominated economy demonstrates few signs of transitioning to a globalised high-finance economy. What we see in Pakistan neither represents a peripheral form of capitalism, nor a pre-modern form of capitalism. Rather, as argued by Jean and John Comaroff (2015), 'What if we posit that, in the present moment, it is the global south that affords privileged insight into the workings of the world at large?' Perhaps most surprisingly, as an economic elite operating in a rapidly developing economic environment, the experience of Pakistan's wealthiest and most powerful members contradicts the widely held expectation that economic growth is leading to increasingly impersonalised and globally standardised economic and political structures across the developing countries of the non-Western world, and offers a contradictory vision for newly middle income countries in the context of modern capitalism.

In the chapters that follow, this book follows the private lives of businessmen like Murtaza to see what they reveal about the role of elites in contributing to and shaping the inequality that characterises the modern world. The first half of this book explores the development of a national elite. Chapter One examines the challenge of accessing elite lives, and the ways in which class and age differences, and gender dynamics, affect the kind of relationship – and access – I was able to develop with the Pakistani elite. It explores how dynamics of class, gender and power shape the interactions of elites with one another, and with outside observers. Chapter Two tells the interlinked story of the emergence of the Pakistani elite with the creation of Pakistan. These stories introduce one of the book's central themes, the interlinking of the elite with the politics of the nation, and specifically, with various political regimes, both civilian and military. Focusing on several pivotal moments of crisis in the relations between the ruling classes and the state, this chapter identifies the strategies of competition and collaboration that have enabled the Pakistani elite to gain and secure economic and political advantage over the past eighty years despite extreme political and economic instability. It explores the evolving relationship between Pakistan's elite factions and the state – both bureaucratic and military. In doing so, it contextualises the elite life histories that emerge in the chapters that follow. Readers without a particular interest in Pakistan should jump directly to Chapter Three.

Chapters Three, Four and Five use stories of marriage, family-making and socialising to examine the construction of power through interlinked elite networks. Chapter Three examines the fractures in the elite class between old and new class entrants, and the institutions where elite networks are both carefully fostered, and rigorously policed. Chapter Four focuses on marital alliances as a key strategy of inter-familial alliance making, while Chapter Five examines the importance of elite networking and socialising to the preservation of power. Chapter Six examines specific cases of how elite businessmen have used their marital, social and economic networks to engage in, and strengthen, a 'culture of exemptions' that allows them to circumnavigate the restrictions of the state and its laws and regulations to reproduce their own position of privilege and advantage. The concluding chapter returns to the role of the global elite within an increasingly interlinked global capitalist structure, and highlights what the story of elites in Pakistan reveals about global capitalism and the international global elite. In doing so, it gathers and sharpens the questions of power, privilege, political turbulence and global wealth that have inspired this book.

Notes

Parts of this chapter were previously published as: R. Armytage (2019), 'An Evolving Class Structure? Pakistan's Elite and the Implications for Pakistan's Political Economy'. In M. McCartney and S.A. Zaidi (Eds.), *New Perspectives on Pakistan's Political Economy: State, Class and Social Change*. Cambridge: Cambridge University Press, and have been reprinted with permission.

1. Sanyal's theory informed and contributed to a small but growing group of scholars who argued that capitalist modernity occurs in varied forms, both in vernacular and more universal iterations (see for instance, Comaroff and Comaroff 2015).
2. See for instance, Craig and Porter's (2006) account of the Pakistani business elite. Craig and Porter (2006) document how the business elite serve as patrons to the civil servants in their sphere of influence, including departmental bureaucrats, the police and even the courts, so that these groups owe their loyalty to individual businessmen as well as to the State, but use highly pejorative terms in doing so. More recently, Leslie Sklair (2016) described a global capitalist class 'working consciously to obfuscate the effects of the central crises of global capitalism, namely the simultaneous creation of increasing poverty and increasing wealth within and between countries, and the unsustainability of the global capitalist system.
3. It is important to differentiate between the top wealth earners and wealth owners. This research uses the term 'the 1%' to refer to the nation's top wealth *owners*.
4. For more detail on the career trajectories of retired senior military personnel, and their ongoing involvement in military-linked corporations, state employment and other positions of influence, see Staniland et al 2018.
5. Bourdieu (2013) defined distinction as a particular sense of style and disposition. He argued that distinction, like all cultural practices and preferences, was the product of

upbringing and education, 'closely linked to educational level, measured by qualification or length of schooling, and secondarily to social origin. . . . tastes function as markers of social class'.

6. Entry into many elite groups is determined by possession of a particular sense of style and disposition that Bourdieu (2013) terms 'distinction' and 'taste'.

7. Staniland et al (2018) found that the military governed more directly than in previous regimes under General Zia's leadership with retired military personnel occupying a substantially higher percentage of federal ministers and provincial governors after 1988 than before.

8. An earlier version of some of the ideas in this section was explored in Rosita Armytage, 'Alliance of State and Ruling Classes in Contemporary Pakistan'. *Economic & Political Weekly* 51, no. 31 (2016): 108–14, and are re-examined with the permission of the publisher.

9. Scholars measure class in different ways using a number of different indicators, and there is significant variation between disciplines, within disciplines, and across country contexts. Durr-e-Nayab's (2011) definition of class in Pakistan expands upon purely economic indicators of class to include level of education obtained, ownership of items representative of a certain standard of living in Pakistan and type of employment. These additional categories, though still limited, can be used to broaden an outline of the economic status and styles of life experienced by Pakistani individuals and families.

10. Language highlighting the desirability of 'nimble and flexible capital' (see: Deshpande and Nurse 2012, 78), 'nimble responses', and warning of the dangers of economic policy that 'constrains the flexibility and potency of macroeconomic tools' (Prasad 2009, 1, 19) has become widespread within both academic business literature and within the popular media since the early 2000s. A number of anthropologists have begun writing about widespread perceptions of capital as unhinged from particular localities (Ho 2009, Inda and Rosaldo 2008), but have also noted that these conceptions of the transition 'from socially embedded to disembedded and abstracted economic forms' is a fallacy (Maurer 2006, 15, 19).

11. A similar set of dominant class interests was later articulated by Pranab Barhan (1984), Partha Chatterjee (1986) and Sudipta Kaviraj (1989) in relation to India. Each conceived of a relatively autonomous state that supervised and mediated between dominant classes. These dominated classes competed with one another – one faction of the elite gaining ascendency over the others at various points – but still sought to align their interests as part of a dominant coalition. Adapting Gramsci's concept of the 'passive revolution' for the post-colonial Indian context, Chatterjee and Kaviraj separated the idea of the 'state' from the elite factions of which it was comprised, assigning the state not only autonomy, but independent agency, under 'the supervision of elected political leadership, a permanent bureaucracy and an independent judiciary' (Chatterjee 2008).

12. Conceptions of a state–elite alliance by Alavi and others have, however, been critiqued by several scholars for failing to account for the agency of the working and middle classes in the power structure of the post-colonial state, and for failing to anticipate the growing centrality and influence of institutions such as the military and the media. Aasim Sajjad Akhtar (2008) developed a revised Alavian analysis of class structure in Pakistan that offers a clear-sighted analysis of power structures and the institutions and individuals who dominate them. Akhtar (2008, 3) demonstrated that Alavi's three propertied classes remain both powerful and central to Pakistan's ruling coalition. He also argued, however, that there have been qualitative additions to the ruling coalition, namely the intermediate classes and religio-political movements/clerics.

13. The 2007 'lawyer's movement' was a protest held by Pakistan's lawyers against the unconstitutional dismissal of the Chief Justice by military dictator Pervez Musharraf.

14. Scholars diverge on the significance of upper-middle class movements in Pakistan. However, Jaffrelot (2015, 371) sums up the situation aptly when he states that 'Since 2007, lawyers have assumed the role of the quintessential opposition force, coming out against both civilians and the military in the name of the rule of law. But the extent to which this new actor can alter Pakistan's political and social situation remains to be seen'.

Chapter 1

MIDDLE-CLASS WOMAN IN AN ELITE MAN'S WORLD

e⁀

A few nights into my fieldwork, I sat in the smoke-filled home of Abid and Kaleem Afridi in a wealthy Lahori neighbourhood. Together with their friend Shahid, we sat and brainstormed a list of high-profile businessmen I should seek to interview. Abid and Kaleem, in their early and late thirties respectively, were businessmen from an economically and politically powerful family in Khyber Pakhtunkhwa (KP). The brothers divided their time between their family home in KP, and their homes in Islamabad and Lahore. Their friend Shahid, was the owner of a large manufacturing firm and the son of a prominent Punjabi political leader.

As the three men chain-smoked and scrolled through the address books on their mobile phones, identifying the friends and acquaintances they could call on to meet with me, I furiously scribbled first one, then two, then five pages of names. Between the three men, together with the social contacts of those they knew well, was an enormous repository of personal social contacts at the highest level of Pakistani business and politics.[1] This list reflected the three men's shared understanding of the wealthiest and most successful businessmen in Lahore, and became the first version of my ever-expanding list of businessmen to meet for my research.

I spent a great deal of time in the large second home of Abid and Kaleem in Lahore during my fieldwork. During this time the two brothers travelled between their primary residence in Islamabad (where their wives and children lived), their village and extended family home in Khyber Pakhtunkhwa and the eight-bedroom Lahore home, often departing for various meetings or family obligations and leaving me to coordinate my meetings and write-up my fieldnotes in one of the armchairs in their home office with Jamil, the cook/house-keeper, a driver and an armed security guard. At various intervals, one or both of brothers would arrive back in Lahore where I was living without warning and demand we go for coffee or lunch, or sit and chat in their home office as they fielded phone calls, chain-smoked and intermittently yelled out to Jamil for omelettes, paratha and endless rounds of chai. The two brothers and their younger cousin Shahzar became three of my closest informants and most valuable cultural guides, as well as close friends. Each took it on themselves to seriously consider each of my questions, even when they clearly found my interests odd, or the answers patently obvious.

Between October 2013 and January 2015, I conducted fourteen months of ethnographic fieldwork in Lahore, Islamabad and Karachi. Though I engaged in interviews with over ninety of the country's most powerful, influential and wealthy business people and politi-cians, their families and friends and the government regulators tasked with monitoring their behaviour in business, the vast majority of my time was spent conducting participant-observation – hanging out with and observing the many elites who became both my informants and my friends. Most days I spent large amounts of time meeting someone for lunch; sitting and chatting in living rooms, offices, or cafes; sharing my informants' chauffeured commutes to their factory sites; visiting factories and talking with the owners and managers and professionals who ran them; attending long drawn out nights of drinks and conversation with various groups of friends and asso-ciates in their homes or private clubs; and intermittently attending large parties or weddings. The vast majority of my informants were male, ranging from 24 to 87 years old.

As with most fieldwork, my access to informants centred on the relationships I developed with a few key gate-keepers to the social worlds of elite Lahore, Islamabad and Karachi. The close friends and informants I made in these cities opened the door to my interviews in each location, and they and a number of those I interviewed, in turn invited me to their offices, factories and homes, and to cafes, dinners, birthdays and weddings. It was at these social gatherings where much of my best participant-observation was undertaken.

Given my interest in understanding how economic power is acquired and protected, and the estimates of my new friends on the revenue streams of their peers and associates, I settled on a baseline for inclusion in my study, with the requirement that the business families included in this research generate a minimum of US$ 100 million in revenue per year (with the inclusion of a few families who had lost this level of wealth, or were near to achieving it).[2] Above this baseline, my informants estimated that around 100–200 families – a specific sub-class within the elite – dominate the nation's highest revenue and most profitable businesses. All 92 of the businessmen I interviewed came from families on this list, as did many of the others I socialised with informally.[3]

As my research progressed, it became clear that in addition to owning and managing major business interests, many of my informants were also current or former politicians. Others, like Abid and Kaleem's friend, Shahid, had a close family member in politics, no more distantly related than a brother, first-cousin, or uncle.[4] Many of the businessmen I came to know funded, or were otherwise engaged in, the backstage processes required to support local and national election campaigns, or the deal-making strategies of their close relatives in politics. Consequently, seeking to understand the relationship between big business and privilege, I also interviewed a number of politicians and senior bureaucrats, and received insights into the relationship between big business, politics, the formal structures of the state, and power and privilege. It became clear that the economic and political processes of the nation, and the individuals who directed them, were so deeply intertwined through social and kinship ties that it was impossible to delineate business at this scale from formal politics or the operation of government.

My secondary group of informants were the government regulators and lawyers tasked with representing and prosecuting allegations of corruption among elite business. Accessing these people was made easier once, after six months in Lahore, I moved to Islamabad where most were based. The people I interviewed in this category were staff or former staff of the National Accountability Bureau (NAB), the Securities and Exchange Commission of Pakistan (SECP), the Competition Commission of Pakistan (CCP), the Capital Development Authority (CDA), the Department of Industry and Production, senior counsel of the Supreme Court and a number of private lawyers representing the interests of high-profile cases against business empires. Most of these individuals were upper-middle class and firmly outside the elite social circles attended by the business and political elite. Consequently, though I socialised with a number of lawyers at elite gatherings, my meetings with regulators and other civil servants were confined to semi-structured interviews in their places of work, casual discussions in the car rides to and from their offices to the court house and observation of their interactions at the courts.

The help of the Afridis was invaluable in establishing me in Lahore, and in starting the round of introductions which snowballed to allow me to meet a large cross section of the nation's urban elite. Alongside the ease and generosity with which my new friends sought to help me, however, lay a whole suite of assessments about me, and my position and status, that informed their willingness to assist and spend time with me. These assessments had a profound impact on my ability to access their lives and those of their peers, and resulted in relationships considerably different from those anthropologists usually experience when researching poor or marginalised subjects. The inversion of this traditional power dynamic in the research relationship, and the background of political instability in which my research occurred, shaped every aspect of my fieldwork in Pakistan.

Ethnographically Researching Elites

Elites are often intensely private groups that are difficult for researchers to access (Gilding 2010; Jabukowska 2013; Pina-Cabral and de Lima 2000, Shore 2002; Smith 2013). The challenges of access are even more pronounced in traditionally closed societies (Abbink and Salverda 2013), and in contexts riven by distrust and political instability (see Green 1994; Robben and Nordstrom 1995).

Within sociology, geography and political science, disciplines with a long history of relying upon elite informants, it has widely been noted that the construction of power dynamics between the researcher and the researched is rooted in social identities of gender, ethnicity and class, and the dynamics between them. The literature on researching elites within these disciplines focuses largely on the heavily structured world of formal interviewing.[5] Though there is also a significant body of research on elites from within sociology, political science and historical studies,[6] and more recently, the emergence of a popular genre critiquing Western elites,[7] elites across the world remain understudied using anthropological and ethnographic methods which attempt to understand these groups *from within* (Abbink and Salverda 2013).

The long-term nature of ethnographic fieldwork differs from these accounts in that it provides critical insights into the reproduction of elite power, which are unavailable through other research methods, as it substantially erodes the ability of informants to present a façade of their life: discrepancies between what is said and what is observed emerge as intimacies are shared, and the lives of the researcher and the researched intermingle. However, a particular set of methodological challenges remain for anthropologists working with elites.

Relying on ethnography and participant-observation, anthropologists spend a great deal of time and analytical effort in assessing and understanding the behaviours, attitudes and beliefs of their informants, and in interpreting what they reveal about their societies. Beyond noting that it is critical to develop rapport with our informants, however, we spend much less time examining the ways that our informants evaluate and determine the role we will play in their own lives, and how their assessments determine the aspects of their lives to which they permit us access. The issue is particularly salient for powerful and elite informants whose influence, networks and education make them particularly effective in crafting their self-representations; how they are represented to members of their own and other classes; and in modulating how they portray themselves to a researcher or observer.

Osburg noted that anthropology's assumptions about 'studying up' often leave anthropologists ill-equipped to handle many of the situations they encounter. He noted that:

> Building rapport is usually portrayed as the anthropologist winning the trust of the reluctant locals and as something the anthropologist does, rather than something that is done to him or her. (Osburg 2013: 299)

His observation echoed much of my own experience of researching powerful men. It was often they who decided the tone and nature of our relationship. I could encourage or set limits on the terms of this relationship, but rapport could only be built with willing subjects who had made a conscious calculation on whether to entertain the relationship, and whether or not it was worthwhile for them to do so.

Halfway through my fieldwork, by which time he had shared many of the intimate details of his life, including much that was illegal, I asked my close informant Abid why he felt he could be so open with me. Abid answered using the Urdu nickname he had early on translated from my own English nickname:

> Gulabo [Rosy], first, I am an excellent judge of character. I know the sort of person you are. Second, you cannot hurt me. If you ever used my name and details, I would deny everything and tell everyone you made it up. I have a big family and many friends here, and you are just by yourself . . . I also had my friends in the intelligence agencies run a background check on you.

Beyond his own sense of impunity, Abid's answer revealed the inter-linking power dynamics which determined my ability to access the lives of some of the nation's most powerful businessmen and politicians. It also revealed the ways in which a number of my informants assessed and evaluated my position within the worlds they dominated. In a few sentences, Abid affirmed his confidence in his own judgment; the extensive networks of elite businessmen, politicians and senior government of which he was a part; and his clear-sighted assessment of my role and vulnerable position within his society. Abid made it clear: as a foreign, unmarried female, I had very little power within his world, and my research was possible because he, and others in his extended network, permitted it. Like most of my informants, he was aware of his power and influence – and of my relative lack of it. My informants had assigned me my 'proper place in the social order' (Warren and Hackney 2011: 9), though as this chapter explores, my proper place sometimes shifted.

Gaining and Restricting Access

The businessmen, and occasionally women, I interviewed often invited me to their homes, where we had long and disparate conversations on stiff velvet upholstered couches while snacking on samosas and sandwiches, drinking tea in china cups brought in by staff on silver trays. At other times, introductions from existing contacts led to formal meetings in nondescript fluorescent-lit offices. A number invited me to meet them for interviews over lunch at their private clubs, or over dinner with their friends and associates. Others I met invited me to tour their factories, enabling me to witness an array of production standards, technology and worker conditions. Some of these factories reflected the highest standards of modern production and technology. At these sites factory owners proudly explained the innovations in their imported Japanese or German machinery, the types of items that could and should be bought more cheaply from China, and the importance of hiring local workers to minimise the likelihood of interference by local extremist groups. In other locations around Lahore and in KP, thin barefoot workers grimaced, faces streaked with dirt and grease as they worked on ancient looking machinery, the hems of their shalwar kameez trailing dangerously close to swirling machinery and open flames. In Karachi, I visited factories in the Korangi Industrial Area accompanied by a vehicle of four private armed guards at the insistence of a Karachi-based businessman, the guard vehicle in almost comic contrast to the white Honda in which I followed with the driver of a middle-class friend. Also in Karachi, were the visits to gleaming high rise office buildings where the owners of investment companies casually made stock trades during the intermittent pauses in our conversation.

I had originally intended to focus on only the active heads of each business empire – the patriarchs – but this was initially difficult. [8] Instead, my emerging friendship with Shahzar, the cheeky, UK-educated, 24-year-old cousin of Abid and Kaleem, opened doors to the younger, third generation of businessmen in Lahore, and his 'batchmates' from Pakistan's most prestigious private boys' school, Aitchison College (discussed in more detail in Chapter Three). These introductions provided a very different view of the structure and functioning of family business, and valuable insights into the lifestyles of the younger generation of elite men. This younger group were often quite willing to discuss their difficulties proving themselves in business, as well as their experiences with dating, *rishtas* (marriage proposals) and the process of identifying a suitable spouse. Many of these men also spoke openly about their relationships with their fathers and mothers, and the contrast between their lives as students in North America or the UK, and their lives in Pakistan.

Yet it was Shahzar's socialite girlfriend, Maryam, a member of the old Established Elite, who provided access to most of the social events I attended in the first months of my fieldwork. Maryam brought me along to the gatherings she hosted in the self-contained suite within her family home, invited me to the weddings of her friends, and on a number of occasions, brought me to the homes of her friends' grandparents, genteel and welcoming people whose families had taken over manufacturing industries abandoned by the British after independence. These social events provided a much-needed chance for participant-observation and a relief from the social firewall that seemed to have blocked my hopes of establishing social interactions with the older business owners I interviewed during the day.

Five months into my fieldwork, during a short trip to Islamabad, an old acquaintance invited me to accompany him to the home of a friend he thought may be able to help with my research. His friend, Kamil, was a charming man in his fifties from one of the most respected old families of Karachi, a political insider and a self-proclaimed 'wheeler and dealer'. Kamil invited me to the dinner party he was hosting later that week, and not wanting to miss the opportunity, I extended my stay in Islamabad. Over the course of the dinner party, I was invited to two more events, and met half a dozen of the country's leading businessmen, politicians, senior bureaucrats and media owners. Recognising the advantage of being situated nearer to this group, and the social capital I had instantaneously acquired as a guest of Kamil's, I decided to relocate to Islamabad for the second half of my fieldwork. My network grew exponentially. On several return trips to visit business families and social clubs in Lahore and Karachi, I found that the doors to the patriarchs of the family empires that had remained so steadfastly closed to me during the first five months of my research, miraculously opened with the introductions of my new friends.

As I came to know many of these businessmen better, I visited their homes and attended their parties, dinners, private clubs and weddings, socialised with their families, friends and colleagues, had countless meals, cups of chai, and glasses of whisky, and had many share their stories as they became my friends and highly valued advisors. Some of my best fieldwork was conducted after midnight, when the mood was at its most relaxed and open, and the men and women at these gatherings spoke more openly and self-reflectively than they would ordinarily do in the interviews held in their offices in the exposing glare of day. My fieldwork now shifted between the formal interviews I conducted during the day, and the social events I attended most evenings. On most days, I would conduct an interview, then meet one of my close informants for long drawn out cups of coffee at a local cafe or in one of their homes, and then attend a social event, dinner or party in the evening.

The Geopolitics of Fear and Distrust

The period in which I conducted this research was a particularly turbulent time in Pakistan, characterised by a number of major terrorist attacks, military blocks and operations, large-scale *jalsas* (demonstrations) and government shut-downs. My research was also informed by the security challenges that differentiate conducting fieldwork in Pakistan from most other sites in Asia. Violence and conflict were pervasive, though notably peripheral, features of the political environment of Pakistan throughout my fieldwork in 2014. On many days it was easy to forget that Pakistan faced a high-level threat from both terrorism and organised crime.[9] But on other days, it was all my informants could talk about and all anyone I knew in Pakistan could think of.

In June 2014, in the middle of my fieldwork, the Tehreek-e-Taliban Pakistan, also known simply as the Taliban, delivered the following threat across the Pakistani press and international media (i24news 2014),

> We warn all foreign investors, airlines and multinational corporations that they should immediately suspend their ongoing matters with Pakistan and prepare to leave Pakistan, otherwise they will be responsible for their own loss. We hold Nawaz Sharif's government and the Punjabi establishment responsible for the loss of tribal Muslims' life and property as a result of this operation. We will burn your palaces in Islamabad and Lahore.

The statement was delivered one day after the Pakistan military had begun a military operation to eliminate terrorists in Pakistan's region of North Waziristan. The military responded to the threat by sending large numbers of troops to patrol the neighbourhoods of Islamabad, Lahore and Karachi. Overnight the suburban and manicured streets of Islamabad were filled with roving armoured trucks, additional army checkpoints on major roads and uniformed soldiers wielding semi-automatic rifles.

On the day this announcement was made, I received a text message from Kamil whose bi-weekly dinner I was due to attend that evening: 'Dear friends', it read,

> I am looking forward to seeing you all at dinner tonight. Due to the closure of Ataturk Avenue, please approach my street from the Serena Hotel. Apologies for the inconvenience.

His laissez-faire attitude was something I encountered in almost all of my informants and many friends in the middle classes as well. Though the military operation and corresponding terrorist threat consumed the evening's conversation, the imminent threat indicated by the Taliban and the enhanced military presence it had prompted were evidently not something Kamil viewed as an adequate reason to cancel the evening's event. Violence, terrorist attacks, military blocks and operations and large-scale jalsas that shut down the operation of government were commonplace, often a nuisance, but something my elite informants felt they could circumvent.

This instability had a pervasive effect on the lives of all Pakistanis, and affected the attitudes, aspirations and plans of almost everyone with whom I came into contact. Matthew Hull (2012, 128–9) aptly summed up this attitude in his research on the Pakistani bureaucracy, noting,

Instability is a fact of Pakistani social life that all sorts of people . . . used to explain their actions to me. "Who knows what will happen tomorrow?" is a refrain I often heard.

However, at times, the tensions of the political and security environment became so distracting that, like many of my Pakistani friends, I would wake up and before doing anything else, scan the news and Twitter feeds of my friends in the media for new security developments. Some nights I couldn't sleep imagining shifting configurations of Taliban, Al Qaeda, or government security forces, breaking into my apartment. In the light of day, these concerns seemed foolish and paranoid, until a number of my middle class Pakistani friends, often those working in the media or in other professional roles that required them to speak out against the military or the security forces admitted their own fears of night-time intruders. As attacks on schools, assassinations involving the friends of my friends, and attacks on middle class families in the Shia community occurred throughout my fieldwork, these fears became more grounded.

Consequently, my methodological approach and ability to build rapport with my informants was also powerfully informed by the security challenges that differentiate conducting fieldwork in Pakistan from most other sites in Asia. Concerns about the interference and surveillance of foreign governments, most notably India and the United States, were widely held and used as a primary rationale for the heavy presence of Pakistan's military and intelligence agencies. Suspicion about the real motives of foreign researchers in the post 9/11 security context was common, as has been noted by other anthropologists conducting research in Pakistan. Conducting fieldwork in rural Punjab, Martin (2015: 10), for instance, noted that many of his informants were so concerned that he may be a spy, that his first host found a pretext to ask him to move out (Martin 2015: 13).

Similarly, questions, jokes and uneasy remarks about the 'real' nature of my visit in Pakistan were a prominent feature of my first five months in the field. Several American spies had been discovered in Pakistan in the years preceding my fieldwork, and my interest in 'hanging out' and asking questions raised a number of eyebrows. Consequently, a high degree of openness regarding my purpose and objectives in Pakistan was necessary in order to disassociate myself from widespread concerns regarding the presence of foreign spies in Pakistan.

In discussing ethnography as a research method, Gary Alan Fine (1993) distinguished between three levels of researcher transparency:

'Deep cover' where the researcher does not disclose their role or purpose as a researcher, 'explicit cover' where they announce their role and research objectives to those they study as fully as possible, and 'shallow cover' where the researcher is open about their role and the general objectives of the research, but vague about the particular goals of the research. He argued that 'the line between being "informed" and "uninformed" is not clear . . . and that all research is secret in *some* ways' (Fine 1993: 277).

In conducting my own research, I was explicit about my role as an academic researcher without getting into the specifics of my research questions. I identified myself as a researcher not only to my research subjects, but to anyone in Pakistan who asked. I explained that I was studying the nation's most successful business families and seeking to understand how they had become so successful. Even if I had wanted to maintain 'deep cover' and conceal my position as a researcher among the broader population as other anthropologists have done in certain instances (see Hoang 2015), I could not have done so. The rarity of foreigners living in Lahore or Karachi (though more common in Islamabad), meant that the first question I received when meeting someone new inevitably related to my purpose for being in Pakistan. Further, given that the selection criteria for my informant group was their position as elite businessmen, and not their engagement in illegality or other morally grey areas, there was no need to conceal my research goals more broadly. My informants introduced me to one another variously as 'a researcher', a 'scholar' and most often, as 'a friend from Australia writing a book on business'. Many were also careful to highlight what I was not: not a journalist, not an American, not working for an aid agency and not a diplomat. Each of these negations differentiated me from most of the other foreigners working in Pakistan, and highlighted that I was neither associated with the negative history of US engagement in Pakistan, nor seeking to advocate for an aid agency, advance a diplomatic position, or use people's names in a journalistic exposé.

Later in my fieldwork, as consistent themes of inequality, class, privilege and illegality emerged, I shifted to a more explicit cover. Despite initial trepidation that my focus on these themes would deter some members of the elite from speaking with me, most remained very willing to discuss these issues, to share their analyses of the contributing factors and to provide examples from their own lives – or more often, the lives of their peers – that proved or provided nuance to my hypotheses. In contrast to other scholars (see Mears 2011) who feared an explicit cover might compromise their project, my own informants appeared unfazed by the critique embedded in my analysis. The reasons for this lay largely in the assessment of most that responsibility for the inequality from which they benefited lay elsewhere: businessmen often noted the corrupt activities of politicians; politicians often noted the unethical accumulation of wealth by businessmen; senior bureaucrats laid the blame on both; and all laid blame on the inefficiency and immorality of a vaguely defined 'state'.

The Hermaphrodite Anthropologist?

Critical in my ability to navigate these challenges, and to ameliorate the difficulties of conducting participant-observation with elites, was my position as a foreign female. When I first presented my research plan to my university faculty, an esteemed visiting professor attempted to dissuade me on the grounds that as a woman, I would be unlikely to gain adequate access to the lives of powerful male informants. If I did, he qualified, I would endanger myself by associating with powerful men used to getting what they wanted – not only in business, but also, he implied, sexually. He concluded that I would be better off shifting my focus to elite women. His assessment, though perhaps intuitive, proved incorrect for a number of methodological reasons that are worth examining more closely.

Being a foreign female researching Pakistani men shaped my positionality as a researcher in almost all areas of my fieldwork, but not in the ways the visiting professor had anticipated. Male anthropologists have often recounted that they were granted positions of status within the communities in which they resided, and were often able to use this newly acquired status to enhance their access to their subjects (cf. Hart 2001). In contrast, as a woman researching men, I was integrated into gender hierarchies that presupposed my junior status in social relations with men as a matter of course, and consequently, I was able to avoid the critical appraisals of status, power and social influence elite men used to identify other men's acceptability and rank in the social hierarchy.

As many female scholars have done before, I embraced my identity as a woman to build rapport with both my male and female informants. Yet, unlike other feminist scholars 'studying up' (see, for example, Allison 2009; Ho 2009; Hoang 2015; Mears 2011), I did not have the option of transforming my bodily self and entering into the life-worlds of my informants *as one of them*, nor could I emphasise the similarities between me and my informants to build rapport (cf. Jabukowska 2013; Mazzei and O'Brien 2009). My informants did not 'see me as local' (Hoang 2015: 191), nor was I able to 'transform' myself into one of my subjects (Mears 2011: 266). Neither did my informants seek to locate me in their own social milieus or hierarchies, as is often the case with native anthropologists conducting research with elite compatriots (cf. Jabukowska 2013, Ashraf 2018). As with researchers occupying the positions of interloper or foreigner (see Herod 1999; Herzfeld 2000; de Lima 2000), my outsider status enabled me to observe elite affairs in ways my informants would never have permitted their class peers. It was my position as an outsider so deeply different to my informants – female/male, middle-class/elite, academic/businessman or politician, Australian/ Pakistani – that eventually granted me access into the elite social circles where much of my research was conducted.

My access to this group was no doubt aided by the novelty of my status as a foreign female researcher in a place where few foreign researchers conduct long-term fieldwork unrelated to either terrorism or foreign aid. As a foreign female researcher much younger than most of the men attending the small urban parties that were a mainstay of my fieldwork, I served as an interesting addition to their carefully cultivated guest lists. The cultural capital most of my informants identified with conducting academic research,[10] and the social capital I acquired by being introduced as the friend and guest of several socially and politically prominent individuals also facilitated my entrance into these elite circles. Being both outside of business, outside of the Pakistani class system and a female in a male-dominated business and social universe, I was an unthreatening non-competitor, and an attentive listener to the exploits, strategies and relationships my informants had developed in order to succeed.

The level of access I was able to achieve as a female researcher is not as surprising as many fellow scholars working in other areas presume. Anthropologists working in many contexts, including Pakistan (see Ashraf 2018), have similarly found that women are able to gain access to both male and female forums in a way that male researchers cannot (Altorki 1982: 170; Brandes 1987; Brandes 2008; Mathur 2016: 27; Nader 1972: 114). Stanley Brandes (1987: 146) aptly conveyed this view, stating that female fieldworkers 'are transformed during fieldwork into something akin to social hermaphrodites, accepted into the worlds of both men and women'. Indeed, anthropologist Hanna Papanek (1971: 518), working in Pakistan in the 1960s and 70s argued:

Paradoxically enough, however, women researchers in societies where indigenous women are secluded often have a much higher degree of "role flexibility" than do men, and have access to both the men's and women's worlds in varying degrees.

This role flexibility allowed me to engage in strategically 'deploying gender' (Mazzei and O'Brien 2009) in various fieldwork contexts. In the small gatherings of politicians and elite businessmen to which I was regularly invited, I conformed to the clear gender delineation of assertive elite men and quietly observant upper-middle class women. In the many political debates and discussions to which I was privy, I was sometimes tempted to demonstrate my own knowledge, before I realised I was not expected to contribute in a substantive way to these discussions – nor was it desirable to my informants that I do so. Rather, it was important that I was generally aware of domestic politics and that I maintained the appearance of an interested but passive attendee, focused on and deeply interested in whatever was being discussed but content to listen rather than seeking to wrest the limelight from the male conversant. When appropriate, like the other female guests, I was expected to know the right kind of question to prop up the status of the male speakers and ensure the conversation progressed.

In other social contexts, my membership in alternative status groups prevailed, causing my informants to rapidly re-allocate my 'proper place in the social order'. For instance, in visiting the rural family home of one of my closest informants, my identity as a foreigner and a guest trumped the strict gender segregation observed within the family residence. As a female, I was welcomed into the women's section of the home and introduced to my informant's elderly grandmother and aunt, and as a foreign guest, I was invited to eat with the men of the family in the *hujra* (men's house) – the sole woman. Because I was safely positioned outside of their business and social circles many of my informants also felt that they could discuss personal dilemmas with me that would have been too sensitive to discuss frankly with other members of their social networks. Consequently, despite the differences between me and my informants, or rather, *because* of these differences, I was able to successfully enter parts of my informants' lives using participant-observation.

My position as a female researcher was not, however, always advantageous. Being female both facilitated access to the lives of my informants and at times necessitated that I withdraw from them. As my primary role was often to listen attentively while asking seemingly innocuous but often quite personal questions about my informants' marriages, families and relationships, in a few instances I found myself on the receiving end of offers to engage in a romantic or sexual relationship. In one instance I was asked to accompany an informant on a business trip to the United Kingdom, with the implicit offer to become a long-term mistress. The offer, though courteously proffered, involved a power differential beyond our 25-year age gap and his influential position in elite society. In explicit recognition of my inferior economic status, the informant noted that in addition to the enjoyment I would take from his luxurious style of travel, it would give me a chance to visit my mother through a flight he had accurately assessed I could not at that time afford. The offer was not forcefully put and caused very little awkwardness when I politely declined. In another instance, however, after a businessman had made repeated offers for me to 'come and party in Dubai', the precariousness of my position as a researcher was brought home to me. Discussing my apprehensions with Abid, he advised:

> Keep your distance from him now. You've got what you need [in terms of introductions], but don't do anything to offend him. One negative word from him and no one in Lahore will meet with you.

As a result, I had to distance myself and decline invitations to events I very much wanted to attend. The doors that my positionality as a younger unmarried woman had opened, required, in this instance, that I diplomatically close them. In these regards, my positionality as a female researcher clearly differs from that of male colleagues who are not usually subject to the same power imbalance when subject to romantic or sexual advances. The power imbalance between myself and my often-older male informants meant that as a younger female I was also more physically vulnerable, especially when conducting interviews in homes or private offices. This vulnerability was, however, substantially ameliorated by the chain of social verification that accompanied my introduction to new informants. Each businessman felt himself to be responsible for the quality of the person to whom I was introduced. As such, I was in effect given their assurance that by meeting alone with a new contact I was not subjecting myself to undue risk. Ultimately, I concluded that the vulnerability of comparative physical weakness is something that I – and all women – face in their daily lives in any context, and that the same precautions of personal safety employed elsewhere should also be employed in my fieldwork.

However, despite the access to elite men's social worlds and work-places I was able to achieve, many of my subjects tightly managed (and even prevented) my access to the women in their families. Many of the businessmen I came to know well initially promised to introduce me to their wives. Despite multiple reminders on my part and our frequent social interaction, the opportunities rarely materialised. Indeed, my relationship with their husbands precluded my entrance into elite women's lives rather than facilitated it. Knowing of my efforts to meet elite women, several months into my fieldwork, a business professor at the Lahore University of Management Science asked cheekily, 'Have you met any of their wives yet?' Before erupting into mirthful laughter and answering his own question, 'No. Of course you haven't. And you won't. Their wives are already very insecure, and meeting you would just make it worse'. I came to understand why later in my fieldwork, as many of the businessmen I knew admitted to having relationships outside of their marriages. Only a few men – usually an older cohort of more religiously-observant patriarchs in their sixties, seventies and eighties – introduced me to their wives. At the few social gatherings I attended where wives were also in attendance, the wives congregated in separate areas from the men, and talked among themselves. Consequently, while I was often introduced to my informant's girlfriends or mistresses, when I was invited into many of these men's homes I found myself entertained in the largely male areas of the home, firmly removed from the family area.

A number of female scholars have noted pressure to dress and behave in a manner which mirrored the standards of appropriate dress held by their informants,[11] and unwelcome critiques on their appearance, as defining aspect of their fieldwork.[12] For Allison (2009), Hoang (2015) and Mears (2011), their ability to conduct fieldwork as a 'local' required them to closely resemble their female informants and to be perceived by their informants as similarly attractive. My own research differed in this regard as my research did not depend on my appearance in any obvious way. Despite this, the men and women I befriended frequently compared my appearance to elite Pakistani women; commented on my body or my clothes; appraised my weight, height, facial features and skin tone; and (depending on their own positionality) either critiqued my choice of clothing or commended the modesty of my attire. Men I interacted with in social situations felt no qualms in either telling me I was too skinny and needed to eat more, or approvingly looking me up and down, and comparing me to their wives who had 'let themselves go'. Elite women were often more critical.

In a talk on fieldwork, Goffman made the remark, 'You have to open yourself up in ways you're not in ordinary life. You have to open yourself up to being snubbed' (Goffman and Lofland 1989: 128). I grew very familiar with being snubbed by elite Pakistani women. Among women, it was initially my clothing that became the major marker of critique, and an indicator that I had failed to accurately ascertain the difference between wealth and status, and to differentiate between groups within the elite. Early in my fieldwork, when invited by a young socialite to the garden party of the 24-year-old daughter of one of Lahore's most prestigious old families, I quickly realised the conservative dress that I wore to my interviews was inappropriate in this context. Guests in tight jeans, stilettos, cropped jackets and short dresses stopped by mini burger stations and had their glasses of champagne refilled by roving waiters. Despite having switched my usual *shalwar kameez* for black trousers and a long, flowing top, my loose clothing and flat shoes looked shabby and out of place. As the host and her friends had almost exhausted the champagne supply, I found myself in the centre of a semi-circle of beautifully dressed young women looking me up and down while commenting, 'your clothes are too baggy', 'you need to wear something tighter' and 'you dress as though you were very old'. Perhaps most telling was the comment of one young woman that 'Lahore isn't a conservative place. You don't need *shalwar kameez* here. *Everyone* wears jeans in Lahore'. When I pointed out that I had been attending meetings all week in offices where the few women present wore headscarves or burkas, they openly scoffed and refused to believe me. The interaction had revealed the almost complete incongruence of the social worlds that they occupied with the offices in which their fathers, brothers and husbands worked.

As I grew more familiar with the various groupings of elite in Pakistan, I altered my self-presentation to better conform to my informants' perceptions of an attractive and cultured woman. This involved highlighting a very specific form of elite femininity both outwardly and in my comportment. Clothes needed to be fashionably tailored or ready to wear from specific stores. Yet, unlike the tight clothing worn by the young women described at the Lahori garden party, my work researching men made it critical that my clothing remained uncompromisingly modest to reduce possible interpretations that I was sexually available. As I began to be invited to the sought-after elite weddings of Lahore, Shahzar's girlfriend, Maryam, offered to let me borrow from the stock of ready-made samples at her bespoke wedding wear boutique at which she was a designer and co-owner.

This kindness instantly transformed me from hopelessly unfashion-able to one of the best-dressed guests at these weddings. Most of these wedding outfits cost around 600–1800 US dollars and could not, I was firmly advised, be worn twice among the same crowd. Now fashionably dressed, I experienced an instant and noticeable rise in both status and popularity at these events, as demonstrated by the approving smiles and nods wedding guests now sent in my direction. Most importantly for my research, a number of the guests at these events thereafter demonstrated a much greater interest in my research and willingness to meet with me socially.

Beyond my predominantly male informant group, however, I managed to befriend a number of women who enriched my research immeasurably. Several of these women were members of the Lahori Established Elite, willing to share their insights on the difference between the 'Old Money' and 'New Money' families who at times intersected with their social world.[13] Several were businesswomen in their own right, and others the highly educated daughters of elite businessmen, several of whom became valued friends. Though the daughters I befriended were almost wholly excluded from decision-making in the family business, the insights they provided into the lives of women within these families were invaluable and helped provide balance to the men who shaped the overarching conclusions drawn during my fieldwork. Their insights and experi-ences particularly helped to inform this Chapter and Chapter Three. However, the women with whom I most frequently interacted were middle-class girlfriends, or the upper middle-class female friends of elite men, women outside of their own class who nonetheless fulfilled an important role within their social circles. I also socialised with a number of both the platonic female friends of businessmen, usually, like me, single professional women in their thirties, as well as a significant number of much younger girlfriends and mistresses from rural areas living in women's dormitories while they studied in Islamabad and Lahore.

Restrictions, Gossip and Rumour

Beyond the gendered components of my interactions with infor-mants, a further implication of 'studying up' was that my informants sought to control their life narratives, and the aspects of their lives to which I was given access, in multiple ways. At times, this was done without my knowledge, at other times I was explicitly asked not to delve further into specific issues. One such example was the hearing of a legal battle involving one of my informants at the Supreme Court of Pakistan. Although I had already found personal contacts at the Supreme Court enabling me to circumvent restrictions on the attendance of foreigners at public hearings, I was explicitly asked by the defendant– or rather, politely instructed – not to attend the hearing, missing a potentially valuable source of information on the activities of an informant and a chance to observe their interaction with the state. These restrictions unavoidably shaped my understandings of the lives into which I was given access.

Beyond these exclusions, my main challenge became that of researching money and power in a context where both were routinely exaggerated, disguised, or hidden entirely. Rumour and gossip circulated continuously among my elite informants and pervaded all political and economic interactions. Consequently, they became an important aspect of my fieldwork. Gossip can be understood as a voluntary, 'informal and private transmission of information about one or more persons between two or more other persons' (Hannerz 1967: 36). As such, it provided both me and my informants with information on the partnerships, deals, animosities, conflict, affairs and marriages of elite peers and competitors. Such information also served as a useful means of assessing current alliances and rivalries in a rapidly shifting political environment. As Hannerz (1967: 38) notes, 'gossip is often information which deals with the discrepancies between "impression" and "reality" concerning a person', and consequentially provides very valuable information for the ethnographer seeking to go beyond face-value key informant interviews.

The skill of many of my informants in curating their public image, meant that I sometimes had difficulty disengaging fact from the art of a good story, self-aggrandisement, or exaggeration. I dealt with this in part by seeking to triangulate and verify or refute the information given to me through other informants, media sources and official records. The real value of these accounts, however, lay not in my attempts to transform pieces of information into established facts, but in what these pieces implied about elite group boundary-making, and about the image my informant group sought to maintain and promote with other elite insiders.

The Religion Taboo

Though all of my informants were Muslim, most among those from long Established Elite families – except a number of those from Khyber Pakhtunkhwa (KP) or conservative political families in Lahore – adhered to the religious obligations of Islam selectively. Their profession of faith co-existed with their neglect of daily prayers, drinking alcohol and for some, engaging in extra-marital sexual relationships. Many of my informants from KP were abstemious and interspersed their daily routine with their obligations for prayer. Working from the second home of the Afridis during large parts of my fieldwork, I had the opportunity to witness Abid's observance of the five daily prayers, excusing himself whenever the call to prayer came through on the reminder set on his mobile phone. For many others though, prayers were engaged in much less frequently, and several told me in lowered voices that they did not follow the practices of Islam at all. One privately admitted he did not even believe in God. Pakistan's Penal Code prohibits blasphemy under a section widely known as the 'blasphemy laws' including the penalty of execution. Beyond the legal sanctions, accusations of blasphemy have frequently resulted in extrajudicial killings within communities. A number of these killings have been widely celebrated among sections of the population, reflecting both strong public support for the law and what Martin (2015, 19) has described as a public 'political debate [that] tended to focus on the individual morality [defined in Islamic terms] and piety of leaders rather than on issues of social equity'.[14] As a result of the very real dangers involved, and my tenuous position as a foreigner, discussions of faith – most particularly a lack of faith – were dangerous both for me and my research subjects, and I did not pursue them. As a result, the lived realities of religion and faith in elite lives did not form a key component of my fieldwork and does not feature heavily in this book. Despite Pakistan's reputation as a highly religious country, the practice of religion was rarely discussed in social forums. In addition to the dangers described above, I was led to believe that this was because many of my informants practiced a relaxed version of Islam that did not involve strict observance of prayer or the avoidance of alcohol. As will be explored in the chapters that follow, a number of my informants lamented that their wives had become 'very religious',[15] or spoke of the respect their mothers had acquired within their communities for their deep religious knowledge. For most of the men within my informant group, however, being Muslim was a part of their identity that they addressed in specific and discrete acts that did not necessarily infringe upon their daily lifestyle choices. Several of the elite families who had recently transitioned into the elite from the middle classes, were however, much more religiously observant.

The religious tenet almost unanimously observed, however, was avoidance of pork, prohibited in Pakistan, and observance of *Ramzan* (known elsewhere as Ramadan). Ramzan was scrupulously observed among the social circles of the business elite with whom I inter-acted. Most of my informants fasted. Notably, the regular circuit of parties held throughout the other eleven months of the year came to a complete standstill during Ramzan and were instead replaced with countless *Iftaris*, gatherings defined by the Iftar meal used to break the day's fast. Iftaris occurred directly after sunset, involved a short prayer, large quantities of food and usually ended with the crowd dispersing fairly quickly after the meal had been consumed. During this one month, the elite parties conducted throughout the rest of the year stopped completely. Most of the elites I knew also abstained from the consumption of alcohol, and many became more observant of the obligation of the daily prayers. One businessman told me with a chuckle, 'During Ramzan we all become good Muslims!'

Ramzan served as a personally important religious ritual, and for some an opportunity to salve their conscience regarding religious permissiveness during the rest of the year. Observing Ramzan and the social engagements generated by Iftaris and Eid celebrations also, however, enabled elites to transform religious ritual into another opportunity for social networking and social consolidation, both with the members of their own elite social group, and with select more socially conservative but influential public figures.

* * *

Late in my fieldwork, a young male informant I had come to know well indicated my *shalwar kameez* with a sweep of his hand and said admiringly, 'you look like a proper woman, but you act just like a man'. The freedom of movement, independence and confidence he attributed to me, were in his mind very clearly masculine traits. The statement also reflected the shifting deployment of gender traits my informants routinely assigned me – at times typically female, at others, much more fluid. Occupying this more fluid social position, I was often able to shift back and forth between the traits many of my informants associated with women and with men. As simultaneously a female and an outsider I was given greater access to elite men's worlds than either a Pakistani woman or a foreign male researcher would have been likely to receive. Yet, while I was occasionally welcomed into women's areas of the home, I was usually kept apart from the home-lives men shared with their wives.

Engaging in long-term participant observation with powerful and at times distrustful informants, revealed the ability of powerful elites to deftly manoeuvre among the varied social, political and familial roles they occupied – and to effectively shape very different public and private personas. In keeping me away from certain events and familial relationships, the moments of ethnographic insight from which I was excluded revealed the soft underbelly of elite power – the personal weaknesses and relationships they did not want to be scrutinised – or jeopardised.

Notes

An earlier version of parts of this chapter was originally published as: Armytage, R. (2018). 'Elite Ethnography in an Insecure Place: The Methodological Implications of "Studying Up" in Pakistan'. *Focaal: Journal of Global and Historical Anthropology* 82, (2018): 80–93, and is reproduced here with the permission of the publisher.

 1. This initial list was focused on the Punjabi elite of Lahore – those of whom each of the three men were aware, and particularly, those with whom they had some direct connection. Shahid's political connections meant he personally knew many of the people on this list, but as he told me, 'I hate asking for favours. They must always be paid back, and they hang over you until they are'. Consequently, after he had introduced me to several businessmen, I didn't ask for further introductions.
 2. At least three quarters of my interviewees were estimated by their peers to vastly surpass my economic baseline for inclusion. I had initially attempted to measure profit but asking this question provoked concern, evasiveness and scepticism as to the goals of my research. I quickly discovered that most of the businessmen I met with were reluctant to disclose their revenue with me. Given the lack of current data on wealth and assets among businessmen, and the prevalence of major tax evasion, my research made it necessary to rely on peer perceptions. I asked ten family patriarchs from my informant group – representing different cities and different ethnic groups – to create their own lists of the most successful and wealthy business families in Pakistan, and to estimate their revenue. This perception list proved a valuable way of categorising perceptions of wealth and prestige within the business elite, and enabled me to compile my own list of elite business families. Surprisingly, the estimates of these business patriarchs were uniformly similar – my first indication of the high level of awareness elite businessmen had of the activities, and successes and failures, of their peers. In addition to these lists, other informants routinely asked who else I had interviewed or planned to interview, and though I did not disclose the names of those on my lists, many proceeded to recommend others I should meet with, often fairly uniformly estimating their annual revenue. Again and again, elite businessmen recommended the same group of 'most successful'.

3. Other sources, such as Shahid-ur-Rahman's (2006) well known publication, *Who Owns Pakistan?*, list 44 business groups as owning the nation's largest businesses, with combined assets on par with the budget of the state of Pakistan. Many of the families identified by Rahman are also included in this study. Research conducted by Cheema et al (2013), also found that dynastic politicians belonging to approximately 400 families have been instrumental in shaping policies, programmes and legislation in Pakistan over the past three decades.
4. The overlap between business and political families has also been noted by Lyon and Mughal (2016), among others.
5. See for example, Conti and O'Neal 2007; Elwood and Martin 2000; Gilding 2010; Harvey 2010; Herod 1999; Rogers 2010.
6. See for instance, the critical work of Bourdieu 2013 [1984] and Mills 1956.
7. See Freeland 2012; Rothkopf 2008.
8. My level of access to each age group – and level of status and authority – shifted as I developed relationships with higher status individuals. The higher the status of the person making the introduction and requesting meetings for me, the higher the level of status and influence it was possible for me to interview. I began interviews with basic background questions about my informants' companies and their history, the challenges and opportunities they had found in their industry and in working in Pakistan, their experience of working with government and their hopes and plans for the future. Towards the end of the interview I asked more intimate questions about their experience of schooling, their children and how they had met their wives. I interviewed many of these people two or more times and on these subsequent visits I asked more about their private lives: their experience of marriage and family life; their relationship with their parents and parental expectations in business, family and marriage; their friendships and rivalries; and sometimes, if it was hinted at, about extramarital affairs. I also asked about their relationship with the State, often expressing sympathy for the regulatory constraints and bureaucratic hurdles businesses face. Many proceeded to talk about how they had circumnavigated these constraints through both legal and illegal means. Some interviews started and ended on the hour, in others I found myself still in someone's living room three hours later feeling I had reached saturation point as they showed no sign of ending our discussion. During one interview with a businessman, conducted in a chauffeured car during his daily one hour commute to the factory site, we focused almost entirely on South Asian fiction as we discussed the issues of wealth inequality, upward and downward social mobility, corruption and illegality, and a double standard legal system, with the experiences and decisions of central characters in our favourite books.
9. Organised crime consisted largely of the kidnapping of members of the nation's elite, or of attacks against particularly prominent and outspoken elements of the media.
10. See also Bourgouin 2013; Harvey 2010; Jabukowska 2013; Mikecz 2012.
11. See Bourgouin 2013; Jabubowska 2013; Rogers 2010.
12. See Allison 2009; Hoang 2015; Mears 2011.
13. The Pakistani elite define Old Money or the Established Elite and New Money or the Navay Raje (new lords), in ways that do not necessarily correlate with the *length* of time a family has held their wealth. For the Established Elite, those families who acquired their wealth either prior to Independence from the British, or in the first few decades of the new nation of Pakistan, the terms Navay Raje, and New Money are often applied to families who have acquired money rapidly, and who spend money and display wealth in an ostentatious manner. I explore the shifting nature of these elite categories in detail in Chapter Three.

– Chapter 2 –

CREATING AND PROTECTING AN ELITE CLASS

Almost all of the major business families occupying Pakistan's upper economic strata today engaged in rapid upward social mobility from the professional or trading classes into the economic elite during one of five major historical events: the Anglo–Indian wars (1766–1849), Partition (1947), the separation of East and West Pakistan (1971) and the nationalisation of private industry (1972). Each of these events drastically shifted the political and economic direction of the country, destroyed the fortunes of many, and prompted previously unexpected marital alliances. They also both consolidated the power of certain families, and created new groups of super rich with the corresponding economic clout to direct the tide of policy-making. These families had their own impact on the broader political and economic development of the country, using their wealth, campaign funding and vast social and political networks to direct the flow of wealth and at times the course of national economic policy-making, or to step under or around it altogether.

The recurrent crises that have typified Pakistan's short history have also meant that most of today's wealthiest business families lost much, if not all, of their wealth in various political crises. Despite these losses, many re-emerged to rebuild their empires through the assistance of their social and familial networks and their ability to ally themselves with the dominant regime of the day. And in each crisis new groups emerged to fill the gap left behind by those families unable to recover.

Allying with the Coloniser

Pakistan's first group of business elite emerged prior to the country's formation, and for many their economic rise occurred in tandem with their support for, or role in, the British colonial regime and its expansionist war efforts. Indian merchants played a major role in equipping the British military, and feeding, clothing and servicing the British and Indian armies in both the 1857 mutiny and the period surrounding it (see Roy 2016), and later during World Wars I and II. These major conflicts created both severe local shortages of basic goods required by the British army and regime, and a new set of demands for war-related production. These needs were met by indigenous merchants and bankers (Roy 2016), and the traders and merchants who served the British during this conflict, profited enormously.

Syed Babar Ali,[1] one of Pakistan's largest and most successful business owners, with a keen historical memory and aptitude for storytelling, recounted to me the close relationship between his own family's rapid upward rise with the fortunes of the British military,[2]

> My family's first business was the enterprise that my grandfather started in Firozpur, across the border in India. It was a store that catered to the needs of the British army. Firozpur was a cantonment, a place where the British army was stationed outside the city. After the 1857 war (what the British called "the mutiny", and the Indians called the first war of Independence), they had these British regiments stationed in strategic places all over India, to make sure that there was law and order. Firozpur was one of the important cantonments in Punjab, and my grandfather set up a shop to meet their needs – food, uniforms, shoes, polish, etc.
>
> My grandfather Syed Wazir Ali passed away in 1900 and then my uncle and father kept the business going. We stayed on servicing military cantonments until 1947. And it kept on growing because they did a good job. They had business all over India. Not in every cantonment, but they were what is called army contractors, and they had more contracts than any other contractor. At any one time they were looking after eight or nine cantonments. And during the Second World War, of course, the business ballooned. They were supplying not only at the Burma front, but also the Middle East. You may know that in the North African campaign, the British captured some 80,000 Italians as prisoners of war (POWs). They were kept in a POW camp in Central India and we had the contract to take care of these Italians: their food, clothes, etc. There was a camp for the Germans in Northern India and we looked after that one also'.

The upward economic mobility of many other major business families was also deeply intertwined with the war efforts of the British empire in the decades that followed, as evident in the meteoric economic and social rise of one of the nation's founding figures, as recounted to me by his great-grandson,

> My great-grandfather was thirteen years old when he heard about business opportunities in Yangon. He managed to get to Yangon on his own. His uncle was there, and he went to his uncle and worked with him as a peon. The rest of the time he worked part-time selling jute on the street. He developed a reputation as an honest man, good to deal with. In his late teens he started his own company. It was a business buying and selling jute and he became a jute trader.
>
> By the time World War I broke out he had become very good at trade. He bought up 70–80 per cent of the world's jute, all on credit for future trade, all on the basis of trust. Jute was used at that time in the trenches in World War One. My grandfather made millions. He set up industries in Yangon and both my grandfather and father were both born there.
>
> My family stayed there right up until the Japanese invaded [1942]. Then they ran away during the night. Hundreds of foreigners ran from the Japanese, and many died on the way. After the Japanese invaded, they escaped and went to India. My great-grandfather sent his family ahead of him and arrived after a few months having left all his business behind. They had already established business in India and had extended family there. In India he established another major enterprise and traded back and forth across the country, as well as in Burma and the area that is now Bangladesh.
>
> He was a risk taker. In the lead-up to World War II he again acquired most of the world's jute and again made a killing. The jute mill he established in Dhaka was one of the largest in the world.

Merchant families like Syed Babar Ali's and the family story recounted above enabled the British to maintain fairly normal trading conditions in the zones under their control. In linking their own economic fates to the needs of the dominant political and economic powers of the time, these families established themselves as independently wealthy business elites, with deep ties across both the British colonial empire and India's Muslim community of traders and professionals.

Jinnah's Personal Network

In the lead-up to partition and independence from colonial rule, Muhammad Ali Jinnah, leader of the All India Muslim League, sought to build a cohesive group of political supporters and financial backers from among the Muslim business community of India to fund the independence movement and their vision for a separate Muslim state. Recognising the enormous vacuum of industry that

the new state of Pakistan would encounter at the moment of partition, Jinnah began actively seeking investors for the new state long
before it came into being. He sought these investors from among the
friendship and broader social circles he had cultivated throughout
the 1930s and 1940s in his work as a lawyer, and later, as the leader
of the Muslim League.

Jinnah's existing relationship with the trading community in
India's state of Gujarat, personal popularity and extensive network
within the Urdu-speaking upper caste elite,[3] was a critical factor in
the willingness of Indian investors to fund the Pakistan Movement.
Later, his personal requests and assurances of the value and safety of
business investments within the new state of Pakistan also became a
key factor in the willingness of these families to undertake the risk
of relocating their already successful businesses, along with their
families, to re-establish their lives in a new nation.

The friendship between Jinnah and the Gujarati businessman,
Adamjee Dawood,[4] illuminates the importance of personal relationships, alliances and obligations, in establishing what was at that time
Pakistan's non-existent industrial sector. Jinnah and Adamjee first
met in 1928 while Jinnah was serving as a barrister and President
of the All India Muslim League. Adamjee hired Jinnah to represent Muslim interests in India against a proposed tax on charitable
Muslim endowments (*wakf*), an act of taxation the Indian Muslim
community perceived to be highly discriminatory. Jinnah won the
case, and the tax on Muslim charity was removed by the national
government (Jamasji-Hirjikaka and Qureshi 2004). Adamjee had a
huge amount of respect for Jinnah for both his skill as a lawyer and
his commitment to serving the Muslim community. And Jinnah had
a huge degree of confidence in Adamjee both in terms of his capacity
as a businessman and in his ability to generate political support
from among the economically powerful Gujarati community: he
personally nominated Dawood as a Member of the Muslim League
Parliamentary Board in 1936 and enlisted Adamjee's assistance in
raising funds from the Calcutta Muslim Chamber of Commerce for
campaigns related to the Pakistan movement on multiple occasions.
Along with other members of the Gujarati trading community,
Adamjee hosted multiple events for Jinnah and his campaign with
the wealthy and well-connected Memon, Bohra and Khoja Gujarati
trading communities, along with other Muslim League members
and government officials, with the goal of introducing 'the Gujarati
Muslim trading communities to League politics' and garnering
their support for an independent Muslim state. Dawood went on

to become one of the largest and most influential industrialists of the new state (Papanek 1972). The role of the business community was critical in the lead-up to the establishment of the new state, and Jinnah recognised this.

When Pakistan was founded, Jinnah repaid the support of these Gujarati traders through prioritising, incentivising and facilitating their migration to Pakistan, along with other individuals deemed vital for the running the new state. Together with senior bureaucrats and politicians from Delhi and Bombay, wealthy Muslim trader families from Gujarat, and those who had earlier settled in Burma and across Africa, were encouraged and facilitated to relocate to Pakistan. These skilled immigrant families became known as the *Muhajirs*, meaning 'immigrants'. In contrast to the horror, violence and loss experienced by many of the middle and lower classes who migrated to Pakistan at independence,[5] the relocation of the Muhajirs was, for the most part, ordered, planned in advance and undertaken largely without substantial financial loss. Using their personal connections within the Indian bureaucracy, these elite immigrants successfully made personal petitions to ensure they received land and compensation in Pakistan equivalent to what they had previously possessed in India. As a result, the state policy of compensation carried out by evacuee property boards ensured minimal economic losses in the migration process for this group of businessmen and bureaucrats as they exchanged their property in India for equally grand homes in Lahore and Karachi (Kaur 2006).[6]

As Jinnah had predicted, partition with India left the new state of Pakistan with an enormous vacuum of industry as almost all of pre-partition India's factories and industrial complexes remained in the land that became India. To accelerate the growth of urgently needed vital industries, the government incentivised the newly arrived traders of Gujarat to enter into industry by providing them with powerful economic inducements in the form of large publicly-funded loans, grants and tax exemptions. The scale of demand for the broad array of goods required by the new Pakistani population meant that the profits gained by the nation's traders-turned-industrialists were massive.

Government policy ensured imports were largely unrestricted between 1947 and 1952, and anticipating a commodity price boom, the rupee was overvalued[7] in industrialists' favour so that large machinery and other goods were relatively inexpensive to import. Pakistan's decision not to align with India in devaluing the rupee following the British devaluation of the pound sterling, made it uneconomical for Indian manufacturers to import raw materials such as cotton and jute from Pakistan. As punishment for not taking India's lead, and to ensure Pakistan did not benefit from importing significantly cheaper Indian imports, India imposed a trade ban on Pakistan in 1949. Because a huge range of basic commodities had previously been manufactured within the area that was now India, the loss of the Indian market created additional opportunities and incentives for industrialists to enter unfamiliar markets in almost every area of industry and manufacturing in both West and East Pakistan. It also significantly reduced Pakistan's reliance on India. The new state, however, was heavily reliant on this group of wealthy traders; their fortunes were directly tied to that of the national economy, and as a result, they were positioned to extract a disproportionate array of economic and political privileges. For those with inherited assets and strong personal connections to those in power, Pakistan was a land of opportunity.

Those with the closest and most established relationships with Jinnah were immediately incorporated into the Pakistani state both in vital political positions as ministers and advisors, and in prominent industrial positions. The favours Jinnah enlisted from his closest friends and the benefits he ensured they received are clearly evident. The Isphani[8] brothers were close family friends of Jinnah who had relocated to East Pakistan at Jinnah's personal request and established Orient Airways one year before partition. When it was nationalised in 1955, one of the Isphani brothers went on to serve as the new state airline's first Chairman.[9] Mahomedali Habib,[10] also a close personal friend of Jinnah, established Habib Bank for Muslims in Bombay in 1941 at Jinnah's urging, and again relocated it to Karachi in 1947 at Jinnah's personal request.[11] Habib Ibrahim Rahimtoola,[12] also a close associate of Jinnah and a prominent Muslim businessman in Bombay, served as Pakistan's first High Commissioner to the United Kingdom in 1947 at Jinnah's request, then later as Governor of Sindh (1953–55). The advantages provided to these Muhajir businessmen and politicians both directly by Jinnah, and later, as a result of the personal relationships they established within the new state bureaucracy, were instrumental in assuring the dominance of a new class of predominantly Muhajir industrialist-elites[13] in the first two decades of the new state.

Table 2.1. Background of industrial families by community and pre-1947 business headquarters.

Industrial House	Community	Family Origin/Area	Settled	Business Headquarters Location pre-1947
Adamjee	Memon	Kathiawar/Jetpur	Karachi	Calcutta
Dawood	Memon	Kathiawar/Jetpur	Karachi	Bombay
Saigol	Punjabi Sheikh	W. Punjab/Chakwal	Lahore	Calcutta
Valika	Dawood/Bohras	Bombay	Karachi	Bombay
Colony	Punjabi Sheikh/ Chinioti	W. Punjab/Chiniot	Lahore	Lahore
Fancy	Khoja Ismaili	Kathiawar	Karachi	East Africa
Bawany	Memon	Kathiawar/Jetpur	Karachi	Rangoon
Crescent	Punjabi Sheikh/ Chinioti	W. Punjab/Chiniot	Lyallpur	Delhi
Beco	Punjabi	E. Punjab	Lahore	Batala
Wazir Ali	Syeds	W. Punjab/Lahore	Lahore	Lahore
Amins	Punjabi Sheikh	W. Punjab	Karachi	Calcutta
Nishat	Punjabi Chinioti	W. Punjab/Chiniot	Lyallpur	N/A
Hoti	Pathan Landlord	Charsaddah (KP)	Charsaddah (KP)	Charsaddah (KP)
Fateh	Marwari	Gujrat	Karachi	
Isphani		Iranian	Karachi	Calcutta
Karim	Bohras	Bombay	Karachi	

Sources: Reproduced from Amjad (1976). (i) Papanek G., op. cit., p. 49; (ii) Papanek, H., 'Pakistan's Businessmen', *Economic Development and Cultural Change*, Vol 12, No. 1, October, 1972.

The Emergence of an Alliance in Business, Politics and the Bureaucracy

Karachi was established as Pakistan's first capital and most of the Muhajir community settled in the city, leaving Punjab predominantly populated by long-term native Punjabis. As businessmen with long experience in undivided India, the Muhajirs' choice of city was strategic. Karachi was both the centre of government, and the nation's principal port and centre of the import trade – the basis of the business empires of most of those who had immigrated (Papanek 1970).

The trader population knew from extensive experience of engaging with government in India that proximity to government, and the development of personal relationships with government officials, was critical for the success and expansion of business. Personal petitions and bribery had long been an important determinant of the provision of permissions and licenses in united India, and they became a prominent feature of relations between government and business in the new nation as well (Papanek 1970). Personal petitions, bribery, entertaining and socialising with government officials, were perceived to be an established component of major business in Pakistan. By the 1950s, the business community in Karachi had successfully diverted a hugely disproportionate allocation of government resources to the city: Karachi was allocated over 50 per cent of the national water supply and public housing between 1955 and 1960 despite being home to only two per cent of the total population (Papanek 1970).

The degree to which the Muhajir immigrant population dominated economically within the rapidly growing economy of Karachi, and in the emerging industrial areas of Lahore and Lyallpur (now Faisalabad) in Punjab, is evident in Table 2.1. Only three out of the sixteen largest industrial families had lived on the land that became Pakistan prior to 1947; the remainder were immigrants from the areas that became Indian Punjab and Gujarat, or Indian traders with established histories in Africa. In the first few decades of the new nation, the indigenous Punjabi elite were removed from the centre of government and posed no economic challenge to the economic and political rise of the Muhajir industrialists.

Economic Policy for the Few

Pakistan experienced an economic boom in the early 1950s as a result of the Korean War (1950–53). International demand for jute, weaved to form the outer shell of the sandbags used in trenches, had generated huge fortunes for the few Pakistani families already holding an oligopoly on worldwide supply, and had siphoned large amounts of export capital into Pakistan. But following the war boom, and the sudden drop in world demand for jute, export earnings dropped dramatically.

To facilitate domestic industrial growth and production the government tightly restricted imports between 1953 and 1959 as part of an import substitution policy designed to create domestic demand for locally-produced goods across all areas of manufacturing, and to lure new investors into industrial production by significantly increasing the profitability of domestic industry (Papanek 1962). A further impact of the import restrictions was that it severely restricted the opportunities for new families to enter into large-scale business. By preventing those in business from acquiring the new machinery and raw materials they required to expand their operations, only those families who already had large-scale production infrastructure, or who had strong personal connections with government bureaucrats willing to provide them with import exemptions, were able to operate large-scale industry. These families were guaranteed enormous profits and market dominance, often across several industrial sectors, with very little competition. Profits were so high that some industries were recorded as having annual returns of 100 per cent on investment (Papanek 1962).

A major component of the government's strategy to facilitate domestic growth was the establishment of publicly owned, and semi-publicly owned, lending banks and industrial corporations. As the government had limited funds available in the early 1950s due to the absence of domestic taxation and very low levels of foreign aid and lending (Khan 1999), these institutions provided a means to support industrial investment through channelling the limited funds available to targeted industries and government-favoured firms. By the mid-1950s, a significant component of central government funding was being dispersed through the Pakistan Industrial Finance Corporation (PIFC).[14] Business owners carefully cultivated relationships with bureaucrats in the PIFC and in the Pakistan Industrial Development Corporation (PIDC) to secure the approvals needed to expand their industries and establish new ones, to advocate for the continued import controls that benefited the large established houses by driving up the cost for their products on the domestic market. And large business holders were able to manipulate bureaucrats to operate in their favour at very low personal cost by paying small bribes, or employing their relatives (Amjad 1976).

The government incentives provided to industrialists were wildly successful in spurring industrial growth. Between 1950 and 1958, the manufacturing sector grew at over 19 per cent. And yet, because wealth was distributed among such a limited number of families, per capita gross domestic product (GDP) experienced no significant increase in this period. While there were over 3,000 individual firms in 1959, only seven families controlled a quarter of all private industrial assets and one-fifth of all industrial assets in total[15] (Papanek 1967).

The Rise of Military Influence and a New Configuration of Power

The politics and business strategies engaged in by the indigenous elites of Punjab were very different from those engaged in by the

Muhajirs, as were their family backgrounds. While Karachi became the city of immigrants and business, Lahore remained an established city of 'old families', many with agricultural and landowning backgrounds from within Lahore or the neighbouring districts. Many of those who had relocated to Lahore following independence had moved only very short distances, many from areas as close as Amritsar, only 50 kilometres away in India.

Conflict between the largely indigenous landed elite and mainly Muhajir business houses had been constant between 1947 and 1958. Both industrial factions actively competed for influence with bureaucrats and policy makers, and the implementation of policies most advantageous to their own political and economic interests. The military coup d'état of General Ayub in 1958 temporarily put an end to the political stalemate: his authoritarian regime eliminated elections, and with it removed the landed elites' dominant role in formal politics and their ability to redirect national economic policy. However, the military government also felt the need to take drastic action to remove the bureaucracy from the 'unwholesome' influence of the business community in order to preserve its 'administrative integrity' (Hull 2012, 40). Ayub's Planning Commission decided to relocate the nation's capital from Karachi to northern Punjab in the early 1960s. A newspaper at the time referenced the commission report declaring that,

> Close contact between the business community and personnel of the Administration of Karachi has not done any good to either. Too much of social contact between those who want things to be done to suit them and the officials cannot lead to healthy results. It is desirable both for the business community and the administration that the capital should be away from the commercial centre of the country.[16]

While reducing the political influence of the landed elites and weakening personal ties between business and the bureaucracy, the government's economic policy remained strongly in support of large-scale business. By the 1960s, however, the continued overvaluation of the rupee had reduced the competitiveness of Pakistani exports. Rather than devaluing the currency, which would also have reduced the buying power of Pakistani importers, Ayub implemented an 'export bonus' to subsidise the manufacturing cost of items sold for export, allowing these items to sell at a rate competitive on the international market. In practice, as this only applied to exported goods, it had the effect of creating multiple exchange rates, keeping the cost of imports low and making otherwise overpriced exports internationally competitive. Ayub also significantly decreased restrictions on imports by reducing the number of items that required import licenses.[17] This made it significantly easier for business people to import the machinery and raw materials needed for many areas of manufacturing (Khan 1999).

To further stimulate industrial growth, the regime offered tax concessions to encourage investment in the less developed areas of Punjab, making the enterprises of the business elites of Punjab competitive with those of the Muhajir business community in Karachi. This policy led to massive investment in manufactured goods such as jute and textiles, prompted huge economic growth (Khan 1999) and dramatically enhanced the fortunes of the major business houses involved in these largely monopolistic Punjabi industries. The result was the emergence of a new group of large-scale Punjabi industrialists (Blood 1994).

Simultaneously, however, the Ayub regime sought to curtail the political influence of the landed indigenous elite through far-reaching land reforms (Blood 1994). Ayub's land reform policy imposed limits on the amount of land that could be owned by one individual and on how the land could be used. He also implemented stern measures against the hoarding of agricultural items that had earlier been used by landowners to artificially decrease supply, raise prices and increase the costs for the industrialists who bought their raw materials. In turn, hoarding had significantly increased the cost of essential items paid by the consumer. Though it angered landowners, this policy further increased the support of major business houses for the military regime (Blood 1994).

The policies Ayub implemented in support of industry prompted the business class to make a lasting shift from reliance on the bureaucracy to consolidating affiliations with powerful political actors – including the military. Individual capitalists began to cultivate relationships with specific politicians who they hoped would support their preferred policy and regulatory reforms in return for generous campaign funding. The business elite also began to serve as a powerful support base for military rule, and helped legitimise the role of the military in politics and policymaking going forward (Khan 1999). The relationships established during Ayub's regime laid the groundwork for the business elite to serve as one of the military's primary constituencies for support and sources of funding over the next six decades.

In tandem with his efforts to reduce the privileges of landed elites, Ayub significantly increased those provided to the military.

He did this by making four million hectares of land in West Pakistan available for public acquisition, and reserving a large proportion of this land for sale to civil and military officers. This broadening of land ownership created a new class of medium-sized farmers with close ties to the military (Blood 1994) and significantly expanded the military's influence in agricultural production. Simultaneously, the ability of the bureaucracy to place economic or political restrictions on the military was severely curtailed, as Ayub mounted a rigorous campaign to investigate and punish bureaucratic corruption – and scapegoat problematic individuals. The result was a significant and permanent increase of military influence in all areas of governance.

By the early 1960s, despite being cut out of much of the economic growth of the 1950s, the landed class had become increasingly vocal in demanding the government redirect resources in their favour. Despite their exclusion from the benefits of industrial policy, they had retained strong support among their constituencies, and were well positioned to return to positions of elected power in the forthcoming elections due to rising public dissatisfaction against the concentration of wealth associated with Ayub's regime. This shift in public sentiment caused many in big business to regard the landed elite as the greatest threat to their interests and continuing accumulation of capital (Amjad 1976). The threat posed to the existing business community was further compounded by Ayub's late attempts to appease the landed classes through the provision of large subsidies on agricultural machinery such as tractors, tube wells and fertilisers – subsidies designed to enable the landed class to finally expand into industry. These subsidies resulted in a number of new landowning families entering industry in Punjab and Sindh for the first time.[18]

Rising Wealth Inequality

By the late 1960s, the legitimacy of the military-state had become increasingly tenuous. The government had distributed licenses to large capitalists in order to secure their support, enabling major industrialists to amass licenses that they were then able to distribute to others with whom they needed to cultivate relationships and patronage (Khan 1999, Kochanek 1983). As a result, the regime found itself heavily dependent on its industrialist support base and unable to enforce necessary limitations on an increasingly politically-dominant industrial class.

By the late 1960s, highly concentrated industrial development and monopolistic business had stifled competition and precipitated a steep decline in economic growth and standards of living in both East and West Pakistan (Amjad 1982).[19] Despite the hardships experienced by much of the population, the profitability of large industry continued to increase for industrial owners and for the landed families newly invested in industry, as the real wages of workers significantly declined. Public dissatisfaction with the concentration of wealth among a very small number of families drastically increased. By 1962, workers' strikes were frequent and increasingly militant (Shaheed 1979). Over 10,000 workers in Karachi congregated for the general strike of 1963, protesting low pay and pushing for greater freedom for labour unions. Though they were successful in extracting promises of pay increases, many owners were not forthcoming on this promise once work resumed, leading to a fresh wave of protests and worker strikes. When an economic study conducted by Mahbub Ul Haq, Chief Economist of the Pakistan Planning Commission, was publicly released finding that only 22 families in Pakistan controlled two thirds of all industrial assets, 80 per cent of banking and 70 per cent of insurance in Pakistan (Haq 1968, Haq 1976), the grievances of the urban working classes found a rallying point. The term '22 Families' became common parlance, and with it public dissatisfaction against the concentration of wealth among a very small number of families rose dramatically.

Seeking to end the disruptions to business, the business elite pressured the government to ban workers' strikes and protests (Shaheed 1979). Despite these measures, by 1968 politicised labour leaders had mobilised large sections of the industrial labour force against industrialists and the severe inequities in their favour generated by Ayub's regime (Alavi 1974). Worker unions allied themselves with militant student movements, each becoming both increasingly violent and effective as a coordinated anti-government force.

The industrialist–worker conflict reached a boiling point when workers forcibly confined industrialists (*gherao*) in their factories until their demands were met. By 20 March 1969 industrial factory owners faced such violence from the united workers' movement that they asked for protection from the military regime, and requested that it deploy both the police and the army to force workers to resume production. Over 800 workers were arrested (Shaheed 1979). The move was widely unpopular. Recognising the shift in public opinion, a number of political parties campaigned against Ayub on the grounds of the massive social inequality he had come to represent (Amjad

1976). As strikes continued, the military moved to strategic points across Karachi on 24 March, and in response to enormous pressure Ayub Khan submitted his resignation the same day (Shaheed 1979).

Despite the public rage directed towards Ayub's military regime, he was immediately replaced by a successor military regime which offered no immediate change in industrial or worker policy. As workers continued to *gherao* industrialists, General Yahya Khan retaliated by retrenching 45,000 workers and jailing large numbers of labour leaders, workers, students and political activists (Shaheed 1979). The Industrial Relations Ordinance of 1969 was implemented by Yahya Khan's short-lived government to mollify factory workers and cajole them into returning to work by ostensibly giving factory workers the rights they had campaigned for: workers were allowed to form trade unions, to engage in collective bargaining and to strike. In practice, however, the Ordinance continued to reflect the interests of factory owners through a series of restrictions and caveats: 75 per cent of all unions were restricted to representing the workers of only one employer, effectively preventing industry-wide action across companies. Nationwide industries deemed 'essential' like railway construction and postal services were prohibited from forming unions at all. The result was the creation of many separate, and thus severely weakened, trade unions across all 'non-essential' industries (Candland 2007). The growth of these weakened trade unions bene-fited the industrial class significantly: workers were partially molli-fied in having their unions restored, and yet the unions posed little threat to ongoing industrial operations.

Civil War

Simultaneously, tensions had been mounting in East Pakistan where East Pakistani elites had been systematically excluded from accessing the benefits of massive industrial development in West Pakistan, and denied equal political representation with West Pakistanis. National industrial policy had massively disadvantaged East Pakistan, sup-porting West Pakistani businessmen to establish factories and indus-trial complexes in East Pakistan but failing to provide indigenous Bengali businessmen any equivalent loans or financial and taxation privileges. The use of East Pakistani exports to fund development projects in West Pakistan became a major focus of public discontent in East Pakistan and a rallying point for the growing Bengali nation-alist movement.

By the late 1960s public dissatisfaction in East Pakistan over the economic inequality they experienced with West Pakistan had been exacerbated by the national government's imposition of Urdu language over Bengali. The policy generated mass public outrage and led to increasingly widespread demands for Bengali self-rule. Eventually recognising the force of the opposition that had emerged within East Pakistan to West Pakistani rule, the Ayub regime sought to provide concessions to the Bengali elites and industrialists his regime had earlier excluded from national economic growth. But his concessions came too late: by the time they were offered, East Pakistani elites could no longer quell the rage of the broader population who had suffered West Pakistan's attempts to systematically entrench their disadvantage and eliminate Bengali identity. The violent civil war that followed, and the appalling atrocities wrought by the West Pakistani army on the Bengali population eventually ended with Bengali victory and the creation of the independent state of Bangladesh in 1971.

The loss of East Pakistan caused both major political and economic instability in what remained of Pakistan. Many West Pakistani elite business families were forced to quickly abandon property, family homes, industrial factories and manufacturing complexes in the violence that ensued in East Pakistan and most of these assets were never recovered or compensated. For those West Pakistani industrialists with substantial assets in East Pakistan, the effect of the civil war on their wealth and lifestyle was devastating. Prior to 1971, six industrial houses – Adamjee, Dawood, Bawany, Isphani, Amin and Karim[20] – controlled 40 per cent of all industrial assets in East Pakistan, and 32 per cent of production of the large-scale manufacturing sector.[21] Four of these houses (Bawany, Amin, Isphani and Karim[22]) lost everything they owned in the civil war and eventual independence of Bangladesh[23] (Amjad 1976), and the others incurred major losses. The account mentioned earlier in this chapter, provided by a grandson of one of the nation's founding businessmen, described his own experience of the onset of the civil war in Dhaka,

> My grandfather employed 2,000 people, and many of the country's largest businesses in East Pakistan were in our hands. Then in 1971 the army came to our house in Dhaka and asked us to leave. They told us we had to leave because we were not safe. We left everything behind. The army escorted us onto our own jet plane, and we were cast out. We abandoned everything.

In the wake of Pakistan's defeat in the civil war with East Pakistan and the emergence of the independent state of Bangladesh two shifts in national power politics occurred: Zulfiqar Ali Bhutto[24] came to power, and the Islamist political parties began to exert strong political pressure as a war-defeated nation sought to re-identify with its ethno-religious roots. The charge of the Islamic parties that the excess and irreligiosity of the ruling elite had led to the breakdown of the nation found a great deal of salience among the middle and working classes (Jalal 2011). In response, Bhutto integrated religious rhetoric into his populist ideology, linking socialism with Islam (Jaffrelot 2015, 11) and pledging to establish an Islamic socialist economy that would address Pakistan's vast social and economic inequality.

In the first six months of the populist regime, however, workers' strikes in response to ongoing poor conditions and wages had re-emerged to such an extent that the industrial elite again threatened the government with a united closure of all major industrial establishments if they did not do something to prevent the workers' protests (Shaheed 1979). In 1972, as Karachi workers protested against not receiving their pay, industrial owners locked angry workers out of their industrial sites and called for police protection.

The police responded by opening fire on protesters, killing three workers. As workers led a funeral procession with the body of one of the dead workers, police and military again opened fire killing another ten workers. The killings prompted a massive general strike involving the closure of 10,000 industrial sites in Karachi for ten days (Shaheed 1979). The strike was called off only after labour leaders managed to successfully negotiate with the Karachi city government for the provision of power and water to the residential colonies, and the opening of a health facility for the city's workers, services neither the industrialist owners nor the government had been willing to provide up until that point. The successful negotiation of unions and workers resulted in a significant shift in the balance of power between the nation's elite and industrial workers (Shaheed 1979).

Intra-Elite Conflict and the Reconfiguration of the Elite Alliance

President Bhutto sought to redress his early failure to either improve conditions for workers, or to redistribute the profits of industrialisation by nationalising most of Pakistan's major industry. His programme nationalised all industries deemed vital for the nation's development, including iron and steel; heavy engineering; heavy electricals; petrochemicals; cement; public utilities; the assembly and manufacture of motor vehicles; tractors; public utilities; gas and oil refineries; life insurance; vegetable oil; banks; shipping companies; and banking and finance. Many of Pakistan's most successful business families had their factories nationalised almost overnight and most incurred huge financial losses from which a number never fully recovered (Amjad 1976). The programme ensured that almost all of the major industrial families whose assets had not been lost in Bangladesh lost a significant component of their businesses at this time, and it severely damaged and in some cases destroyed the fortunes of the largest of Pakistan's remaining industrialists. The major exceptions to the decimation of the elite business class were those families primarily invested in textile manufacturing, as these were among the few large-scale industries that were not nationalised. As a consequence, those families whose diversified portfolio included textiles managed to retain some of their assets during this period.

Table 2.2 below documents the devastating effects of nationalisation on Pakistan's largest industrialists.

An exception to this trend, the current patriarch of a major conglomerate owner in Karachi, Ashraf Mirza, provided his own explanation of how his family had managed to escape nationalisation,

> When Bhutto nationalised major industry in the 1970s, he also nationalised our industry, but our company was allowed to keep working, ostensibly

Table 2.2. Percentage of business assets lost during nationalisation.

Saigol	68.8
Habib	69.8
Amin	62.9
Valika	66.1
Fancy	89.7
Beco	100
Colony (N)	49.5
Colony (F)	77.1
Adamjee	40
Zafar-ul-Ahsan	71.3
Ghandara	67.7
Reyaz-o-Khalid	90.9
Dawood	12.9
Ragoonwala	100
Hyesons	19.6
Wazir Ali	14.6
Haroon	23.6

Source: Adapted from Amjad (1976).

because it did not meet the threshold of the size required to be nationalised. In reality, however, it was probably the result of two other factors. Firstly, we kept our factories running through the labour union riots of the 1960s, which made the government team in charge of nationalisation predisposed towards us. Secondly, before we came to Karachi, Zulfikhar Bhutto was a tenant of my grandfather in Bombay. Once we moved to Karachi, we then lived just a few doors down from him in Clifton. Being a small society, people of that class were all friends, or at least in the same circles.

For most, however, Bhutto's nationalisation shattered both the wealth and confidence of many of the country's largest business families. The shock of the financial loss, the speed at which it occurred and the inability of many industrialists to recover caused an ongoing lack of confidence and trust among the business community regarding the government's ability or trustworthiness to protect private business interests or to ensure the basic property rights necessary to encourage investment. Because Bhutto himself came from an elite family with deep ties across elite society, his nationalisation programme was felt by many to be both a personal betrayal and an indication that investment would not ever be secure within Pakistan. Many of the elite families whose businesses were destroyed during this period, either by the loss of assets in East Pakistan or Bhutto's nationalisation programme, thereafter remained hesitant to reinvest.

Some companies, like Ashraf Mirza's described above, did benefit from the decimation of many of the nation's major business groups. A number of medium-sized business groups found themselves able to scale up and compete in the domestic market for the first time now that so many of the largest industrial groups had been eliminated. Moreover, many families working in textile manufacturing now found themselves among the wealthiest in the nation, with more wealth available for future investment opportunities (Amjad 1976).[25]

Reconsolidating Elite Business Interests

In 1977 General Zia, Bhutto's Chief of Army Staff, staged a coup d'état with the support of a number of powerful conservative religious groups. Zia immediately imposed martial law, suspended elections, introduced Islamic law, reversed Bhutto's socialist economic policies, increased public funding to the military, and expanded military involvement across government.[26] Recognising the need to appease each of the nation's various power blocs, he sought to implement policies that would promote and protect each of their separate economic interests. To minimise possible opposition, Zia actively incorporated both industrialists and the landed elite into his military regime by including them as members of the National Assembly (see chart below). In his efforts to ensure the loyalty of the business elite, Zia also brought a number of industrialists into key advisory roles within his government, where they not only influenced economic policy, but also won large government contracts for their private businesses (Shenon 1991, Burki 1988).

Perhaps more typical among this group of new elites, is the class trajectory of the Sharif family, and specifically of Nawaz Sharif,[27] the former Prime Minister, in exemplifying the shifting class boundaries of the elite. Sharif came from a middle-class Kashmiri–Punjabi family, who owned a small factory in Amritsar prior to independence, and it is reputed that one of his uncles worked in a steel furnace. At partition, Nawaz Sharif's father, Muhammad Sharif, immigrated the 200 kilometres from Jati Umra near Amritsar in the state of India, to Lahore. By the 1960s, the Sharif family owned a few medium-sized factories, including ice making facilities and a water pump factory (Qureshi 2015). In 1969, Muhammad Sharif, along with his six brothers, established the Ittefaq Group iron foundry. Nawaz Sharif was educated at Saint Anthony's High School and Government College in Lahore and received a law degree from Punjab University. Following his education, he entered Punjab provincial politics, joining the Punjab advisory district council. He initially joined politics in the late 1970s when he became a member of Asghar Khan's Tehrik-e-Istiqlal. In 1976, when Bhutto nationalised the steel industry, the Sharif family business empire, Ittefaq Group, was also nationalised and much of the family's emerging wealth was lost.

When General Zia's military regime assumed control of the country in 1978, Sharif was appointed Finance Minister for Punjab. In 1985, he was appointed Chief Minister of Punjab. In the same year, General Zia returned to the Sharifs the iron foundry that had been nationalised under Bhutto (Baker 2005), enabling the family to rebuild its fortune. His close relationship with General Zia was a personal relationship based on the specific benefits each could provide to the other at a particular political and economic moment. During the 1980s as Sharif rose in seniority within Zia's regime, Ittefaq Group expanded from ownership of five mills to thirty businesses, including those in steel, sugar, paper and textiles earning annual revenues estimated at $400 million. The distinction Nawaz Sharif embodies, along with those of his peers who acquired their wealth from the 1980s onwards, is more Punjabi than English. He wears shalwar kameez and *sherwani*

(South Asian waistcoat) rather than suit and tie, speaks mostly in Urdu and Punjabi and is publicly viewed as representing a socially conservative worldview.

Nawaz Sharif's rise to power indicates the shifting face of the business elite in Pakistan, away from the established families with ties to the British, to a new group defined by more local and ethnically-based markers of distinction, and by close mutually-supportive relationships with the military. He is indicative of the social shift slowly occurring among the nation's business elite having emerged from the classes below the elite to become a member of the top tier of the economic strata in only one or two generations. Though some Navay Raje elites have sought to attain Anglicised forms of distinction from the private clubs and schools of the Established Elite, assimilating with this group and shedding the stigma of the Navay Raje, Nawaz Sharif typifies the new group who are slowly discarding the English dispositions and indicators of status.

In an effort to both strengthen the economy and appease the industrial elite, Zia's government attempted to re-privatise the nation's still publicly-owned manufacturing plants (Husain 2000). Industrial licenses were reinstated to most former industrial owners, strengthening the traditional alliance between the military–business bloc once again. Zia's strategy of co-opting powerful political and business families by incorporating them into his government was at least partially successful. However, he lost some of the goodwill he had fostered among these elites by increasing income tax revenues in 1988, introducing agricultural income tax[28] for the first time, and by failing to privatise all of the industries that had earlier been nationalised (Candland 2007). His efforts to privatise Pakistan International Airways, for instance, resulted in only 10 per cent of the publicly-owned company being divested (Candland 2007). He further angered a number of influential business families by deregulating a number of monopoly industries, including the sugar, pesticide and fertiliser industries; removing subsidies; and ensuring that the price system became more responsive to the market, lowering the guaranteed profits these industrialists had come to expect.

But Zia's policies were widely viewed as advantageous to emerging smaller businesses. After years of loaning only to large-scale industrialists with close personal ties to government and senior bureaucrats, Zia broadened access to government finance and credit, in keeping with his priority of reducing the disparity of wealth across the country, and allowing small-scale enterprises to expand at a scale not previously possible (Husain 2000). As a result, new industries led by smaller-scale producers in leather manufacturing, sporting goods and surgical goods began to flourish, creating a much more diverse industrial environment (Husain 2000).

However, resentment among large sections of the elite grew during Zia's regime in response to his inability to fully meet elite demands, his targeting of particular elite families in politics, and his implementation of Islamic law which severely curtailed many of the social freedoms – and events – elite Pakistanis had enjoyed up to that point. These religious policies and the freedoms he gave to conservative religious parties had a lasting and permanent impact on Pakistani politics as these groups became exponentially influential. Yet by crushing his political opposition, he also severely limited the opportunities for the elite to organise resistance to his policies. Under the surface, in private forums, however, sections of the elite (particularly those with pre-partition multi-generational wealth) allied themselves together in opposition to his repressive and deeply conservative regime.

Shifting Power to Punjab

One of the major impacts of Zia's regime on big business in Pakistan was the acceleration of the shift of wealth and power it facilitated away from Karachi to Punjab, through a range of policies preferential to the province, the stronghold of Zia's own military supporters.[29] By 1982, for the first time in Pakistan's history, the annual incorporation of companies in Punjab exceeded that of Karachi (Rehman 2006). Punjabi business groups surged ahead creating larger and more profitable enterprises than those established in Karachi, leading to a permanent regional shift in corporate power to accompany a Punjabi dominated bureaucracy, parliament and military. As noted by Jaffrelot (2015, 133), by 1983,

> 55.8 per cent of the staff [senior civil service] were Punjabis, 11.6 per cent were from the NWFP [now KP], 20.2 per cent urban Sindhis (a large majority of them Muhajirs), 5.1 per cent Sindhis from rural areas in the province and 3.1 per cent Balochis. In state-owned enterprises, the proportion of Punjabis was estimated to be 41 per cent and urban Sindhis 47 per cent, compared to 6 per cent from the NWFP, 3.5 per cent from Rural Sindh and 1 per cent from Balochistan.

The Punjabi families who rose to prominence in business were often relatives of senior Punjabi military officers and bureaucrats with high-level personal connections in the bureaucracy, as these relation-ships enabled them to negotiate with ease the many bureaucratic obstacles imposed by the state (Alavi 1990).

Zia's role in the shift towards Punjab angered many of Karachi's industrial elite. As Punjabi recruits to the army also grew rapidly under Zia, his regime began to be viewed as vastly inequitable in its favour towards Punjabi agriculturalists, businessmen, bureaucrats and soldiers (Noman 1989). His pro-Punjab policymaking exacer-bated existing resentment from other states towards Punjabis and against the central government. Zia's economic policies were deeply unpopular with the Muhajir business community, and opposition against these policies, and Zia's leadership more broadly, steadily grew among this group (Noman 1989), leading to increasingly viru-lent demands for a change in government.

Appeasing Big Business and Undermining the 'Established Elite'

Pakistani politics underwent frequent political shifts after General Zia was killed in a plane crash in 1988. Between 1988 and 1999, civil-ian rule oscillated between the leadership of the Pakistan People's Party led by Benazir Bhutto and the Muslim League led by Nawaz Sharif. Throughout this time, overarching economic policy remained fairly consistent, despite largely cosmetic revisions to specific gov-ernment programmes and policies with each change in leadership. The economy fared badly under both governments, and, as a result of the frequent shifts between their regimes, GDP growth decelerated as manufacturing and agricultural production slowed, and massive fiscal debt emerged (Husain 2000).

Both leaders sought to create alliances between the two powerful business communities of Karachi and Punjab. Having strong family ties with the landed Sindhi elites, Benazir Bhutto sought to quickly secure the support of the Karachi business elite by enlisting Karachi busi-nessmen to frame the budget for her new administration (Candland 2007). She also established the Board of Investment (BOI) to manage and establish industrial policy guidelines, and insisted on chairing the Board herself (Candland 2007). The BOI increased new investment limits, streamlined the licensing regime, and provided a range of incen-tives and benefits to certain 'key industries' including engineering, fertilisers and the electronics industry – measures designed to benefit and appease both the Karachi and Punjabi industrial elite.

Coming from a large industrial family, Nawaz Sharif also implemented a broad range of generally pro-big business polices (Husain 2000, Dawn 2013). His economic policies focused on privatisation and deregulation in an effort to further simplify the license regime, facilitate easy access to credit and grant additional tax incentives to industrialists (Husain 2000). His popularity in his political stronghold of Punjab was further consolidated by the popularity of his brother, Shahbaz Sharif, a long-time Chief Minister of Punjab.[30] The Sharif family demonstrated a strong bias in favour of their voter stronghold in Punjab as evidenced by the prioritisation of large infrastructure development projects in Lahore and across the province at the expense of development in other parts of the country.

By 2001, the relationship between Muhajir and Punjabi elites had settled into an accommodation under the clear dominance of Punjabi business, bureaucratic, political and military power. When General Musharraf assumed leadership of the country by military coup d'état the same year he was initially welcomed by many elites for his apparent support for Westernisation and socio-cultural liberalism. Some have even argued that the nation's liberal elite was willing to support Musharraf's brand of 'liberalism', where their lifestyles were protected, at the cost of democracy' (Zaidi 2007, 4). Musharraf's regime was further fortified by high levels of support and economic backing from both the United States government and a number of other Western governments (Ahmed and Stephan 2010).

However, it quickly became apparent that Musharraf actively sought to diminish the power of the old elite in myriad ways. First, he sought to diminish the established landowning political class through direct attacks on their political capabilities. In the first election after his coup d'état in 2002 he prevented many secular politicians from running and rigged the election in favour of pro-military politicians and parties. Secondly, he implemented a new law requiring all politicians to hold a university degree to run for elected office, a policy designed to remove most of the nation's established politicians. What he had not expected was that these dynastic families would respond by shifting their loyal rural constituent bases directly to their young university educated sons and nephews. The move disqualified a generation of politicians but Musharraf was entirely unsuccessful in his attempt to dislodge dynastic politics (Cheema et al 2013, 5).

Though Musharraf sought to weaken much of the political class, he recognised that he needed the support of their constituencies and sought to tie the success of some of the most politically powerful families to his own. In this he was partially successful. A significant number of established and opportunistic politicians defected from their own parties to join Musharraf's newly formed Pakistan Muslim League-Quaid (PML-Q), an outcome reflecting the opportunism engrained in remaining successful in Pakistani politics and business. Those families who refused to join his party were targeted on corruption or other criminal charges and arrested, and many had their assets confiscated (Jaffrelot 2015, 345). The attacks also hurt many major business families involved in politics, as is discussed in greater detail in Chapter Six.

Musharraf's relationship with the major business families not involved in politics was significantly less turbulent. Throughout his leadership the economy grew by almost 50 per cent and the per capita income of the population increased by nearly 25 per cent (Dawn 2007). Large industrialists and investors generated high profits: Real estate investment, in particular, flourished, rapidly creating upward economic mobility for those with real estate expertise and the close military relations required to secure preferential access to subsidised land-holdings. Musharraf promoted Pakistan as an attractive location for foreign investment, highlighting the period of relative stability and security his government had been able to ensure in both diplomatic and business circles. Consequently, he was widely popular with the business elite. Further, though he came down hard on corruption, he made no serious efforts to increase elite taxation, instead relying on foreign aid and loans to finance the regime (Husain 2015). The working class, however, continued to be exploited in aid of greater elite profit making: The profits of the business elite were further aided by the maintenance of consistently low workers' wages (Dawn 2007).

However, Musharraf also sought to replace the dominance of certain old elites with a new elite class comprised of military personnel and those with close personal military ties. He set about transforming the senior ranks of the military into a reconstituted elite political class by reinforcing the economic privileges of military personnel. Each of the previous military dictators had begun a process of allocating privilege to military personnel, but Musharraf significantly enhanced these privileges: He increased the land allotments to active and retired officers to reward them for their service and placed a large number of military personnel in senior bureaucratic posts, in an attempt to 'renew' the political class with military staff (Jaffrelot 2015, 344). In 2008, after attacking the judiciary, suspending the constitution and imposing a state of emergency, fearing impeachment, Musharraf resigned.

From 2008, under the short-lived leadership of several Prime Ministers, the economy again faltered, entering into periods of stagflation, until Nawaz Sharif began his third term in 2013. From 2013 until his defeat by Imran Khan in the General Elections of 2018, Sharif advanced the interests of the business community, and relations between the civilian regime and the military steadily worsened.

Sharif improved the electricity supply to major industry, offered massive tax cuts to large companies, improved the investment climate by increasing security crackdowns on militant and terrorist groups operating in the country, entered into several major transportation infrastructure projects in Punjab and the Islamabad Capital Territory, and negotiated major Chinese investment. The business environment fostered during this period improved dramatically as a result of these partnerships and investment, and the economy grew at a steady 5 per cent per year during Sharif's last term. To date, the flagship programme of this Chinese investment is the Chinese–Pakistan Economic Corridor (CPEC), valued at over US $ 62 billion. The plan is intended to rapidly modernise Pakistani infrastructure and strengthen its economy through the construction of modern transportation networks, numerous energy projects and special economic zones, and is likely to involve Chinese enterprises infiltrating all areas of Pakistan's economy.

Sharif's term also resulted in a serious tension between the civilian regime and the military, as Sharif asserted himself on foreign policy and national security, traditionally the domain of the military. Among other shifts in policy, Sharif demonstrated a softening towards India and a willingness to engage in trade negotiations which would likely have resulted in huge economic benefits for Pakistan. The Supreme Court's investigation and indictment of Nawaz Sharif on corruption charges in 2017 is widely believed to have been orchestrated by the military as punishment for overstepping into the remit of the military and attempting to undermine their traditionally anti-India policy.

The high spending involved in developing transportation infrastructure has improved the quality of life for many Pakistanis in urban Punjab and the Islamabad Capital Territory, continuing a long pattern of uneven national development that has entrenched Punjab's advantages over the Khyber Pakhtunkhwa, Sindh and Balochistan provinces, in turn fuelling the nation's ethnic tensions. It also created an enormous fiscal deficit and foreign debt burden. The new Prime Minister, Imran Khan, has inherited this debt, and he may be forced to accept a massive IMF bailout with strict pre-conditions and constraints on both the economy and the state at large. The alternative is a continued reliance on the Chinese, and additional Chinese loans, but many Pakistanis are also worried about the looming prospect of Chinese neo-colonialism.

Consolidating the Elite Dominated State

The inequality embedded in Pakistan's political and economic structure has been widely noted in the scholarship on Pakistan. The economist Ishrat Husain (2000) aptly described the conundrum many economists and political scientists have sought to understand or address when he described an elite-dominated and exploitative economic and state structure that replicated itself despite seemingly radical shifts in political leadership,

> the forms of government – democratic, nominated, directly or indirectly elected, dictatorial – did not matter. Nor did the professed ideological inclinations of the government in power – liberal, conservative, Islamic, leftist . . . The same constellation of landlords, industrialists, traders, politicians, military and civil bureaucrats, and some co-opted members of the religious oligarchy and professional and intellectual groups dominated the scene under every single government . . . The stranglehold of this elite group, accounting for less than 1 per cent of the population, on the affairs of the state has remained unscathed. (Husain 2000, pxiii–xiv)

Successive governments have attempted to document the informal economy and implement tax reforms that would eliminate widespread tax evasion among the elite. However, opposition among the elite, particularly industrialists and agriculturalists who had the most to lose from tax reforms, impeded all meaningful implementation. The tax code has remained, in the words of a prominent economic analyst, 'moth eaten, riddled through with exemptions' with the 'tax bureaucracy . . . as uninterested in pursuing documentation and implementing a transparent sales tax as it ever was' (Husain 2015).

Pakistan's separate ruling classes, representing business, military, bureaucratic and political interests, have undergone cycles of competition, conflict and cooperation throughout the nation's history. Changes of government and subsequently policy have alternately destroyed and resurrected elite business prospects. Throughout these tumultuous years, a small group of families has continued to retain their position as a business elite despite fluctuating attacks from bureaucratic, military and popular constituents.

Notes

1. Actual name used with permission.
2. Other scholars have noted that these traders and merchants were primarily Hindus and Jains (cf. Roy 2016), though as accounts like Salman's confirm, Muslims were not entirely absent.
3. The ancestors of this group had risen to prominence as a result of the land grants and benefits provided under the Mughal empire from the sixteenth and eighteenth centuries. British colonisation in the nineteenth century removed much of this power and autonomy and endangered the privileged position of this group (Jaffrelot 2015, 9).
4. Actual name. This information is drawn from already published secondary sources.
5. The migration experience of the business and political elite to Pakistan was starkly different to that of the majority of the migrant population. The chaos, violence and carnage of Partition created dramatic shifts in fortune for many Muslims in the middle and lower classes. Certain Hindu and Parsi families of Lahore, for instance, were reported to have sold their lands to Muslim families for a fraction of their true value in response to widespread rumours that land vouchers would not be honoured in the new states, or that non-Muslim landholdings would simply be confiscated without regard for legal ownership. The converse was also reported to have occurred with Muslims in India selling their lands well below cost before fleeing to Pakistan in a significantly worse financial position.
6. There is very little scholarship on this process of compensatory land claims in Pakistan, however scholarship on the claims of the Hindu elite who had migrated from Lahore to Delhi provides important insights into the migration experience of elite individuals during Partition.
7. See Kugelman 2103.
8. Actual name.
9. The Isaphani's relocated from Calcutta to Chittagong in East Pakistan in 1947 at Jinnah's urging. ISAPHANI. 2013. Available: http://www.ispahanibd.com/about-us/ [accessed 15 June 2015].
10. Actual name.
11. Jinnah's relationship with Muhammadali Habib, founder of Habib Bank, was reportedly so close, that the Habib family who had been Khoja Ismaili followers of the Aga Khan later converted to Isnasheri Shia Islam, of which Jinnah was a follower, and became key figures in the Khoja Isnasheri community.
12. Actual name.
13. In contrast to the enormous opportunities Muhajirs gained for economic accumulation and the assumption of political leadership, the experience of the indigenous elites of the areas that became Pakistan was one of loss. Partition with India caused huge dissatisfaction among the strong and fiercely independent local Muslim leaders of Sindh, the North West Frontier Province (NWFP) and Balochistan. The local leaders of these provinces had always exercised strong control in their area, largely unimpeded by British colonialism; had separate cultures, languages and customs; and possessed a deep aversion to central control by the Punjabi dominated state staffed largely by bureaucrats and politicians from Northern India (Jalal 1985). These indigenous leaders found themselves marginalised in the apparatus of the new Pakistani state, excluded from major industry and expected to conform to the rules of a central national government they had not participated in creating.
14. PIFC was established as a public–private venture, with 51 per cent of shares owned by the government, and 49 per cent by private investors, bankers and insurance companies. Though initially established to lend only to public companies listed on the stock

market, its lending mandate was significantly expanded in 1952 to include private industry.

15. Amjad identifies these seven as Adamjee, Dawood, Saigol, Valika, Colony, Fancy and Bawany. (The names are given in a descending order according to net assets owned). The next nine industrial groups i.e. with assets more than Rs. 50 but less than Rs. 100 million controlled 13.8 per cent of assets and 9.1 per cent of sales of the private corporate sector. He estimates the following twelve houses to be: Fateh, Crescent, Isphani, Beco, Wazir Ali, Hussain, Amins, Nishat, Karim, Habib, Hyesons and Hoti'. ibid. (Amjad 1982).

16. Cited in Hull 2014, 40.

17. The items imported on license declined from 90.3 per cent of total imports in 1960/61 to 39.5 per cent by 1964/65 (Amjad 1982).

18. In Punjab, the Qizalbash, Noon, Qureshi and Abbasi families set up industries for the first time, and in Sindh the Talpur, Soomro and Jatois families entered industry (Amjad 1976).

19. As India enhanced its defence capabilities between 1958 and 1973, Pakistan allocated increasingly large amounts of the national budget to counter the presumed threat (Looney 2004). India and Pakistan went to war in 1965, and as punishment, foreign aid was sharply curtailed (Khan 1999).

20. Actual names.

21. 'Three houses (Adamjee, Isphani and Amin) accounted for 69.1 per cent of total jute production with Adamjee holding the dominant position with 48.9 per cent . . . In East Pakistan, the production of the six houses were concentrated in the jute industry and accounted for 81.5 per cent of the total. Paper contributed 14 per cent and cotton textiles and shipping 3 and 2 per cent respectively' (Amjad 1976).

22. Actual Names.

23. The Saigol, Valika and Colony Groups had no investment in East Pakistan.

24. Bhutto came from an elite Sindhi family: his father was a powerful government official in the Indian princely state of Junagadh, and his family had thrived under the British colonial regime.

25. Houses which moved up the ranking were Hoti (from eighth to fourth), Bawany (from eighteenth to eighth), Hussein (from thirteenth to ninth) and Nishat (from twentieth to fourteenth position). Gul Ahmad, Arag, Rahimtoola, Noon, Shahnawaz and Monnoo moved into the top twenty after nationalisation (Amjad 1976).

26. Defence spending increased on average by 9 per cent per annum during 1977–1988 while development spending rose 3 per cent per annum. Over the decade of the 1980s defence spending averaged 6.5 per cent of GDP (Burki 1988).

27. Nawaz Sharif served as Prime Minister from 1990–1993, again from 1997–1999 and most recently from 2013–2018.

28. In March 1988, the planning minister declared that 'imposing an agricultural income tax is a test of our government's credibility . . . we cannot have a just or efficient tax system as long as we have one class in society which is exempted from paying tax' (Noman 1989).

29. Prior to this, Karachi Muhajirs had dominated the nation's political, economic and military institutions despite their representing only 8 per cent of the total population.

30. Shahbaz Sharif was Chief Minister (CM) of Punjab 1997–1999, and again 2008–present (with a brief period standing down when Najam Sethi was the caretaker CM in 2013).

– Chapter 3 –

OLD MONEY, NEW MONEY

One of the businessmen I came to know well, Raheel Mukhtar, differed from most of the elites included in this study in that he did not meet the economic threshold I had set for inclusion in my research. His business, Mukhtar Steel Foundry, generated half of the minimum revenue earned by the other business and political families included in this study. Instead of earning over $100 million in revenue per year as the other elites included in this study had done, his company earned just $50 million per year. The Mukhtars were, however, rapidly moving into the ranks of the nation's elite. They exported steel to companies in the USA, Brazil, Central America, Europe, Africa and South East Asia, and their revenue – and profits – was rapidly increasing year on year.

Unlike many of the Established Elites I came to know, Raheel was deeply religious and conservative. His family engaged in major international business, partnership and trade in accordance with Islamic banking and finance principles, meaning they did not borrow money, engage in financial speculation, or enter into transactions of debt and interest. Having been made aware of his religiosity by our mutual acquaintance, I had arrived for our interview in a simply embroidered traditional black shalwar kameez, with a matching *dupatta* modestly draped across my chest. With hand to his heart, and a greeting of 'As-Salaam-Alaikum', he immediately complimented the modesty of my outfit. Sitting on the plain couch of his small and minimalist office, decorated with several framed prayers in Arabic calligraphy, he recounted his family narrative in the almost sing-song tone of a well-worn fairy tale,

Our family is very, very conservative. Borrowing is prohibited in the family business. No one has stakes outside the family business. All our family members have separate homes, but they are all within the same housing compound . . . Deep, deep love keeps us together. We do not call each other cousins. We call each other brothers. Part of the reason that we have all stayed together is that the daughters of my paternal grandfather all married the sons of my maternal grandfather.[1]

Our business was established in 1880 by two brothers, Imran and Raza. When they were both little boys, they apprenticed with a man who passed away when the boys were only thirteen years old. He left behind the tiny shop in which the boys had worked with him. The boys settled with their employer's widow, and eventually they became the owners of the shop. Then they invested and became steel foundry men.

In the early 1900s, the now grown up boys bought a piece of land. The 1930s were full of troubles and our family business had troubles too. Small and medium businesses were struggling. In the late 1930s the brothers split the business, but both kept working in steel. Then came the new Pakistan, with new horizons, and new opportunities. A highly respected Lahori businessman, close friends with our family, advised us to set up business in Karachi. So, three of the six Mukhtar brothers went to Karachi to set up factories, and the other three stayed in Lahore. Both were very successful. The businessman also convinced the elders in our family to send the boys to Aitchison [the most prestigious boys' school in Pakistan]. We began Aitchison in 1962. But we were misfits. Among 100 sons of chieftains, there were only two or three students, like us, coming from the masses.

Today, ninety per cent of the Aitchisonians who now sit in Parliament are known to me personally. The majority of Pakistan's sugar factory owners are Aitchison alumni, and as a result, they are also our customers. But we have retained our values. We are middle class even to this day – though all our boys go to Aitchison.

Raheel's family narrative is informative in regard to class dynamics on three counts. Firstly, Raheel's unselfconscious depiction of his family as 'middle class' reflected the difference in values and lifestyles he observed between his own family and other members of the elite, despite their rapid ascension into the economic 1%. Secondly, his family narrative highlights that the decision of the elders in his family to send both him, and later, his own sons and nephews to Aitchison College, was a pivotal moment in the family's class trajectory. His acknowledgement of the fundamental role Aitchison College played in the network his family had developed with the nation's sugar producers (a highly lucrative and politicised industry on account of the ability of sugar factory owners to mobilise large voter blocs as major local employers), and with the nation's parliamentarians demonstrates the critical role of a few select forums in providing access to – and gatekeeping – the nation's economic and political decisionmaking spaces. Despite seeing his family as 'outcasts' in the Aitchison school environment, he recognised the critical importance of developing and maintaining close ties with its student body and alumni – the nation's most economically and politically influential.

Schooling an Elite

Aitchison College was inaugurated by the British in 1886 as the Punjab Chief's College with the explicit purpose of transforming the children of Punjab's nobility into loyal British subjects and effective colonial administrators. By the time independence from the British was achieved in 1947, English colonial culture, and its impression of exclusivity and 'eliteness', had been institutionalised and engrained in elite colonial Indian society. When the British left, the Pakistani elite who had risen to economic prominence under the colonial regime adopted and occupied many of both the physical and ideological spaces the British left behind, and British schools and clubs functioned with a high degree of continuity. Despite having been excluded and marginalised under the colonial regime[2] the appropriation of their institutions by elite Pakistanis involved very little adaptation of the outward symbols or structures of British power and high culture with which they were imbued. Rather, the Established Elite who took over the leadership and membership of British clubs, and sent their children to the formerly British schools, actively sought to maintain a high level of both symbolic and operational continuity within these institutions.

Britain's occupation and domination over the peoples of undivided India brought with it specific notions of high culture and a set of exclusive institutions designed to keep Indians out, and to protect and preserve appropriate forms of British high culture. These institutions catered, firstly, to the desire of many colonisers to separate themselves from Indian society,[3] as evidenced by the carefully segregated realm of the British club,[4] and secondly, the need to create a class of Indians who would help the British expand and govern their empire, as exemplified in the British-run schools established for the Indian elite class (Rahman 2012).

The overtly racist desire of the British to culturally dominate upper class Indians, was captured succinctly by British historian and politician, Thomas Babington Macaulay[5] in his 1835 summation of the role elite Indians were expected to play within British colonial society,

> We must at present do our best to form a class who may be interpreters between us and the millions whom we govern; a class of persons, Indian in blood and colour, but English in taste, in opinions, in morals and intellect.

The domination and subjugation that English colonisation exerted on Indian society also did not exclude the Indian upper classes, nobility, royalty, or business moguls. While colonisation involved explicit coercion against the Indian masses, its oppression often took subtler forms of symbolic violence[6] when levied against the Indian elite. Elite Indians were to serve as an intermediary class, representing and administering British interests, whilst shielding the British rulers from the majority of the population, and the Indian cultures they represented. Elite Indians associated with the British regime were often provided with land, cash payments and the bestowal of official titles to guarantee their support for the colonial regime through their leadership in local forums. These inducements could not, however, fully disguise the transition of many of these leaders into largely powerless agents of the British and implementers of their colonial objectives. Colonisation stripped the nation's rulers, professionals and upper castes of their autonomy, imposed limitations on their ability to control the Indian lower classes, and coerced these elites into becoming subjects of the British empire, subject to its laws and to the edicts of its administrators. Elites were simultaneously materially rewarded and politically disempowered. They were excluded from decision-making roles but induced to support and implement the wishes of the rulers on whose funds they were made to rely.

Over time, the types of 'distinction' (Bourdieu 1984) favoured by the British, along with many of their dispositions, became part of the lived experience and culture of the Indian elite. These colonised subjects became a 'newly emergent, translocally produced and oriented elite'.[7] They were not simply engaging in what Homi Bhabha (1984) has described as 'mimicry' by imitating English lifestyles, rather, the lifestyle was 'in one sense fully their own already, part of their habitus'.[8] In the act of performing the rituals and mannerisms of the colonial British upper classes, the Pakistani elite appropriated a version of Englishness that differed from its original form. Former colonial subjects assumed the places that their colonisers had left behind, feeling themselves to be, in the words of Bhabha

(130), 'almost the same but not white', and seeking to eliminate the status differential 'between being English and being Anglicised'. In the process, the colonised elite reinvented the culture they had appropriated, exaggerating certain aspects and entirely removing others. They created what Bhabha (131) termed a 'fetishised colonial culture', one that sought to redress the status differential that existed under colonisation by appropriating the institutions and styles of the group that had dominated them.

The New Lords

Like all social classes, however, the Pakistani elite continues to evolve, with new groups of wealthy emerging to contest the upper echelons of political power, and cultural authority. The Pakistani elite define 'Old' and 'New Money' in ways that do not necessarily correlate with the *length* of time a family has held their wealth. As each new privileged group emerged in association with various civilian and military regimes, the Established Elites actively attempted to exclude prospective competitors in business and other fields from the informal social forums in which business and politics is largely conducted. The oldest and most prestigious elite families have served as gatekeepers of various elite institutions – private clubs; the school board of Pakistan's most exclusive boys' school, Aitchison College; exclusive parties; and as arbiters of appropriate and inappropriate marriage.[9] By gatekeeping these institutions, a small number of established families were able to ensure that those families not deemed suitable were denied entry to the social forums where decisions were made and resources allocated – regardless of their level of wealth.

Many of the families who have risen to prominence in these political and economic shifts have come to be known by the pejorative 'Navay Raje'[10] meaning literally 'new lords'. The terms 'Navay Raje' and 'New Money', are often also paired with the term, 'paindoo', an Urdu term for 'villager', connoting a lack of sophistication. The more recently a family acquired its wealth, the more negative the association of the Established Elite, and the more critical the descriptors used to explain their rapid rise to wealth. The terms Navay Raje, paindoo and New Money are most often applied to families who break one of two taboos: the taboo against acquiring money rapidly; and that of spending money and displaying wealth in an ostentatious manner. Both of these social rules replicate the norms dictating class structure in colonial Britain: a prohibition against attempting to rise above one's station (unless undertaken discreetly and cross-generationally); distaste for ostentation; and an aversion to those who have not acquired the full suite of elite dispositions. 'Old' or 'Established Elite' families are widely associated with the category of *khandani*, which though it literally means 'of family', is used to imply respectability, and indicates a family has origins as senior government officials in colonial India or earlier claims to state patronage – some, as with the business families noted in Chapter One, also had ties to the independence movement.[11] As noted by Maqsood (2017), these ties enabled certain elite families to associate themselves with progressivism in the subcontinent, and to present themselves as aligned with a largely liberal worldview. Families belonging to the khandani Established Elite also tend to associate education with social refinement (Maqsood 2017), to place a high value on ensuring the education of their members, and to favourably compare themselves to 'paindoo' or New Money families who did not hold comparable levels of liberal education.

The economic rise of new groups, who embody some but not all of the characteristics associated with the 'Old Elite', have made these categories particularly nebulous, as the Mukhtar's more gradual ascent into the elite classes demonstrates. A split emerged largely between families who acquired their wealth prior to, or in the first few decades of the new Pakistani state, the New Money families who transitioned from the middle classes into the uppermost tier of wealth from the 1980s, and a slowly emerging third category of upwardly mobile middle-class families who are now achieving partial – and at times, almost complete – integration with the Established Elite through their adherence to Established Elite educational values and social norms.[12] As Navay Raje elites obtained influential roles in business, politics and the military, the Established Elite began to employ screening techniques that encouraged prospective new entrants to absorb, or perform, as many of the class attributes of the Established Elite as possible through rigorous processes of socialisation in schools and social clubs. The patterns of upward mobility experienced by these new families – both those who sought to fully adapt to the 'old elite' lifestyle, and those like the Mukhtars who have retained their middle-class adherence to religion and conservative social values, are instructive in understanding how change takes place among the elite class, and further, how tensions characterise the relationship between 'new' and 'old' elite families.[13]

Munir, an established Karachi elite, had transitioned from the middle classes into the elite in the early 1950s in the first stages of Pakistani industrialisation, benefiting from the subsidies, tax exemptions and interest-free loans provided by the state to the Muslim trader class who had immigrated at Partition. His family was now firmly positioned among the ranks of the Established Elite. His views on the intra-elite class divide exemplified a common attitude among the Established Elite to New Money groups,

> The difference between Old Money and New Money is this: The Old Money have culture, depth, human characteristics. They work hard; they value education. The New Money are into fast-cars, fancy things, ostentatious displays and all that is instant.

Munir's statement embodies a number of contradictory sentiments typical of the attitudes of the Established Elite to those they designate as New Money. He defines his own class as having the attributes Bourdieu (2013) describes as 'distinction': 'culture', complexity, values, work ethic and (presumably the best of) human characteristics, whereas the New Money are defined by their lack of subtlety, their inability or unwillingness to behave according to norms of reserve, refinement and understated elegance required of those from the established families. Nowhere does he refer to the specific period in which these families acquired their money, but he specifically locates their values as being focused on the 'instant', juxtaposing the hard work of his own social grouping with the instant gratification of these new entrants. Established Elites often recounted stories of the lack of ethics evident in the behaviours of Navay Raje elites in business, deriding the scale of their bribery, or their lack of distinction. These failings were evident, they argued, in a large array of attributed behaviours, from ogling women, to speaking English with a regional accent, or to being too religiously conservative.

What Munir objected to most in relation to the families he saw as New Money was their patterns of expenditure, and what he presumed to be their lack of education. The conspicuous consumption he associated with New Money was to him and to the Old Money society to which he belonged, distasteful, garish and grounds for exclusion from elite society. To Munir and others from his background, the expenditure patterns of New Money families signified much more than bad taste: they served as a proxy for a whole range of values, attitudes, morals and personal histories at odds with the inherited wealth and mannerisms of established families. 'New' and 'old' in this context were indicators of social positioning and a richly nuanced assessment of the social positioning of each family.

Some of Pakistan's most powerful political families today have emerged from the middle class, but further investigation reveals strong family or marital ties with the military, bureaucracy, or the Established Elite (as evident in some of the marital alliances explored in the next chapter). Pakistan's most successful real estate mogul, Malik Riaz, for instance, is famous for his lower middle-class background, and his dramatic rise into the economic elite, largely on account of his entrepreneurial prowess. But closer inspection reveals family connections with senior military leadership that it appears he was able to leverage to acquire large portions of undeveloped land at very low prices. He has been described in the media as a 'mythological creature' who 'travels in his private jet, lives in seven-star mansions, parks a Bentley in his porch and drives with a fleet of SUVs with a battalion of armed private commandoes that should match the prime minister's protocol' and further, as 'the most powerful person in Pakistan' (Mateen 2013). Malik Riaz is reputedly the fourth highest taxpayer in Pakistan and possibly the wealthiest. He is also one of the most controversial figures among the economic elite. Riaz has openly admitted to bribing members of the military, the Inter-Services Intelligence agency (ISI), politicians and the bureaucracy (Reuters 2016), and rumours regarding his exceptional and rapid ascension to becoming the wealthiest man in Pakistan abound. Growing up in a middle-class family who had fallen on hard times, working as a low-level clerk, and transitioning to one of the wealthiest businessmen in Pakistan, he is closely associated with the Navay Raje.

More interesting than 'the truth' of Riaz's rise are the varied responses he generates among Established families compared with families in the Navay Raje. Members of the Established Elite often described him as the antithesis of the elite gentleman, recounted tales of his corruption and attributed his rise from economic obscurity to extreme wealth to his underhanded relationship with the military. From many others in the elite, however, particularly among those whose own wealth had emerged post-1978, I heard admiration for his enormous charitable work across the country, and strikingly, for his ability to have propelled himself from being born into the lower classes to becoming one of the richest men in Pakistan.

Perhaps more typical among this group of new elites, is the class trajectory of the Sharif family, and specifically of Nawaz Sharif,[14] the former Prime Minister, in exemplifying shifting class boundaries. Sharif came from a middle-class Kashmiri–Punjabi family, who owned a small factory in Amritsar prior to independence. It is reputed that one of his uncles worked in a steel furnace. At partition, Nawaz Sharif's father, Muhammad Sharif, immigrated the 200 kilometres from Jati Umra near Amritsar in the state of India, to Lahore. By the 1960s, the Sharif family owned a few medium-sized factories, including ice making facilities, and a water pump factory (Qureshi 2015). In 1969, Muhammad Sharif along with his six brothers, established the Ittefaq Group iron foundry. Nawaz Sharif was educated at Saint Anthony's High School and Government College in Lahore and received a law degree from Punjab University. Following his education, he entered Punjab provincial politics, joining the Punjab advisory district council. In 1976, when Prime Minister Zulfikar Ali Bhutto nationalised the steel industry, the Sharif family business empire, Ittefaq Group, was also nationalised and much of the family's emerging wealth was lost.

However, the family's fortunes shifted again with the change in government. When General Zia's military regime assumed control of the country in 1978, Sharif was appointed Finance Minister for Punjab. In 1985, he was appointed Chief Minister of Punjab (BBC 2013). In the same year, General Zia returned the family's iron foundry, earlier nationalised under Bhutto (Baker 2005), enabling the family to rebuild its fortune. During the 1980s as Sharif rose in seniority within Zia's regime, Ittefaq Group expanded from ownership of five mills to thirty businesses, including those in steel, sugar, paper and textiles earning annual revenues estimated at $400 million.

Nawaz Sharif's rise to power reflects the shifting face of the business elite in Pakistan, away from the established families with ties to the British, to a new group defined by more local and ethnically-based markers of distinction, and by close mutually-supportive relationships with the military. He is indicative of the shift among the nation's business elite to previously middle-class families who have risen into the top tier of the economic strata in only one or two generations. Though some Navay Raje elites have sought to attain the Anglicised forms of distinction still performed and cherished in the private clubs and schools of the Established Elite, Nawaz Sharif typifies the new group who are slowly discarding the English dispositions and indicators of status.

This intra-class division among the elite was most notable in my friendship with the Afridis. Though Abid Afridi possessed an extensive and powerful social network in his home province of KP, and among various divisions of the security and intelligence agencies, his ethnic background and relatively newer wealth prevented him from being welcomed into the socially-insular, Punjabi-dominated elite circles of Lahore. Having assumed control of the family business at 18, Abid had not attended university overseas like his younger brother and cousins, and when speaking English his accent and sentence construction were notably regional. Unlike the members of established Lahore, he was not a native English speaker. Neither was his grandfather a member of their social worlds. Consequently, despite his success in the corporate and business sectors, or even because of this success and the fact that he had economically surpassed most in those circles, he had not been welcomed into the forums in which Old Lahore socialised and conducted business. He had responded to this social exclusion in Lahore by embracing his Pakhtun identity even more strongly, dressing solely in *shalwar kameez* and *chappals* (sandals), growing his beard and loudly speaking Pashto in the city's most expensive restaurants whenever possible.

In contrast, his brother Kaleem, a popular and charming man in his thirties, derided the Established Elite and the social snubs he had experienced by embracing the ostentation Munir and other Established Elites attributed to New Money: he drove imported luxury vehicles – carefully selected as one of a kind in Pakistan, casually flicking his car keys to valets across Islamabad and Lahore, and by entertaining the attentions he attracted from Established Elite women. Showing me the flirtatious messages and photos he had received from Established Elite women on his mobile phone, he boasted that despite their pretensions, the women of these families – both married and unmarried – frequently pursued him. 'These women', he told me with a grin, 'talk and act one way in their own circles, but talk and act completely differently with me'. In telling me and others these stories, he disparaged the group of elites he felt to have rejected him through circulating a counter-critique of his own.

Their cousin, Shahzar, had been slightly more successful in penetrating the social circles of the Established Elite – though this too was possible only up to a point. Though also a member of the Navay Raje, the Afridis had called in a broad range of favours to ensure Shahzar was admitted to Aitchison College. He was, as a result, included in the younger generation of Aitchison alumni and their circle of female friends. Shahzar's girlfriend, Maryam (introduced in Chapter One) was from an established, old Lahori family, and a member of a highly educated and socially liberal crowd. She was sure that her parents must know of her relationship with Shahzar, but believed that they turned a blind eye, expecting her decision to date a 'New Money' Pakhtun to be a phase she was going through as she prepared to find a more suitable match for marriage. Though the Afridis were much wealthier than Maryam's family, and most of her social world, Shahzar and his cousins remained outsiders in established Lahore.

A Thoroughly English Vetting Process

Among many Established Elite groups, the possession of a form of 'high culture' is critical to obtain entry to the social forums in which the elite socialise, do business and determine marriage partners. Status and high culture are assessed and carefully policed by conformity to a very specific style of life, comportment and distinction which has long been intertwined with colonial-era British culture. In the act of performing the rituals and mannerisms of the colonial British upper classes, the Pakistani elite appropriated a version of Englishness that differed from its original form. Writing specifically on the Filipino elite, Johnson (2013, 185) describes the acquisition of colonial culture by colonised people as something that is,

> acquired and experienced as "second nature", not just because it is lived in and through the body ... [but as] something that had to be repeatedly and self-consciously claimed, an act of appropriation of that which is already one's own but [which] is not recognised as such by others.

Johnson's analysis captures the ambivalence of the colonial experience, whereby the colonised acquire the culture of the colonisers in a deep bodily way that is experienced as natural and yet is not recognised by the colonisers as being legitimately possessed or owned. In the process of being seen as Anglicised rather than English, the colonised Indian elite reinvented the culture they had appropriated. By the time independence from the British was achieved in 1947, English colonial culture, and its impression of exclusivity and 'eliteness', had been institutionalised and engrained in elite colonial Indian society.

Among the Established Elite in Pakistan today, most visibly for men this taste includes a European style of dress, seamless use of clearly enunciated English, private home art collections of nationally esteemed artists, and almost invariably a penchant for Scotch whiskey. This mimicry is particularly evident in the physical spaces of Established Elite private social clubs and schools, where clothing (and uniforms), architecture, landscaping, and consumption all replicate the style, taste, and ritual of upper and upper middle-class colonial Britain. The Established Elite has adopted many of the arte-facts and symbols of the very culture that had earlier oppressed and excluded them.

The Right Sort of Person

The Principal of Aitchison College, Shamim Khan,[15] sat in his waist-coat and trousers, shrewdly observing me from behind his large wooden desk in the school's colonial era buildings on a cool day in 2014. Already in his mid-70s, he had been called back to his post from retirement as a result of corruption allegations and in-fighting amongst the school's Board of Governors and the need to restore leadership in the interim,

> There is a trade-off between maintaining standards and keeping people out, or opening up the doors and reducing quality. There is a Moghul history here and it can't be replicated. We are balancing the needs of tradition and those of the 21st century. I do this ruthlessly. Studying English, Urdu and Shakespeare here gives you status. I am ruthless about the entrance exam and I personally select each student. We are the only school that has this much land and these facilities. And we take the intellectual best.
>
> We have 3,000 students now, but I intend to reduce it to 2,000. Each year thirteen students are admitted on full scholarship. Many of the current scholarship holders are what we could say are the "well-connected poor". The scholarships are intended for the intellectual best, but during the four-year gap in my tenure many were admitted as a result of their connections, rather than their academic excellence as intended!

Aitchison and other elite private schools are designed to provide students with a skill set not available within the public-school system. The elite private schools of Pakistan do not follow the national curriculum, teach the same subjects as children in English and American schools and follow a Western style of pedagogy involving more interactive classes with a greater focus on critical analysis than the rote learning style followed in most of Pakistan's publicly-funded schools (Naviwala 2016). The school is particularly important in socialising students in gentlemanly behaviour modelled on largely colonial era manners, etiquette, and customs. It teaches not only academic subjects, but in the traditional English public-school tradition, includes an equal focus on academics, sport, and extra-curricular activities like drama, with the goal of shaping an individual to be as capable of effortlessly attending a formal dinner as succeeding in business or politics.

In addition to the international curricula, students are provided with superior resources, facilities and teaching staff, access to which ensures the skills they acquire are superior to those of the vast majority of the population without this access. The acquisition of this superior level of education and extensive social and professional network ensures the superior ability of its alumni to hold political office, to own and manage large domestic and multi-national corporations, and to serve at the highest levels of the judiciary, because it ensures that its graduates acquire the specific skills required to excel in these senior posts.

The prestige of Aitchison College,[16] and the efforts of Pakistan's elite families to ensure the attendance of their sons at the school, goes right to the heart of elite identity in Pakistan. Among the elite businessmen and political leaders included in my research, as many as 80 per cent had been educated at Aitchison.[17] Many of the most senior posts in Pakistani government and politics are also held by Aitchison alumni. Consequently, though members of the elite also attend a handful of other schools, the importance of the school and its alumni network among the most powerful members of Pakistani society means that the changes taking place in Aitchison serve as a powerful barometer of the changes taking place among Pakistan's elite, and of how emic understandings of what it is to be 'elite' in Pakistan are slowly changing in tandem with major demographic shifts taking place within a section of the elite class. The inclusion of families like the Afridis and the Mukhtars in the College has made the school a site of elite class tension.

The role of Aitchison and similar Established Elite institutions as contested vanguards of elite heritage and identity was starkly evident in one instance that emerged during my fieldwork in Pakistan in 2014. The Chief Minister of Punjab, Shahbaz Sharif, brother to former Prime Minister, Nawaz Sharif, and a member of the post-independence, newer elite, appointed a new Principal to Aitchison College. His explicitly stated aim was to eliminate Aitchison's historical nepotism towards admitting the children of established 'Old Money' families over those who performed competitively in the admissions exam. In doing so, Sharif had attempted to replace dynastic qualifications with a system more conducive to the admission of families with more recently acquired wealth. The school Board of Governors, comprised of Aitchison alumni from Pakistan's most established and prestigious elite families, responded by removing the new Principal. In reaction, the High Court of Lahore, itself an upper middle-class domain, instructed the school Board to reinstate the removed Principal

(Express Tribune 2014; Dawn 2014; Daily Pakistan 2015). The battle that took place between the Board of Governors (the old guard of Lahori society), the Chief Minister (a member of the new class of elite), and the High Court (the domain of upper middle class professionals), attests to the symbolic importance of the school as the training ground for the nation's future political and economic leadership.

Seeking Acceptance at the Private Club

Beyond the inculcation of class values imparted by schooling, most among the elite class attend one or more elite social club. These clubs serve as critical forums for inter-elite networking, business deals, and political manoeuvring. Admission to the Established Elite social forums of Lahore, Karachi, or Islamabad requires vetting and an invitation from an insider. Access to these elite events requires that a person have not only economic capital, but also a sufficient degree of what Bourdieu[18] terms 'social and cultural capital'. This encompasses the people one knows and is publicly recognised by; their family history and current standing; and the social assets that promote social mobility – education, intellect, dress and mannerisms, among others. In this sense, the perceived quality of the individual and of the individuals he or she knows and has access to becomes a resource to be utilised to access those with influence or those in a position to offer opportunities.

I had met Aliya, a true Established Elite insider in Lahori society, following an interview with her father, a highly successful clothing retailer positioned within the top thirty firms on the Karachi Stock Exchange. He had obligingly responded to my interview questions and then suggested I would enjoy meeting his daughter, a woman of my own age, who he suggested may be able to give me some insight into the domestic life of a large business family. It was a kind gesture, and deeply appreciated as Aliya became one of only a few female friends I made in Lahore in those first six months, surrounded as I was by an almost entirely male informant group. Aliya neatly summarised the importance of private social clubs as a bastion of Established Elite gatekeeping, in her explanation of the difference between various elite private clubs, and their membership. She explained the difference in the Lahore club scene as follows,

> Gymkhana has a huge membership, doled out to all the civil servants based in Lahore, and access for all the visiting ones. So, not the nicest group of people:

full of corruption, politics and cheating. It's prestigious because of its facilities (fantastic golf course, great tennis courts, swimming etc.) and its history.

Punjab club is far more discreet and selective: Only the old families of Lahore. I think it has a 1,000 person [and their nuclear family] membership at any given time. Uber liberal crowd; Old Money.

Royal Palm opened up as the option for New Money with no social connections. Application for membership is a fee of Rs 2,500,000 [USD 25,000].[19] No one in my family can afford that, or is *willing* to afford it, rather. So naturally you will get your rough diamonds there, with their Filipina maids, bodyguards, and luxury cars.

As Aliya's characterisation of the Royal Palm makes clear, certain venues, though known for their exorbitant fees and the exclusivity such a fee structure engenders, are viewed by many among the Established Elite as garish. It further revealed her distaste for those in government, and her association of government workers with corruption and cheating (see Maqsood 2017). As most among the Navay Raje cannot gain admittance to the oldest clubs of the Established Elite, many chose to join their own set of clubs. As a result, the number of private clubs catering to the demands of newly wealthy families in Pakistan have proliferated in recent years. While the amenities at these newer clubs are often better, the relationships and networks which serve as the primary value of club membership in each venue, are often considerably more circumscribed: they facilitate opportunities to network among the nation's wealthiest New Money families, but generally fail to provide opportunities to meet with Established Elite political families, or with the uppermost professional managers of the major multinational corporations who are permitted corporate memberships at the Sind Club or Boat Club.

The importance of the older clubs in assessing – and verifying – Established Elite credentials was explained to me by the President of the Boat Club, one of the oldest elite clubs in Karachi. He detailed the characteristics he and the selection committee use to assess the applications of potential new members,

The most important factor in our admissions process is family background. We create a shortlist based on academic, social and business background. Reputation is also important, as are more subtle things like body language and mannerisms. Someone on the committee always knows the person who is applying so it is very easy to check. We incorporate the opinion of all committee members. Then the shortlist is looked at by the President, Vice President, and one other member, and those who are approved are invited to an informal meeting with each of the three of us for around thirty minutes. About ninety per cent of candidates wear a suit and tie in these meetings. Then there is a formal meeting held at 7pm and the candidates will wear a full dinner suit. The informal meeting will include the applicant's spouse. Lady members can be admitted, but only if they are single. If married, the woman's membership is cancelled, but her husband's application will be fast-tracked. Family membership for the wives and daughters of members continues throughout the year. But new members will only be admitted once every three years. When the membership period is open, I take a very large number of phone calls!

From those in government we accept the most senior government positions, those at grade 21 or 22. For business people we look very closely at their backgrounds. We take members from the top tier banks. Corporate membership costs 2.5 million rupees per year and is valid for ten years. It is still very selective. We only admit the number one or number two from each of these firms. The applicant will send the company corporate profile as well as the individual's profile. They need to be proposed by someone and supported by a second person.

All the networking people do here is to get social status. It means a lot. And when you're in trouble you need friends in the right places. The Club was established in 1910 by the British, and the old members are highly regarded. It is a good place to hob-nob.

There are many families who become rich in just ten, twenty, thirty years. It's not wealth they inherited, but money they got through smuggling and narcotics. Now they want respectability. They acquire this through getting membership at clubs or being seen in posh hotels. Some clubs don't care as much about a person's background. It costs 1.5 to 2 million rupees for entrance into some clubs (approximately $20K). These kinds of clubs have easy membership rules. The Karachi Gymkhana used to be easy to get into. Royale Rodale and many others are still easy. The admissions committees there will not go into social, academic, or ancestral background. All they like to see is if you will default on your bills. Here the fee is 1 million rupees. We will raise this soon to 1.5 million rupees. The Sind Club is already 1.5 million, maybe 1.7. Both are very selective clubs. Four hundred people applied when we last opened admission. Ninety made it to the short list, and sixty were accepted.

The President's explanation of the club assessment process highlights the critical nature of club exclusivity: membership at the Boat Club and the equally prestigious Sind Club convey status precisely because it is so difficult to obtain membership. Pervez, a Karachi businessman and third generation member of the Sind Club's selection committee, explained to me the criteria he personally used to assess whether applicants were the 'right sort of person',

> We try to distinguish Sind Club membership from money. It's more about being the right sort of person. A good measure of admission criteria is to be found in relation to the club pool. The question I ask myself about a possible future member is: 'Would I be comfortable having that person standing by the pool if my wife was sitting or swimming in a bathing suit?'

Here gender relations – and specifically the manner in which a man interacts with, around, and towards an elite woman – becomes a representative symbol for 'being the right sort of person' and for the whole array of values, attitudes, and behaviours demanded of club members. Pervez was implying that the wrong sort of man, someone with more recently acquired wealth, or from the presumably more conservative classes below, would have been likely to behave in a way that would have made him or his wife uncomfortable, either by gawking, or by acting shocked and perturbed at her level of exposure. Given the rarity with which women's bodies are seen in broader Pakistani society without voluminous layers of cloth, his statement implies that the inclination and ability not to stare at a largely uncovered female form could only be expected of a man of the established upper classes. Elite men, he assumes, are accustomed to seeing women in bathing suits through their education and travels abroad, and, regardless of either, have been inculcated with the upper-class code of ethics which carefully dictates the behaviour of a gentleman towards a lady.

This mismatch of values was evident in the lifestyle and values of the Mukhtars and the Established Elite society to which they were peripheral. The family's sons attended the premier elite educational institution, but they would not have been admitted to its oldest, largely liberal, social clubs – nor would they have wanted to gain such access. The relaxed attitudes of institutions like the Sind Club towards women's dress, gender interactions and alcohol would have been something the family actively sought to avoid.

The code of ethics that strictly determines appropriate mannerisms and behaviour was brought home to me most clearly by the response of my friend Kamil's extended circle towards the indiscretion of their friend, Sohail, a politician and businessman known for both the powerful political family he had married into, and his habit of chasing women other than his wife. Sohail had phoned me past midnight one evening while I was at the gathering of a mutual friend, to invite me to interview him in his home. When, in amusement, I mentioned the lateness of the call to a mutual acquaintance, he responded with silence but visible disapproval. When after several weeks Sohail had failed to respond to my messages to confirm a time for our interview, and I had not seen him at any of Kamil's regular social gatherings, I asked Kamil where he had disappeared to,

We all heard about him calling you past midnight, and it is just not acceptable! We will not allow these gatherings to be an opportunity for him to harass our female friends. We have all blacklisted him. It's temporary, but he must learn that he cannot go on in this manner!

Sohail's behaviour had crossed an unspoken line of appropriate behaviour within Kamil's social group, and had offended their sensibilities of how women – and an unaccompanied woman such as myself – should be treated. The news of his call had, unbeknownst to me, spread throughout the extended social group and been harshly critiqued. His behaviour was framed in moral terms, and the group had decided, collectively, that he would be punished by a shared (temporary) exclusion from their social world.

Maintaining and Blurring Class Boundaries

Historically, specific attributes of cultural capital have been carefully reproduced through schooling and the repeated rituals of elite social interaction: those who were admitted to the social world of the elite fulfilled precisely determined criteria, and those who did not were kept outside, sometimes humoured, but never admitted to the inner sanctuaries. The role of these institutions in maintaining class boundaries was evident in the account my friend, Khurram, a highly educated university lecturer, provided of his inability to transcend his class origins. Khurram, in his forties, recounted his interaction with Salman, one of Pakistan's largest and most successful business owners, and an active board member for both the Lahore University of Management Sciences (LUMS) and Aitchison College as follows,

> I was teaching at LUMS at the time and had been selected to be Master of Ceremonies for a LUMS event. I had been told to arrive early to check the set-up of the event and found Salman sahib there doing the same. We introduced ourselves and then Salman sahib asks me, "So where did you go to school?" I assume he is trying to find out the calibre of LUMS staff so I tell him I graduated from Harvard. And he looks at me like I am an idiot and says again, "Where did you go to *school*?" and I tell him, "Well, before Harvard, I graduated from LSE [London School of Economics]". And now he is looking at me like I am *really* stupid, and he asks me again, "But where did you go to *school*??" And then I realise he is asking about my *high school*, and I tell him I went to Army Burn Hall College, and he looks at me, and then just turned around and walked away. He had absolutely no follow-up question. If I had gone to Aitchison he would have known my father or my uncle, but without that connection, he had absolutely nothing to say to me!

Despite his academic achievement at two of the most globally respected universities in the world, Khurram's attendance at a respectable middle class high school – rather than Aitchison – served as a permanent indicator to the LUMS board member that despite his intelligence and achievement, he did not share his family history, nor his background as a member of Pakistan's elite.

Khurram's experience of exclusion contrasts markedly with that of Zeeshan, a bookish and sensitive Aitchison alumni, also in his forties, who had, as the son of a major Lahori industrialist, found himself the reluctant co-owner of a major industrial enterprise. He told me,

> I hated Aitchison. It is elitist in its beliefs. On the first day at school, with all the students gathered in the Old Hall, the principal announced to us all, "When an Aitchisonian walks into a room, he is superior to everyone else who walks into the room!" It was an ugly speech, and it sums up the attitude there. Having said that, I did make lifelong friendships, and the students there came from all of the provinces. The graduating class went on to become government ministers and to take on other important roles. My father also went to Aitchison. Everyone in my family also wanted my son to go to Aitchison, but he started there, and I could see it killing his spirit. It is all rote learning and not suited to someone like him. He now goes to the New School which follows the International Baccalaureate system. It nurtures his spirit of enquiry.

Though Zeeshan came from an Established Elite family, he chaffed against the constrictions of Established society, and wanted his son to have more freedom than he had grown up with. By choosing to send his son to a newer elite school, he eschewed the 'old boys' network that Aitchison would provide, ensuring his son would mix with similarly wealthy boys, but many from families whose wealth was more recently acquired, many of whom could not – on account of their family backgrounds – gain admittance at Aitchison.

But Zeeshan's choice to send his own son to an alternative elite school comes with risks, as pointed out by Ali, the twenty-seven-year-old son of another Lahori industrialist. Ali straddled the new and old elite: his mother was born into one of the original '22 families' (see Chapter Two), but his father's wealth emerged in the 1960s as they cornered the market on a commodity previously unavailable within Pakistan. Ali had spent the first half of his life living in Canada where his family had fled when their industries were nationalised in the 1970s, but had returned to Pakistan for high school on his father's wishes and had stayed to join the family business,

> I went to the Lahore American School (LAS). When we moved to Lahore, I interviewed at Aitchison College but a teacher hit me on the hand with a ruler during my interview so my mother would not let me go there. All my friends are from LAS, but I would never send my children there. You become

so Americanised: I couldn't even speak Urdu properly until I was nineteen or twenty! It's only in the last three years that people have stopped making fun of the way I speak Urdu. That school is full of spoiled rich kids, Ambassador's children . . . Up until 9/11 there were a lot of Western foreigners there. Now it is mostly Asians and some Westerners. We do very well, but I don't have networks at the top of government like the Aitchison crowd.

Though Ali, straddling both the New and Old Elite, struggled to develop the political and bureaucratic networks he observed amongst the Aitchison alumni, a number of Navay Raje families have entered into the top level of Pakistan's economic and political leadership during the last thirty years. While some have sought to acquire the full suite of dispositions of the Established Elite, and admission into their exclusive spaces, many have retained a more indigenous and regional style of distinction. These families have pursued either a full or partial integration with the Established Elite. Some, like the Afridis, have used their recently acquired money to send their children to established educational institutions with high levels of cultural capital both within Pakistan, and abroad for higher education.[20] By doing so they provided their children with access to an inner circle of peers, school mates and friends not available to their parents. This newer elite also splits their membership between Established Elite clubs – the Sind Club, the Boat Club, the Punjab club – and the newer clubs whose facilities are often better and whose criterion for membership is less informed by family heritage and British-inflected taste and decorum.

Increasingly, however, many of these Navay Raje families, like the Mukhtar's, eschew the English forms of distinction displayed by the old Established Elite, and embody a more religiously and socially conservative ethos than the Established Elite families. Indeed, most of the Navay Raje families I came to know were not the ostentatious group that Munir and others in the Established Elite had characterised them to be, as both the Mukhtars, and my friend, Abid, demonstrated. Rather than acting as the nation's 'new lords', many retain a more modest and austere world outlook more commonly associated with the middle classes, despite the increase in their economic standing. Yet they too prized, sought inclusion in, and benefitted from, the powerful elite network provided by admission to the nation's most exclusive Established Elite educational institution.

* * *

The naturalisation of privilege occurs across all societies. Weber argued that in every structure of domination, those 'privileged through existing political, social and economic orders are never content to wield their power unvarnished and to impose their prerogatives naked', but rather, they 'wish to see their position transformed from purely factual power relations into a cosmos of acquired rights'. Elite schooling enables each elite child to acquire the skills and network to thrive within elite society (Bourdieu 1998), to direct and benefit from the profits of major corporations and industries, and to shape national policy. The 'cosmos of acquired rights' they acquire in this process serves to legitimise privilege.

The nature of what it is to be elite in Pakistan is changing as the elite class expands and fractures, to accommodate new entrants. The result is that the uppermost tier of Pakistan's social structure is inhabited by a mix of culturally incongruent groups of people holding vastly divergent ancestral and educational backgrounds, value systems and mannerisms. As explored in this chapter, the backgrounds of elite families have become more diverse, and the forms of distinction they use to identify one another and to exclude outsiders, are accordingly diversifying. The tensions between these different groups of elites is ameliorated by this gradual expansion of elite symbolic and physical space. Despite these accommodations, at times the tension between new and old elites threatens to undermine the power and wealth of both groups.

Private clubs still perform an important function in maintaining elite exclusivity and excluding middle class or newly wealthy members from the opportunities available to the elite. But even as these forums serve to reproduce the elite, and admit a very limited number of new, adequately appropriate members, they are becoming obsolete with the rise of a new group of ultra-rich Pakistanis, like the Mukhtar's, who eschew the cultural capital of the old elite, in favour of new, regionally relevant, rituals and signifiers of distinction. The result is the bifurcation of elite unity, and an erosion of the protective mechanisms that have effectively excluded the rising stars of the middle class from Established Elite forums since Pakistan's inception.

As new class entrants create fractures in long-established traditions of distinction, the nature and form of elite distinction is being forced to expand and to accommodate these new elites. As will be examined in the chapters that follow, many among the elite are overcoming these divisions through the creation of permanent alliances between families of different social backgrounds – drawing together the prestige of the Established Elite with the wealth of New Money families. As the social forums of the elite serve as the primary selection pool for potential spouses, some among the Established Elite, particularly those whose wealth has declined faster than their status, are seeking to lower the barriers to entry within elite schools and social clubs, enabling families with more recently acquired wealth to enter the social pool from which wealthy spouses are chosen. In the process, these new elites, and the considerable capital and power they possess, have become more acceptable as social peers and prospective partners for the children of the established and post-colonial elite. Yet despite these shifting demographics, changes to the composition of the elite class have failed to substantially redefine the exclusionary nature of wealth accumulation.

Notes

1. Raheel's sister-in-law later told me that the women in their family had become very aware of the risk of congenital defects among the children of close relatives and that they would prefer the next generation marry outside the family network, or a significantly more distant relation.
2. See Jaffrelot 2015, 9.
3. See Ahmed 1997, Chirol and Lyall 1910, Mathur 2016, 41.
4. See Sinha 2001, Orwell 1962 [1934], Chirol and Lyall 1910 for examples.
5. Quoted in Ahmad 1981.
6. Bourdieu and Wacquant 1992.
7. Johnson 2013, 184.
8. Johnson 2013, 184.
9. Marriages in Pakistan extend well beyond the two individuals entering the marriage and have long been documented as a powerful strategy of political dynasty making (Cheema et al 2013, Lyon 2012, Lyon and Mughal, 2016) and as a strategy to increase resilience in the context of extreme political and economic insecurity (Lyon 2012, Lyon and Mughal 2016).
10. The divide is echoed in similar forms between the established rich and those who have newly acquired wealth from other countries. For instance, the divide between the old aristocracy of the White Anglo-Saxon Protestants (WASPS) of the United States (old aristocracy) and the ethnically diverse new billionaire class that emerged throughout the twentieth century (see Aldrich 1989).
11. These families are often known as *ashraf* (see Maqsood 2017).
12. For a detailed exploration of Pakistan's new middle class see Ammara Maqsood's (2017) 'The New Middle Class'.
13. See also Martin (2015, 40–41) for his description of the upward inter-generational mobility of one New Money landlord family from rural Punjab whom he calls the Gondals.
14. Nawaz Sharif served as Prime Minister from 1990–1993, again from 1997–1999, and most recently from 2013–2018.
15. Actual name used with permission.

16. Aitchison College remains the most prestigious private boys' school in Pakistan, providing day and boarding facilities from primary school through matriculation.
17. Just as strikingly, as many as 90 per cent of these elites were members of at least one – often all – of the nation's three most prestigious social clubs.
18. Bourdieu 2013, 1986.
19. In seeking to verify Aliya's claim this amount was found to be significantly inflated.
20. See also Martin's 2015 ethnography.

– Chapter 4 –

MAKING AN ELITE FAMILY

Kinship and family relations are central to the reproduction and survival of elite families globally – in contexts as diverse as Australia[1]
and Pakistan. These ties determine and enable both the succession
of elite privilege, and the accumulation of capital. In Pakistan,
despite the restrictions delineating family from public life, wives and
mothers often hold central roles in building and consolidating relationships with elite families in similar or complementary spheres of
influence, in gathering and distributing information, and in broader
social networking. In Pakistan, however, where political crises are
frequent, marriages increase the ability of families and individuals
to adapt and respond to rapidly changing political and economic
circumstances (Lyon and Mughal 2016, 121). The centrality of women
in managing the domestic economy of intra-family elite relations is
also reflective of a specifically gendered structure of political and
economic power.

My friend Aliya, introduced in the previous chapter, differed from
many of her elite female peers in that she had obtained not only a
bachelor's degree, but also a master's degree in anthropology from
LUMS, and as a result, she was unusually reflexive about her own
society and the sub-culture in which she existed. She had also, unlike
many women of her class, worked professionally for several years
leading up to and following her marriage – despite the consternation
of her parents and the gossip her actions generated within their social
circle. As a consequence of being an elite Lahori native, and of having
pushed the boundaries of its social rules, she effortlessly shifted
between reproducing and succinctly articulating its often-unspoken

value system and mercilessly critiquing the social code and obligations it imposed upon her. During our first meeting at Butler's Café
in the boutique-populated Lahore neighbourhood of Gulberg she
described the gendered division of labour, and expectation of family
roles, within her natal family,

> My two brothers are in the family business, working with my father. My
> brother Hamid was working in the U.S. for a tech firm and he had a great
> career over there. But he was required to come back and work in the family
> business. It was never said but always understood that I would not work in
> the [family] business. It was made clear that it was not an option. I used to
> wish that I could, but there is this unsaid expectation that I would give up my
> work and stay home with my daughter once I became a mother.

She paused a moment from her explanation to encourage her two-
year old daughter, dressed in a white frill covered dress with matching frilly white hair band, to eat another piece of crust-free white
bread sandwich, and then continued,

> I used to be a consultant for some of the major international development
> agencies. I travelled all over rural Punjab consulting on and researching inter-
> nationally-funded development projects – and I loved that. I don't think my
> parents could ever understand it, but they put up with it. My father seems
> very progressive, and he has always encouraged and enabled me to do exactly
> what I want to do, but once I got married, and even more so once I became
> a mother, there was a lot of pressure on me to stop working and stay home.
> I think they wanted me to stop because of the enormous social pressure
> here. You cannot underestimate it. They were worried about what their circle,
> what "the society", would think of seeing me running around all muddy in
> rural Punjab. They worried people would think that I was working because I
> needed the money, that my husband could not provide for me properly, and
> that I would make my husband look bad – and my parents look bad – for
> allowing me to marry someone who was not able to make enough money
> to look after me! We call this the "Begum Sahib"[2] phenomenon. It is the little
> princess image that men in our society try to preserve of their wives and
> daughters. I am not supposed to need to work and no one can understand
> why I would want to.
>   But now I feel sorry for my brothers. They cannot ever leave Pakistan. If
> they did, what would happen to our business? It is all family run and they are
> needed. They cannot decide to move somewhere else like I can. My husband
> Atif and I applied for residency in Canada and we received confirmation that
> our visa application was approved ten days ago. We are going to move once
> Atif finds a job. I want us to go for my daughter, because there are no options
> for her here. If we stay in Pakistan she will grow up just like me. She will go
> to school in Lahore, then go to university overseas somewhere for a few years,
> and then come back and marry some Pakistani from our community and have
> children. I want more for her.

As Aliya's comments demonstrate, the strategies used to create and protect family dynasties – economically and in terms of reputation – differ markedly between men and women, and between the male and female siblings of the same family. Despite her peripheral role to the family business, Aliya fulfilled an important role in preserving and strengthening the various branches of her extended family within the broader world of the Lahori elite. She did this through continuous acts of visiting, coffee dates and socialising with her own natal family and that of her husband, and with the various members of Lahore's Established Elite society. There were no expectations that she would contribute to building the family's wealth or political influence.

Marriages in Pakistan extend well beyond the two individuals entering the marriage and serve as a powerful strategy of political dynasty-making (Cheema et al 2013, Lyon 2012, Lyon and Mughal 2016). They also serve as an effective strategy for increasing family resilience in the context of extreme political and economic insecurity (Lyon 2012, Lyon and Mughal 2016), insulating elites from threats to their power and privilege and as a means for internally policing appropriate elite behaviour. Consequently, marriage serves a critical role in the survival and continued dominance of elite families, with each marriage acting as a link in a chain connecting powerful extended families and allies. This chapter explores the functional purpose of marriage within an elite family, and examines how the elite classes of Pakistan have used marriage to consolidate power within their closest kinship group, through strategies of inclusion and exclusion. The importance of these alliances ensures that selection of a marriage partner is carefully policed by the extended kinship group of both parties, and by the broader elite society with whom they identify.

The Permanent Alliance

Marriages among the elite, as among other classes, are used to create bonds between families and to reduce vulnerabilities to the threats of economic competition and reputational damage. As explored in the previous chapter, descent comprises an important component of the elite distinction used to determine elite social inclusion or exclusion. However, complementing these vertical ties, marriage also extends the family network outward through horizontal bonds across a broader group of families and individuals. It therefore also serves as a defensive mechanism designed to shore up allies and supporters and to incorporate would-be detractors into the inner folds of the family network. Traditionally, kin relationships dictated who would gather and support one another in the case of conflict (Banerjee 2000, 28). Today among the elite, though the nature of the conflicts engaged in often differs, these kin relations are still expected to fulfil the same functions of support. Marriage connects households who may otherwise be antagonistic to one another. It creates permanent inter-family alliances that are not dependent upon shared ancestry.

In analysing political family dynasties in Pakistan, Lyon and Mughal (2012, 112) conclude that,

> Marital alliances incur mutual expectations of support and resource exchange. They also, to some extent, implicate households in one another's public reputations. So, while the most important people affecting a household's honour, or *izzat*, remain those linked by common descent, everyone connected to the household can impact the izzat in some way. Thus, marriages outside unilineal descent groups not only extend political networks, they also increase the number of households who have a shared interest in maintaining the positive public reputations of all linked households (Lyon and Mughal 2016, 112).

The most adroit families assess the limitations of their own power and influence, and seek to supplement these through the creation of permanent kinship alliances – even if this requires alliance-making with those families who have only recently transitioned from the ranks of the Navay Raje. Others seek to enhance the status of their families through marriages to families of similar, or higher, status, as Aliya again illuminated,

> You are measured here by the people you know. Marriage is a way to connect people. Don't underestimate the importance of social pressure in Lahori culture. For instance, my friend is married to Sana Tariq. As you well know, the Tariqs are a very well-known and high-profile business family. So now my friend's younger brother wants to get married, but he feels that he needs to make as impressive a marriage match as his brother did. But how is he going to match marrying a Tariq? If you stay long enough, you will be here for a very high-profile wedding. He is dating a girl from a *very* high-profile business family, with very senior military connections. These connections are critical . . . But most of his interest is out of the pressure he feels to top his brother.

The Criterion of Marriageability

Given the important role of women in networking with other elite families, as well as child-raising, selection of the appropriate spouse is critical. For traditionally conservative or rural families, rules governing marriageable relations serve to regulate the selection process, limiting the pool of potential spouses to within a particular kinship group or *biraderi*.[3] In contrast, for many of the most liberal Established Elite families, marital selection occurs without a formal acknowledgement of the implicit rules determining appropriate partners. Yet even among these more seemingly liberal families, under a veneer of openness, practices of social inclusion and exclusion remain rigorously policed. Various marital strategies are used either to acquire, consolidate, or protect the wealth and political influence of a family: marriages *within* a family group are used to protect and defend existing wealth and power, and marriages *outside* of kinship groups are usually used to expand this wealth and power. In almost all instances, marriages among the elite class retain a high degree of both social and ethnic endogamy, excluding outsiders from the benefits of an elite extended kinship network, and the wealth that marriage confers.

'Did you know Salim is getting married?', Aliya asked me ten months into our friendship during a casual evening of Japanese take-out and domestically-brewed, black market *Murree Beer*,

> His fiancée is 11 years younger than him. I think it's a good match. She is young and beautiful, and he is older and wealthy. Women want wealthy husbands, and men want beautiful wives. That is the way things work. My mother always used to say to me, 'don't get left on the shelf', and she's right. Women pass their use-by date. He is making a good choice by marrying her.

Aliya's framing of the news regarding our friend Salim's marriage was instructive in illuminating her attitudes towards marriage. Her assessment focused on the exchange value of a prospective bride or groom, assessing the value of each on the market of marriageability within her own elite social circles. Notably, her assessment of value for each was gendered, and assessed according to separate gender-specific criteria. Her comment above noted Salim's wealth, and his fiancée's youth and beauty, but beneath this simple assessment, a broad array of other criteria informed her view of their suitability for marriage – and of the many others both inside and outside of their social class who were not so suitable.

Aliya's comments about Salim's choice of marriage revealed a deeper internalisation of elite Lahori gender norms than her candid reflections on the gender roles in her family had suggested during our first meeting. The small gathering in which she shared the news of Salim's upcoming marriage was held in the home of mutual friends our own age, all married, with the exception of two of the male guests and myself. In stating her approval of Salim's marriage to a woman much younger than him, she was also validating her own choice to marry and have children in her early twenties to an older man, and with it, her choice to leave behind her ambitions for a professional life. It may even, in the style of the criticisms I occasionally experienced in Lahore, have been a none too subtle critique of me. As a woman of her own age, engaging in an independent research career, she saw my research as being undertaken at the cost of squandering my dwindling prospects for an advantageous marriage.[4]

Protecting the Family through Marriage

Marital strategies and rules determining marriageable and unmarriageable prospective partners guide many Pakistani marriages, not only among the elite but across social classes in Pakistan, and often vary according to specific cultural practices associated with particular regions or ethnic groups. Marital strategies are divided between consanguineous marriages (between both first and distant cousins) and non-consanguineous marriages. Traditionally in Punjab, most marriages were confined to spouses from within the same biraderi, creating a high level of biraderi endogamy. By ensuring marriages occurred within a biraderi, men 'appropriate[d] their own women rather than exchange[ing] them with other kin groups', and benefitted from the social injunction which determined that 'keeping daughters within one's own biraderi is an index of social prestige' (Alavi 1976, 5–6). Marital strategy was most often structured on the principle of preferential patrilateral parallel cousin marriage, most preferably with the father's brother's daughter (FBD) (Alavi 1976, 5). Parallel cousin marriages between the children of two brothers were viewed as particularly advantageous as these marriages ensured a portion of family wealth, shares in business, or inheritance owed to daughters under Islamic property rights, did not leave the lineage when daughters married. In addition, local custom among Punjabi and Pakhtun families often interpreted cousin marriage with a father's brother's daughter to be the most appropriate form of marriage prescribed by Islam (Alavi 1976, 5).[5]

Across Pakistan's class structure, two-thirds of marriages remain consanguineous, with over 80 per cent of these marriages occurring between first cousins (Hussain 1999, 449). Unsurprisingly, those who do engage in cousin marriage tend to demonstrate a cross-generational family preference for cousin marriage, and to be more likely to be born to parents who entered into marriages with first cousins than those who marry non-consanguineous partners (Hussain and Bittles 1998, 264). Even outside of consanguineous marriages, a significant degree of in-group endogamy remains the norm among most communities – whether defined by class, sect, or ethnic identity, and families tended to pursue a dominant marital strategy to which the majority of family members adhered. When marriages occasionally occurred between marital partners from outside of the kinship group, and sometimes even from separate biraderis, these marriages were usually instigated under an exceptional circumstance (Alavi 1976, 7) that required a new alliance to be quickly fostered. Yet even in these exceptional cases, the importance of ensuring strong and enduring bonds between families meant that families usually sought to marry a set of brothers from one family to a set of daughters from another (Das 1973, 31). This practice quickly produced multiple strands of kinship between families, rapidly drawing previously unrelated families tightly into multi-stranded kinship relationships. Once this relationship between families was established, it was common for these two families to develop an ongoing exchange of marriage partners through successive generations.[6]

For many elite families, cousin marriages remain popular. Of the 90 individuals I formally interviewed, as many as 70 per cent were married to first cousins (with a higher proportion among those over 40 years of age), and the majority of those in cousin marriages had parents who were also in consanguineous marriages with first or more distantly related cousins. Cousin marriages had often been strongly advocated for by parents, aunts and uncles with the explicit goal of tempering, or avoiding, the discord and feuds reputed to plague family businesses in the second and third generation. They continued to be perceived as a means of strengthening emotional and economic ties between sibling-parents, and through this, of strengthening the unity of the entire extended family unit (Nadvi 1999).

However, I also encountered a number of intermittent variations to the preferential family strategy, a 'split marriage strategy' (Lyon and Mughal 2016, 113): within most generations of siblings,[7] one or more sibling was likely to have married outside of cousin structures or biraderis, sometimes pursuing a love marriage, but more often in response to their family's need to foster a specific strategic alliance with an elite family occupying a complementary sphere of influence. These strategies shifted according to a 'pragmatic assessment of what ensures household survival best' (Lyon and Mughal 2016,

121). Today, the rules guiding preferred marital strategies have been significantly relaxed, with some families in a community continuing to select marital partners only from among their kinship group, or father's brother's daughters, but with many others marrying wholly outside of their kinship or biraderi group.

Three Patterns of Strategic Marriage

The family histories and recent genealogies of four of my informants are typical of the marital strategies engaged in by the elite, and are closely linked with each family's upward social, economic and political mobility.

The Split Strategy

The family history of three of my closest informants, the brothers Abid and Kaleem Afridi, and their cousin, Shahzar, is typical of a marital strategy common to business and political families from Khyber Pakhtunkhwa. Abid and Kaleem's father, Salar, died when Abid was seventeen. As the son of the eldest of five brothers, the passing of Salar, the head of the family, created a leadership gap which Abid, as the eldest son of the eldest son, was required to fill, with the support of his uncles. At his father's death he became responsible for his mother, sisters and younger brother, Kaleem. But he was also required to assume responsibility for both the family business that had been led by his father up until his death, and for his female cousins. In keeping with the expectation that a male does not become a man until he marries and fathers a child, it was important to Abid's family that he marry quickly and assume the responsibilities of a man.

It was determined by both their mother and uncles that Abid and Kaleem would marry one of their father's brother's daughters (FBD), to protect both the emotional unity and economic assets of the family. Abid married his uncle Nadir's daughter, Niloufer. When Kaleem turned twenty-five, he married the daughter of their third uncle, Mateen. Their marriages marked the fourth generation to adopt a strategy of patrilineal cousin marriage, and the third generation to marry their father's brother's daughter.

Abid's paternal great-grandfather, born in the 1870s, was an Afghan clay-potter, and emigrated from Afghanistan to Fakra[8] in what is now Khyber Pakhtunkhwa at the turn of the century. Despite his humble occupation, he was known to be one of the best students in his madrassa, and had the social distinction of having memorised the Quran. As a result, he was widely respected in the Fakra community. He had three sons (the number of daughters, tellingly, was not recorded), one of whom was known within the family to have discredited the family by becoming a musician; Taroon, whose occupation no one in the current generation could remember; and a third, Qalandar (b: 1900), Abid's paternal great-grandfather. Qalander followed in his father's footsteps by becoming a religious scholar. To support his family, he concurrently worked as a trader of *tafat*,[9] trading the tafat grown in Fakra with buyers across Asia.

Qalandar had eight daughters and two sons: the eldest son, Arsalan (born in the 1920s), inherited his father's tafat business, shifting from work as a trader, to becoming a land-owning agriculturalist. Arsalan and his brother were the first in their family to complete a secular high school curriculum. As a result of his educational qualification Arsalan found employment as a Land Registrar under the British Administration, and ran his own tafat business on the side. His brother became a doctor. When Arsalan married, he married his uncle Taroon's daughter, Mina (FBD).

Mina's brother, Bazir, had also inherited some of the family tafat industry, and like his uncle and grandfather, he was also trained as a religious scholar. One of Bazir's five sons, Babar, a lawyer, married one of Arsalan and Mina's daughters. All of their children except one, married first cousins on their paternal side. One son, Ali, with unmarried daughters remaining from his father's brothers, married a cousin on his mother's side, the son of one of her brothers. The marriages were carefully designed to both ensure the unity of the extended family, and to ensure the assets of the family's business were secured.

In the 1950s, Arsalan shifted the family's marital strategy. By this time, he had already become a very successful agriculturalist and producer of tafat in KP province, and the family had a great deal of wealth to preserve and protect. For his six children, rather than following the preferential FBD marital strategy of his own parents and grandparents, Arsalan decided to enter into a marriage exchange of his own children with the grandchildren of two brothers, also of the Yusefzai tribe, but outside of his immediate kinship group. One of these brothers was a captain in the British military (later the Pakistani military), and the other a locally-esteemed lawyer. As all of Arsalan's sons were equipped to enter the family business and to become businessmen like himself, marrying them to the daughters of a senior military official and a successful professional significantly expanded the family's networks outside of their limited sphere of influence in agriculture and industry.

The exchange of the sons of one family with the daughters of another has a clear precedent in both Pakhtun and Punjabi cultures. As was common in marital exchanges of this nature, the exchange established an ongoing and permanent bond between the two families that resulted in future marriages between the first cousin offspring of these unions. Arsalan's eldest son, Salar, was twenty when he married in 1955, and his bride, Saba, the granddaughter of the lawyer, was sixteen. Saba's second sister married Salar's brother, Mateen in 1960, and her third sister, Rekhmina, married Salar's younger brother Roshan five years later. Saba's youngest sister, Laila, married Salar's brother, Munir. Much later, Saba's younger cousin, Mahzala, married her aunt's youngest brother-in-law, Salar's much younger brother, Pohand.

Rekhmina and Roshan had one daughter, and much later, when Rekhmina was already in her late thirties, Shahzar was born (late 1980s). Being so much younger than his sister, as well as loud and high-spirited, the family decided Shahzar should be raised by Saba, as she already had experience raising two boys: Abid and Kaleem. Shahzar was raised as the youngest brother of Abid and Kaleem, believing Saba to be his mother, and Rekhmina to be his aunt, up until he was ten years of age. He was devastated upon being told of his true parentage. His devastation was likely compounded by the shift in relations his true parentage effected with his brothers-turned-cousins. The '*tarboor*' relationship (father's brother's son) in Pakhtun culture is traditionally characterised by enmity and antagonism, (Ahmed 2011, 44). In the Yusefzai clan, sibling terms are extended to all cousins except for father's brother's sons, who are known only as 'tarboor' (cousin) (Ahmed 2011, 44), an acknowledgement of the tension and distance present in these relationships. Up until the revelation of his parentage, he had enjoyed the most intimate of Pakhtun relations with Abid and Kaleem, that of a brother.

Traditionally, Pakhtun families sometimes avoid cousin marriages, as they are seen as a weak strategy for reducing the inevitable tensions expected between agnatic cousins (Ahmed 2011, 44). Instead, many Pakhtuns prefer to marry their daughters to those outside of the lineage in order to establish alliances with those sharing similar political objectives. However, Arsalan broke with this prescription of Pakhtun marital preferences, and instead chose to arrange agnatic cousin marriages for his own children, perhaps in an attempt to reduce the tensions associated with splitting the considerable wealth he had amassed by the end of his life. The strategy was not effective: after Salar's death in the mid 1990s, infighting among his younger brothers and his son Abid intensified dramatically. The family assets were divided, and widespread mistrust, along with accusations of theft, dominated not only the relationship between Salar's surviving brothers, but also among their sons, with Abid, Kaleem and a number of their cousins engaging in severe bouts of competition and sabotage with their rival tafat companies.

The Military Connection

Arsalan Afridi's decision to wed his children to a family with strong military connections replicates a strategy that many elite business families continue to pursue in seeking to create alliances between business and political families. The pre-eminence of Pakistan's military in the political and economic life of the country has made the creation of alliances with senior military personnel highly sought after. The influence of the military pervades all areas of political decision-making across the nation, and controls, both formally and informally, a very large – and substantially unregulated – percentage of government funds (see Siddiqa 2007 and Jaffrelot 2015). Unlike the inherited power and leadership of the business elite, the power of senior military officials is based almost entirely on their current ranking, promotion prospects, or status as retired senior members of the military. Consequently, entering a marriage with a Captain who is recognised as ascending the military ranks is a desirable match for the daughters of business families. For the sons of businessmen, marrying the daughter of a General is also advantageous both for the duration of the General's active life in military service and following his retirement. A father-in-law with close ties within the senior ranks of the military may be able to facilitate any number of advantageous military contracts, assist in solving legal disputes and in making introductions and recommendations, particularly following his retirement when the constraints imposed upon the behaviour of military personnel are considerably relaxed.

The value of a military marital alliance was explained to me by a Brigadier and former military attaché over tea in his office,

> If an elite family has a son-in-law in the military, they will feel very safe. You know Sialkot? It is a very rich area and full of industrialists with huge wealth.

We [the military] also have a base there. It is known as "The City of In-Laws" because young officers are sent there and then they find in-laws! The industrialists make sure their daughters meet these young men. The parents are often not very well educated, but they have made sure their daughters are, and they need to find a good match for them. These boys are twenty-two years old, and they have a very good career, and very good prospects – everyone would like to marry them. Inter-marriage between military families is also very common, but the military boys also marry civilian girls, particularly girls from industrialist families. The officer boys try to avoid marrying into the political families because it is not good to be too associated with politicians, it could damage your career. They prefer industrialist girls or even the daughters of bureaucrats with good standing. There is so much competition within the military that it is important to avoid anything that could damage your standing or reputation. But political families want to marry their daughters to military boys 200 per cent! My son is still in college but I've already had many families making enquiries about him regarding marriage with their daughters.

As the Brigadier's account demonstrates, the elite are highly aware of the social value of their own family members as prospective marital partners, and of that of others. His account also highlights the value many elites place on marrying into different spheres of political (including military) and economic influence in order to reduce the threats and vulnerabilities that may arise from reputational or economic weaknesses.

Shifting Marital Preferences: Hypergamy to Kinship Marriage

Marriages that do occur between individuals from separate kinship structures in Pakistan are often used to provide family members with a wider circle of business and social contacts (Nadvi 1999, 154–5). Families whose members predominantly follow a preferential marital strategy will often select one member of the family to serve as a strategic exception. These exceptions to the preferential strategy most often occur when a family seeks to create important alliances with families occupying complementary, and therefore strategically advantageous, positions of power outside of their own kinship group. Though they most often occur within the same ethnic group, if not the same biraderi or zaat,[10] at times marriages are made wholly outside of these groups to create important strategic relationships with families occupying parallel spheres of political or economic influence.

The family history of Hamza and Ilyas, two brothers from a prominent Punjabi political and business family, demonstrates a strategic shift towards a consanguineous marital strategy. Their family's unprecedented adoption of cousin marriage sought to preserve the unity and wealth of the family's third generation to grow up in the elite. When the time came for Hamza to be married in 1980 at twenty-five years of age, his family arranged a matrilateral cousin marriage with Karina, the daughter of one of his mother's sisters. The marriage was the first consanguineous match to be made within his family in several generations, and as such followed no precedent or tradition. It did, however, serve a clear strategic purpose.

Hamza's paternal grandfather was a doctor in Lahore, a very respectable upper-middle class professional, and his grandmother was literate in both Urdu and her native regional language, achievements that positioned her as a well-educated woman for the time. They married in the early 1920s. Their two sons also took on respectable upper-middle class positions, one as a barrister, the other, Hamza's father Mustapha (also born in the 1920s), as an officer in the Pakistani military. By the late 1970s, the war in Afghanistan had become the critical priority for both the Pakistani and United States' governments and huge amounts of American funding was being channelled to the Pakistani military to fight the Soviet Union in Afghanistan. Being a strategic thinker and popular among his peers in the military, Mustapha rose quickly in the military's ranks and made himself indispensable to the military government throughout the following decade.[11] His seniority and success within the military during the Soviet–Afghan war, catapulted him and his family from the military's upper middle classes into the ranks of the wealthy elite.

Having accumulated extreme wealth for the first time, Mustapha and his extended family believed that it was critical to retain this newfound wealth within the family. Despite not having a history of cousin marriage in either his own marriage or that of his parents, Mustapha and his extended family agreed that three of his four children should enter into marriages with the children of their mother's siblings. The decision to marry Hamza and Ilyas to matrilateral cousins, rather than a patrilateral cousin (FBD) as was traditionally preferred among Punjabi families, was not something for which Hamza had an explanation. However, a close review of his family history, and the alliances made between non-consanguineous families up until the third generation, provides possible indications of the motivation for this variation on the FBD norm. Hamza's maternal grandfather was, like his paternal grandfather, a doctor. He graduated from the same school in Lahore as his paternal grandfather in 1880. Both men were highly respected upper-middle class professionals, but they owned no large assets, and were neither members of the elite nor the colonial administration.

Hamza's maternal grandparents had nine reputedly very beautiful daughters, and one son. Recognising the social capital of their daughters' beauty, and their respectable positions within Lahori society, Hamza's grandparents embarked on a strategy of ambitious hypergamy for each of their daughters: one daughter, Karina's mother, was married to the son of a landed feudal family in Punjab; another, Hamza's mother, was married to a rapidly rising officer in the colonial military; another married a senior bureaucrat; and another married the heir of an expanding business empire. The high status nature of each of these daughter's matches with spouses occupying senior roles in complementary power structures – land holder, military, bureaucracy, business empire – ensured that the offspring of these marriages were born into the nation's elite classes, enabling the family to undertake rapid upward social mobility in just one generation. As a result of these efforts, the children of these marriages, Hamza's mother and her siblings, had also gone on to assume prominent roles in each of the uppermost tiers of Lahori society, and within the national elite more broadly. Today, Hamza's family is one of the largest combined political-business families in Pakistan.

Despite the upward mobility achieved by this generation, the status differential between the Established Elite whose wealth had longer histories intertwined with the colonial regime, and of the recently acquired wealth of industrialists or military officers, meant that the more recently acquired wealth of Hamza's mother and her children placed them in a subordinate position to their cousins with parentage in the Established Elite. The marriage of Hamza's aunt to a powerful feudal lord, by far her class superior, ensured that their daughter, Karina, was born into the Established Elite of 'old' Lahori society, thereby granting her a level of social prestige not acquired by her cousins despite their mothers' *economically* advantageous marriages to senior military men and industrialists.

Hamza and his siblings became fully fledged members of the economic elite upon their father's assumption of a senior position within the military, and the substantial economic benefits he acquired during the course of the Soviet–Afghan war, and upon his retirement. Yet the rapidity of this rise in fortune meant the family risked being labelled as Navay Raje by Lahori society. Consequently, Hamza's marriage to his cousin Karina both promoted internal family solidarity, and consolidated Hamza's own status, and that of his broader family network, by tightening the bonds between the military arm of his own family, with the feudal origins of Karina's father. Karina's father's family, while socially superior in terms of their status within

Lahori society, also benefitted from the increase in wealth and political influence Karina achieved through her marriage to the industrial and political side of the family. Two of Hamza's brothers continued the newly implemented preferential family strategy and also entered matrilateral cousin marriages, yet the third brother entered into an arranged marriage with the daughter of a senior member of the military from outside of the extended family lineage, a match so advantageous that it overrode the newly implemented family preferences for consanguineous marriage.

After having spent a considerable amount of time with Hamza and Ilyas, having not been introduced to the brother's wives, over drinks in the brothers' drawing room I asked Hamza if he spent much time with his wife, Karina. He looked at me mournfully over his gin and tonic, and answered morosely,

> Rosita, we have nothing to talk about. And worse, she has become very religious. She spends all her time praying and reading the Quran, and she does not like me to drink alcohol. So we spend very little time together.

The extremity of this constructed gender difference in the lives of the brothers and their wives had resulted in each developing highly differentiated spheres of interest and experience. Hamza's wife, a first cousin whom he had married at the explicit wishes of his mother, was highly conservative, educated only to high school level, and unlike Hamza, who had worked in the UK as a young man before returning to Pakistan, she had travelled little outside of Pakistan. They had very little common ground in terms of educational background, engagement in shared work, recreational interests, or areas of responsibility. Hamza's interest in socialising in the presence of his wife was further constrained by his regular consumption of alcohol, and her severe disapproval of it. Like a number of the businessmen I met, Hamza's alcohol consumption was a considerable source of tension within his marriage, and an area of marital contention that he, and a number of other elite men, used to justify almost entirely separate social and recreational existences.

Despite the clear motivations for the historical marital patterns within his family, Hamza was adamant that his own children would not enter any form of consanguineous marriage. He, like a number of elite men I interviewed in their forties and fifties, had come to see cousin marriage as a matter of some embarrassment. His embarrassment reflected a shift in attitude which coincides with vigorous public information campaigns warning of the increased chance for genetic abnormalities in children born to closely related parents. A number of my informants, like Hamza, awkwardly acknowledged that they know it can predispose future children to genetic abnormalities, stating that they will not continue the practice when arranging the marriages of their own children.

Love Marriage

Kamil was a highly successful 'indentor', a term used in Pakistan to refer to those who facilitate business deals with foreign firms. He also owned one of the nation's largest energy production industries. He was the first businessman on either side of his family, but came from a socially prestigious lineage on both his paternal and maternal side. Kamil's paternal great-great-grandfather and great-grandfather were Nawabs in one of India's princely states prior to 1947, of mixed Punjabi and Kashmiri descent. In contrast to the eminent ancestry on his paternal side, his great-grandmother's father owned a leather tannery in Calcutta, and his great-grandmother's brother was a mid-ranking bureaucrat in the Indian Civil Service. Kamil's great-grandmother came from a significantly lower social standing than her husband, and it is rumoured, Kamil told me with a wink, that she ran away to marry the Nawab against the wishes of both of their families.

The Nawab and the tanner's daughter had seven children: two of the daughters married the Nawabs of separate princely states, and the third married a successful businessman who later emigrated to the United States where he became an exceedingly wealthy landlord. Three of the sons became senior officers in the English army. Majeed, Kamil's grandfather, worked first as a journalist, then joined the British army. He was a childhood friend of Mohammad Ali Jinnah, and when Pakistan became independent, he served as a personal advisor to Jinnah, and assumed leadership of a vital ministry in the new state. Majeed married Naima, a woman from an Established Elite Lahore family.

Naima's father was a respected Ahmedi[12] doctor and educationist of Kashmiri origin living in Uttar Pradesh, and was married to a Kashmiri woman. One of their sons assumed an extremely senior bureaucratic role in an Indian state, the other son became an artist, one sister became a teacher and the other married a military officer who was eventually promoted to General.

Coming from a line of educated aristocrats in Uttar Pradesh, Kamil's grandmother Naima was herself highly educated, holding a Master's degree. Unusually for women of the time, she had also worked before marriage, and after she married, she founded a highly regarded welfare organisation. Her daughter, Sherbano, married three times, the second time to Kamil's father, a prominent and senior member of the military, and the last time, after the children were already adults, to a government Minister. Kamil and his siblings were raised by her third husband, the government minister, a man Kamil and his siblings adored, and each of Sherbano's children went on to follow diverse and highly successful careers in education, business, politics and fashion.

Kamil's background as part of an Old Money, established family, enabled both his mother and him to take significant social risks in their own choices of love, marriage and divorce. For his mother, Sherbano, her decision to divorce her first husband, a marriage that had been arranged by her parents, and to then enter into two 'love' marriages thereafter was highly unusual amongst the Pakistani elite, and would undoubtedly have led to her and her family becoming the subject of gossip among the elite social circle of which they were established members. By breaking the rules of her community, she subjected herself to what was no doubt at times unpleasant gossip, but she was not at risk of expulsion from the elite. As a beautiful, cultured, highly-educated and opinionated woman from one of the most reputable families in the country, her peers more often than not viewed her behaviour as charmingly risqué.

Similarly, Kamil had also bucked the conventions of his social network in relation to marital relations. When he fell in love with an Italian woman while studying in Canada, his parents travelled all the way from Pakistan to dissuade him from marrying her, and when he refused, cut off the stipend on which he had been living. After a year of struggling financially on his own, his relationship with the Italian ended and he was readmitted to the family and its finances. Eight years later he married a Canadian. By this time, he had his own successful career and his parents did not try to discourage him. His wife moved to Pakistan to be with him. After ten years she asked him to come back to Canada with her, but he could not leave his country. With sadness, they agreed to a divorce and she returned to Canada. Still only forty, and unusually for someone among the upper-classes, Kamil made no attempt to remarry. He committed to the life of a bachelor, remaining an excellent confidante, advisor and host to his many friends. Like his mother, his unconventional choice of marriage and later divorce was remarked upon affectionately by his peers, but in no way discredited him.

For most elite Pakistanis who decided to pursue love marriages without the approval of their families, however, the consequences were often severe. One of my closest informants, Imran, the forty-year-old eldest son of a major manufacturing family in Karachi, often lamented his own insistence on ignoring the injunctions of his family in regards to marriage,

> I married my high-school sweetheart. It was the only love marriage in my family. Her family is also wealthy and respected. But they are not on the same level. Both my brother's marriages were arranged. Now the irony is that they are much happier, and I am the one in the "love marriage" wishing I was not!
>
> My wife has been corrupted. My father bought her out and now she is on his side. I gave her more money than she had ever had with her own father, but now she looks at my brother's wives who came from families as wealthy as my own and she sees that their fathers still give them money, along with what my brothers give them. She sees that they have more money than her. My brothers and I give our wives the same, but she wants me to give her more to make up for what her father is not giving her.

Imran was the only one of his siblings, and the first in his family, to enter into a marriage with a woman he had chosen himself. They had met in university, dated through the four years of study and had fallen in love. His family had responded to his demand that he be allowed to marry a wife of his own choosing with reluctance, but succumbed when he informed them of his decision to go ahead with the marriage despite their objections. Immediately following the marriage, however, his father demoted him within the family enterprise to a junior management role in a small and marginal division. In further retribution for his disobedience, and to incentivise the obedience of his other offspring, he promoted Imran's younger brothers into senior positions. Imran's decision-making role on the family board was also significantly reduced, and his share of the family assets cut. Exacerbating his anguish, his family welcomed Imran's new wife into the family while continuing to marginalise him within the family enterprise. In doing so, they not only punished Imran, but drove a wedge of frustration and distrust between the spouses. He frequently lamented his poor choice of wife in the small parties he regularly threw when traveling to Islamabad and Lahore for work, and vocally advocated against marrying outside of family guidance. His unhappiness served as a living emblem of the misfortune and misery associated with ignoring one's parents and making an ill-advised match in marriage.

Religious Miscegenation

Beyond the injunction to follow a family-mandated marital strategy, strict taboos often exist in regards to religious miscegenation. My friend Talat, a senior politically-appointed government advisor in his twenties, had spent many hours in conversation with me discussing the Pakistani upper classes, of which he was an established member, before he added a detail on his own personal situation,

> My parents are organising my *rishta* (engagement) right now. I know the girl, of course, because we all know one another among this circle in Lahore. She used to be the girlfriend of one of my friends. That doesn't bother me, that's how it goes among our circle. My parents always made it clear that I could date whomever I wanted and that they would never intervene, but I knew that when it came to marriage, it would be their decision and I'd have to accept it. It sounds strange because we are such a liberal family – all of these families are liberal – but this is how it is done. My best friend dated a girl from high school for eight years, but when it came time for her to get married, her parents would not allow her to marry him, because they already had their eye on his first cousin, a man whose father was a prominent politician, and much wealthier. She spent the first two years of her marriage crying, but now she is in the social pages of the Sunday magazine every weekend and she is perfectly happy.
>
> I also dated a girl for years, she was from an old family too. Our families knew we were together. We wanted to get married, but when the time came her family wouldn't allow it because my family is Ahmedi.[13] I come from a good family, they liked me, and they respected my parents, but they couldn't allow their grandchildren to be Ahmedi.

Talat's observation on the prohibition against inter-sect marriage, particularly with a group as politically marginalised and structurally disadvantaged as the Ahmedi religious community is in Pakistan today, reveals the hard limits of intra-elite ethnic tolerance: Ahmedis hold few political positions and some Pakistanis refuse to do business with them. Talat had attended Aitchison College with his Sunni Muslim peers, had a long-standing Established Elite background tracing back to the British colonial era and possessed the full suite of elite dispositions. He was impeccably dressed, well-spoken and charming. He was an insider in terms of descent, social circle and educational and professional background, but he was not someone to whom a non-Ahmedi family would ever consider marrying their daughter. To do so would be to endanger the prospects of the next generation and to expose them to serious political and financial risk.

* * *

Marital strategies continue to be one of the most powerful mechanisms employed by the Pakistani elite to expand or protect their economic assets and their social status, to foster inter-elite networks, and to gather information on other elite families. While the majority of marriages occur according to some pattern of endogamy – whether within the family, the biraderi, or the broader ethnic group – these preferences are eschewed when the family's need to develop a broader support base becomes more critical. As demonstrated by the case studies in this chapter, marital strategies shift within families through the generations depending upon the changing economic circumstances of the families involved. Families who have long pursued cousin marriages at times enter into marital exchanges with unrelated families to build important alliances with powerful groups outside of their own kinship network; and families who have long married outside of kinship groups, like Hamza's, at times decide to begin a tradition of cousin-marriage to protect newly acquired wealth from the leakage of assets that may occur with daughters marrying outside of the family.

Though the form of elite marriages changes through generations – shifting from exogamous marriage, to patrilateral marriage, to matrilateral marriage, to individuals from outside the extended kinship group – marriage continues to be seen by elite families and the broader social world they inhabit, as a critical mechanism for protecting or expanding wealth and status. Marital ties are made with the purpose of linking families, and not just individuals, into permanent alliances. While other alliances developed with friends or acquaintances may shift based on changing circumstances, marital bonds are unbreakable. This does not eliminate the possibility of competition or treachery from within the branches of an extended family joined through marriage, but it binds the self-interests of families allied through marriage, so that economic or reputational damage sustained by one member is experienced as a threat to all.

Finally, the sanctions imposed upon family members who fail to conform to the family marital strategy provide a powerful indicator of the centrality of marriage to the expansion and protection of elite power. As marriage is intended to occur only once, the alliances made between families are highly valued and singular strategic choices not to be wasted. Ostracising non-conforming family members, particularly male family members who hold responsibility for continuing both the family line and the business, is a form of sanction that both punishes non-conformity and warns other family members against future transgressions.

Notes

1. cf. Gilding 2004; 2010.
2. The term 'begum' was originally a title for a female royal or aristocrat in Central and South Asia, usually referring to the wife of a lord or official. Today in South Asia, it is used as an honorific for Muslim women of high social status. 'Sahib' is the masculine term for 'master' or someone of high status.
3. A *biraderi* is an extended, patrilineal kinship group that often serves as a strong determinant of community loyalty and cohesion.
4. If indeed she was worried about my declining marriageability, she was not alone. A number of my close male friends and informants asked a number of times if I was willing to stay in Pakistan and be a second wife given that most men in my age group had already married, and that agreeing to be a second wife would give me many more options from which to choose.
5. Alavi (1976, 5) notes that Islamic law neither demands preferential marriage within a patrilineage nor prohibits marital exchanges outside a patrilineage.
6. The particularities of these traditional preferred marital strategies differ among ethnic, regional and biraderi groups.
7. Families of four to eight children were the norm for the business families for whom I developed genealogies.
8. Fakra is the fictional name I give to an actual town in KP.
9. To preserve the anonymity of this family *tafat* is the fictional name I have given for an agricultural product.
10. Zaat or jaat is an occupationally grouped community emerging from, but not fully analogous with, the Indian caste system.
11. Interview data has been fact-checked and verified against archival records.
12. Though today Ahmedis are a highly persecuted religious group in Pakistan, noted in the constitution as 'non-Muslims' despite their professed belief in Islam, in the 1940s and 50s a number of elite Ahmedis held senior and highly esteemed government positions.
13. Ahmedis are a long-persecuted minority in Pakistan, who follow an Islamic religious movement decreed un-Islamic in a constitutional change made by General Zia in 1984. Ahmedis are highly discriminated against across all social classes in Pakistan. Though a number of high-profile Ahmedis, like Talat's friend, remain included in the social circles of the elite, they were severely limited to marriages within their sect.

Chapter 5

THE ELITE NETWORK

e⤳

As we walk towards the stately, illuminated home of one of Islamabad's most exclusive suburbs, trickles of laughter and music drift down to greet us. The cul-de-sac is clogged by Landcruisers, Mercedes and BMWs. Drivers emerge to open the back doors of cars, while the shalwar kameez clad workers of the construction site opposite survey the procession of suits and gowns from where they rest on the stacked bricks of tomorrow's labour.

A white-suited member of the household staff leads us through the fairy-lit and manicured gardens, through the small huddles of men in black suits smoking and drinking whiskey-pani and past the brightly decorated, bejewelled and kohl-lined women perched on couches across each side of the garden's periphery. A waiter appears as if from nowhere and, as I take my wine, he immediately offers to make my friend Kamil something stronger. With drinks in hand, Kamil steers me towards the host: he is one of Islamabad's most well-known politicians and wealthiest businessmen. We are introduced to a group of what the host claims are 'four of the most influential men in Pakistan' and the host disappears to circulate amongst the familiar crowd of faces. The most authoritative of this group introduces himself as a retired naval officer and former advisor to both President Musharraf and President Zardari and assures me he can help with my research on business and politics in Pakistan.

At parties like this the lines between social and business-networks blur as one mingles with the highest tier of Pakistan's commercial, political and military elite; retired senior military, senior bureaucrats and major businessmen engage in shared leisure activities centred around drinking, smoking and sharing insider information based on first-hand experience as well as rumour and gossip gleaned from other members of the elite classes. One of the important functions of these events is to create a space of intimacy between individuals who may be functionally useful to one another. By hosting events that people want to come to, which are known for having interesting and high-status guests, and quality alcohol (a lure in itself given the difficulty of procuring it on the black market), the business, political, bureaucratic and military elite generate trust; and through sharing recreation, develop relationships that transcend instrumental goals and take on genuine qualities of affection and friendship.

This sharing of leisure and enjoyment among men with the objective of fostering intimacy that may facilitate business or political objectives is not unique to Pakistan, or to developing country contexts. Examples of how elite businessmen engage in shared revelry, heavy drinking and flirtations with women as part of a purposeful strategy to transcend the formality of work relationships are explored in both Allison's (2009) research on the interactions of Japanese businessmen in hostess bars and Osburg's (2013) research on the class of 'new rich' businessmen in China. In both accounts, they demonstrate how elite men seek to generate affective ties that will in turn prove advantageous to their business transactions. The experience of elite male networking in Pakistan is, however, differentiated from that engaged in by men in the developed economies of Japan, and increasingly China, in that the instrumental element of these relationships is not only a strategy to maximise profits: it is also a critical means to insulate the elite against the vagaries of the state, and of the insecurity of the economic and political environment.

In the chapter that follows I explore how social relationships between elite men are used to reinforce their power and privilege by creating endogamous social spaces that preclude the entrance of non-elites. This chapter will examine the ways in which elite men foster peer to peer relationships with other elite men through social interaction, and how they make use of these relationships to overcome obstacles to their business and political success. The first part of the chapter explores how elites foster affective relationships with other powerful and influential individuals in business, the bureaucracy, formal politics and the military through endogamous elite male socialising. The second section provides specific examples of how these relationships are called upon to deal with challenges to elite power or privilege.

The Hybrid Roles of Friendship

Anthropologists have long differentiated between relationships which are primarily emotional in nature, and those that are primarily functional and entered into with the purpose of gaining access to desired social or economic resources (Wolf 2001). Wolf (1966, 12) defined an emotional friendship as being one that 'satisfies some emotional need' and which is confined to a small social circle. In contrast, he defined instrumental friendships as those where each member of the friendship serves as 'a potential connecting link to other persons outside'. These concepts have their origin with Aristotle (1976 [350 BCE]), who made clear differentiations between friendships based on affection or virtue, and those based upon utility, and later by philosophers such as Montaigne (1991 [1580]). Both Aristotle and Montaigne exalted affective friendships while denouncing instrumental ones.

In his work on Sicily, a context not dissimilar to contemporary Pakistan in terms of its 'great inequality in the distribution of economic and political power', Boissevain (1974, 24) picked up Aristotle, Montaigne and Wolf's differentiation between affective and instrumental friendships. He argued that for Sicilians, all 'friends are actual or potential intermediaries and patrons. For when a friend is called on to provide protection or assistance . . . the friendship becomes asymmetrical and shades off into patronage'. For each of these scholars, affective and instrumental friendships are clearly separate. A friendship may transform from one objective to the other based on the need one member of the friendship has for assistance.

Mauss's (1966) theory of the hybridity of gift-giving, exchange, reciprocity and obligation, dissolved the binary nature of virtue and self-interest that Aristotle and Montaigne had assumed, by revealing the universal way in which mutual obligation creates social integration and cements relationships. The blended instrumental/affective nature of relationships is, for instance, particularly evident in the Chinese practice of *guanxi*. Guanxi, the custom of gift-giving in Chinese business, demonstrates the hybridity of the gift within interlinked worlds of business and friendship in contemporary China (Kipnis 1997, Smart 1993, Strickland 2010). Smart (1993) explains that through guanxi 'a critical social capital of trust, not just obligation, is created through the repeated exchange of gifts and favours'. Like many relationships, guanxi 'simultaneously creates human feeling and material obligation' (Kipnis 1997, 23).

At each of the events described in this chapter, with a regular rotation of guests, and the sharing of affection and sentiment through partaking in songs, dancing and sharing memories of an idealised Pakistani past, the lines between the affective and instrumental, and work and relaxation, blur. Consequently, the hosting and attendance of intimate dinners, parties and large events with powerful and politically influential elites from each of Pakistan's political parties, major institutions and regions, form a critical component of elite alliance-building. These pleasurable social activities and the sharing of valuable political, economic and social knowledge create an inner circle of trust in which to strengthen existing friendships, cultivate new acquaintances and overcome the distrust that exists between the ethnic and regional communities from which members of the elite originate.

Endogamous Socialising

Returning to the party scene described at the beginning of this chapter, as dinner is announced, the former presidential advisor escorts me to a table resplendent with a centrepiece of overflowing white roses, and I find myself seated to the left of a senior official of the Capital Development Authority, the government body responsible for permit and license-granting among a variety of other city planning matters in Islamabad, Naseer and his wife, Ameena. We each introduce ourselves and Ameena begins engaging us in small talk regarding an upcoming gala event she is organising. She laughs at the men's jokes, and several times references her husband's accomplishments and standing, drawing him into the centre of the conversation. As the plates for the first course are cleared Naseer leans towards the political advisor and enquires after a former President's health. He then asks the advisor to share the former President's mobile phone number and to arrange a meeting between them over the coming week. It is a commonplace exchange. The telephone number to contact is entered into his mobile phone, the waiters serve tea and coffee and the conversation moves on to other issues.

The hosting and attendance of intimate dinners, parties and events with other powerful and politically influential elites form a critical component of how elites create and strengthen relationships with other elites from across Pakistan's business, bureaucratic, political and military/security circles. These pleasurable social activities and the sharing of valuable political, economic and social knowledge create an inner circle of trust in which to strengthen existing friendships and cultivate new acquaintances. The performative elements of these parties enable the business elite, and the political, bureaucratic and military elite with whom they are connected to display their wealth, and their connections. But the display also has an important functional purpose in the generation and production of wealth and influence – these forums provide an opportunity for the elite to identify one another, to reinforce social hierarchy, to share information and to facilitate the introductions that broaden political and business opportunities.

For the Pakistani elite, regardless of their origins in the business, bureaucratic, military or political strata, the political life of the nation is something they are comfortable, familiar and often even intimate with – whether that intimacy involves possessing insider political knowledge by personally serving in a political capacity, or through occupying the same social circles as the elected political leaders who determine state policy. This intimacy with politics is one of the primary ingredients of 'being elite' in Pakistan. The level of access elites have to those in political power, and the extent to which they can either passively or actively influence national and local politics is in large part determined by an individual's wealth and status. Even for those who do not follow politics closely, those with direct and indirect political influence are known to one another, or are only one social connection away. As a result, at its uppermost levels, the country's economic system is closed, and the elite, not legal statutes, create, control and guard their domain, serving as gatekeepers to those outsiders who might seek to gain entry.

A former senior official from the National Accountability Bureau (NAB), the government department mandated with identifying and investigating corruption charges described a friend he recognised as being particularly adroit at the process of cultivating social connections for economic advantage from among a broadly affiliated group of Islamabadis. He noted that a major component of his friend's business was networking through the hosting of small exclusive parties in his home. At each of these parties he would build a guest list around a carefully selected 'target' guest with whom he intended to enter into a business arrangement or to seek a favour in the medium to long-term. He crafted these lists with great care. The former official explained,

> I have a friend who owns the best [home] bar in Islamabad. He calls himself a business consultant, and he works for a number of international companies. His house is a huge American-style mansion. He regularly hosts these garden parties, perfectly catered, with only around twenty people attending each party. These parties are attended by Generals, members of the ISI [national

intelligence agency], senior bureaucrats, any kind of person who it may be helpful to know at some point in the future . . . One or two of his employees will also be present at every party in case they need to follow up, or provide information. He also has an old Islamabad socialite on his payroll, just there to help bring in the right people and facilitate introductions. Usually there will be only one or two people attending each party as his target, the rest are just there to add to the atmosphere. The one target person will be someone from whom he needs a favour. This way he has government officials dining at his home before they even need to consider whether to issue him a contract. The entertaining is not a bribe; the entertainment is just to lure them in.

Cultivating an adequately broad network of individuals with some degree of influence is important for all citizens in Pakistan's unstable state context. Individuals rely on personal relationships to deal with their problems, and those with less power need more powerful patrons to advocate on their behalf (Lyon 2004). For the elite, however, their social network comprises the nation's most powerful and influential individuals. Elite businessmen and politicians actively cultivate friends, associates, patrons and clients, but also a network of allies and supporters with complementary sources of power across the business community, the bureaucracy, political parties and the military who can be relied upon to provide their support in the medium term.

These medium-term or temporary alliances are based upon shared sociality and affection and hold a crucial role in defending and protecting the interests of the elite as a united class. In many situations, these pragmatic or affection-based temporary alliances serve as a shield against the as-yet-unknown uncertainties and challenges that may arise in the absence of predictable and impersonal government laws and regulations (as explored in more detail in Chapter Six). As a result, the ability of the elite to intervene on behalf of those in their network, either by addressing the problem directly or calling on the members of their social class, is both unparalleled within the broader population and – when they deem it worthwhile to do so – enormously effective. By assisting others with power or influence within critical institutions and across well-connected families, Pakistani business elites maintain a network of the country's most powerful and influential individuals, indebted, willing and obliged to assist when threats emerge. These networks serve to insulate elites against outside threats to their assets or position through the diverse assets of those they know and with whom they socialise.

These dense social networks are, however, prone to flux, and require constant careful cultivation. They also require elites to maintain a delicate balance between the affective and the instrumental, being careful not to outweigh the former with the latter. Efforts to blend the instrumental and affective were evident at most of the social interactions I attended between elites, though to greatly varying degrees. As the careful cultivation of the guest list described by the former official above demonstrates, the ability of the elite to generate instrumental friendships creates affiliations that enable individuals to extract specific, tangible favours. The result is that elite power and privilege is routinely reinforced and consolidated through both permanent kinship ties (as explored in the previous chapter), and the partially transactional relationships that blend shared enjoyment and affection with instrumental objectives. These interactions shore up elite power, and configure it in specific ways that reflect not only the desire of elite individuals to pursue economic incentives, but also the desire of individuals to generate and reward affection, help and loyalty.

The Necessity of Alliance Making

Many scholars have explored the means through which elites secure their position of power within society through alliance-making, conflict and competition (Barth 1959, Nelson 2011, Martin 2015, Lindholm 1982, Ahmed 2011 [1980]). Most relevant to the interpersonal elements of alliance-making among political scientists is Khan's (2010) theory of political settlements. Khan argued that elite groups sustain themselves through incorporating other powerful factions into their ruling coalition, as incorporating these groups was more advantageous than absorbing the ongoing costs of engaging in continuous conflict. In this process of absorbing other elite groups, the ruling elite minimised possible threats to their power and contestations over their chosen distribution of resources.

Khan's (2010) theory of political settlements focused largely on understanding the performance of institutions and the ways in which powerful groups, loosely defined, utilise these institutions to advance their own interests. Instead of classes, Khan (2010, 8) examined factions and coalitions.[1] Instead of a state that mediates between the interests of various elites (as Hamza Alavi 1972, cited in the Introduction, had argued), Khan argued that political factions, groups with specific factional rather than class interests (p. 62), directly compete with one another for both political power and economic capital. These groups, he argued, engage in continual processes of conflict and contestation as they each compete for the same resources. The individuals and groups who remain dominant at any given time are those able to inflict the greatest costs upon their rivals, and to absorb the costs rivals inflict upon them. In addition to these processes of conflict, elites survive by incorporating and absorbing other powerful factions into their own ruling coalition. His analysis provides some insight into the way that boundaries are selectively maintained, or made porous, to the greatest advantage of the dominant group. While his analysis provides a means of understanding the processes factional groups use to secure their own power and influence, it provides little room to analyse individual elite interests within these elite factions.

Khan's analysis implies that political factions shift form based upon the specific goal held by individuals at one point in time, and as a consequence his analysis presents a structure of largely temporary and shifting alliances that respond to, and are reconfigured by, changing circumstances. In his analysis, powerful groups engage in conflict with one another to access limited resources, and incorporate powerful opponents when they cannot defeat them. And yet, Khan's conflict-focused analysis does not explain the remarkable level of integration found among Pakistan's elite, across institutional affiliations, nor the resources of time and money invested by this group in cultivating alliances with their economic and status equivalents.

Cultivating a Shared Class Identity

The elite class in Pakistan, though constituting a largely unified social order, is comprised of separate and distinct sub-groups which form a complex and multi-stranded network. These networks are comprised of cross-institutional and cross-lineage ties linking the uppermost tier of politics, business, the bureaucracy and the military – and the economic elites of each of the nation's ethnic communities. The cohesiveness of these disparate groups, with their hold over separate but equally powerful institutions, has been critical in enabling the families that comprise the elite to retain their position of privilege and pre-eminence over the past seventy or more years.

Over tea in his office, Zahir, the owner of one of Pakistan's major media houses, lifted up his phone to show me his phone directory and proclaimed,

> To be successful in business in Pakistan you need affluence, connections, parties, socialising . . . I keep a budget for entertaining and parties. I know everyone. I have all the powerful big boys on my speed dial: the Prime

Minister, the Chief Minister, the Head of Army Operations for the whole of Punjab . . . Anyone who is big enough has access to these devils. My family is responsible for fifteen per cent of the parties in Lahore – for those who matter, that is. It is only a handful of people who host these types of parties. All the "who's who" mingle at these few people's homes.

Though there was some hyperbole in the statement above, Zahir's role in shaping the opinion and attitudes of a large proportion of the Punjabi population, and the political dominance of Punjab in national politics, made him enormously powerful. Like most powerful Pakistanis, his power did not come only from his economic or professional position, but from the cultural capital inherited from his family – and from their reputation in politics, business and importantly, their reputation for entertaining: his family's parties were famous and invitations were sought after. When I was invited to the *mehndi* event of his brother's wedding some months later I could see why: it was spectacularly opulent, with wild and exuberant dancing, boutique-clad guests swathed in silk and chiffon of every colour and at least half of the elite businessmen I had interviewed in Lahore in attendance. Though I had identified and met many of these men through separate contacts, it quickly became apparent that they were all known to one another, had gone to school together, and that many were friends. The dyadic relationships between each of the men I knew comprised a much larger class of elite whose identities, loyalties and political and economic interests were intertwined.

The integrated nature of the various institutional affiliations of the elite was particularly evident at the elite parties I attended in Islamabad. In Islamabad, home to a more recent and transient population of elites, events were often attended by a mix of established and Navay Raje families. A number of businessmen and politicians held gatherings every one to two weeks, while others hosted dinners or evening drinks every few months, or just a few times a year. It was, as several businessmen noted, important to reciprocate in providing entertainment, networking opportunities, food and alcohol. In Lahore and Karachi, the gatherings I attended were often less diverse. The gatherings I attended at the Sind Club and the Boat Club in Karachi (discussed in Chapter Three), for instance, consisted largely of elite business families, with occasional guests from one of the diplomatic embassies in Islamabad seeking to increase bilateral trade, or the representative of a multinational corporation seeking to establish an investment partnership.

In Islamabad my friend Kamil hosted bi-weekly gatherings with a small but carefully crafted guest list. The male guests were invariably among the most powerful people in the nation, including those based in Islamabad, and a regular rotation of businessmen and politicians from Lahore and Karachi visiting Islamabad to meet with politicians and bureaucrats, to lobby, or to conduct business. The most regular attendees at these gatherings included a sugar mill owner, a Federal Minister, the spokesperson of one of the major opposition political parties, a senior television news anchor, and a well-known political columnist reputed for his excellent relationships on all sides of politics and his ability to elicit insider information. With one or two exceptions, most of Kamil's male guests were invited only to every second or third event, ensuring a rotating group of powerful individuals occupying different spheres of influence and holding varied positions of authority. At the larger parties Kamil hosted every few months, the dynamic shifted considerably as a more diverse crowd of people attended, including the vast social circle with whom Kamil cultivated reciprocal hospitality. This group included professionals – doctors, lawyers, art collectors and a range of mid-sized business owners. Belonging to a slightly different tier of elite guest outside of the uppermost tier of business or political decision-making, many of these guests brought their wives or husbands.

The attendees of these events benefitted from their attendance at Kamil's gatherings in multiple ways. Kamil was an excellent host, served a much sought after *nihari*, alcohol was liberally provided, and one guest or another often took it on themselves to start the singing of old Punjabi love songs. Beyond these enjoyments, the opportunity to meet with powerful individuals from across the country, each with separate spheres of political or economic influence in their own region, city or constituency, made events like those held at Kamil's enormously useful in consolidating relationships among a group of variously-affiliated, and ethnically diverse, elite. This opportunity to interact outside of their own institutions and closely-knit kinship and biraderi group, was an important addition to the more homogenous and endogamous relationships they cultivated in settings like the social club.

For Kamil, the attendees at these parties provided him with valuable information on the state of the nation's politics, economy and developments in business – vital information for his own success as an indentor. Much of his work required him to be aware of the developments that may affect the ventures of his clients as they emerged, and his extensive social network kept him appraised of political and economic developments across the country long before they were reported in any formal forums. Further, his knowledge of these issues ensured he would be able to mitigate or eliminate the damaging effects of these developments on the investments of his clients, or capitalise on the opportunities they provided, by calling in favours from his extensive social and professional network.

As the projects Kamil facilitated were implemented across the country – in Punjab, Khyber Pakhtunkhwa, Sindh and Balochistan – it was a requisite that his own network be correspondingly diverse in terms of the ethnic and regional backgrounds of his friends and associates. Working in Balochistan, for instance, a region riven with insurgency movements, he needed to keep abreast of tensions, where they were likely to occur, which individuals may need to be appeased and which local leaders he might need to enlist to ensure their political objectives did not impinge upon his economic objectives. Though the majority of his guests in Islamabad tended to be Punjabi (given the preponderance of Punjabis in senior government, and the proximity of Islamabad to Punjab), the highest tier of the Muhajir, Sindhi and Pakhtun ethnic communities were also often represented. These non-Punjabi elites come from ethnic communities that are comparatively politically and economically marginalised: both they, and the communities from which they emerge, are often disgruntled by the benefits apportioned to Punjab and the related status they receive in terms of government services and infrastructure, and political representation. Yet in social forums like Kamil's, retired senior military, senior bureaucrats and major businessmen from each community mingled in shared leisure activities centred around drinking, smoking and sharing insider information based on first-hand experience as well as rumour and gossip gleaned from other members of the elite classes.

Kamil's purposeful cultivation of a large and ethnically diverse social circle with utilitarian value to his business was by no means unusual, particularly in the government city of Islamabad. But whereas the composition of the guests at Kamil's bi-weekly gatherings were drawn from each of the nation's various political parties, as well as the bureaucracy, and business, with standing invitations to his friends from Karachi, Lahore and rural Sindh when they came to the city, other gatherings focused more on ensuring the inclusion of people holding the particular government positions advantageous to his business interests.

An additional outcome of these gatherings and their mixed composition of elites was that they also served to help dissolve the tensions between elite members of the nation's various ethnic, as well as institutional, communities, and to foster class comradery and a shared ruling class identity. Unlike the criteria used in determining the permanent alliances of kinship and marriage described in the previous chapter, the inter-elite affiliations and temporary alliances created through repetitive social practice, served as a continuous effort to minimise the ethnic and institutional fault lines between the nation's elite, and highlighted their shared class interests and affiliations.

The specific goals of elite social events, and hence the way guest-lists are composed for various social events can, however, vary considerably. In small and intimate social settings, the host may have a more general desire to strengthen his network, or to stay abreast of hard-to-obtain information on new business opportunities or government tenders; insights on political crises and ongoing instability, leadership changes, which deals are likely to collapse; or speculation on how business is likely to be affected by extended government shut-downs, road closures, or increased security measures. At the large party hosted by a prominent politician I described at the start of this chapter, the politician host had invited a cross-section of the capital's elite, drawing on senior bureaucrats, former military and the nation's most prominent businessmen. A singer had been flown in from Karachi, as had the chefs of the country's best restaurants, and the event served the purpose of rewarding the men who had supported the host politically over the previous year, and of generating goodwill among those he hoped would support him in the coming year. Rather than fostering a specific relationship for a particular purpose – which would have been impossible among the 200 guests he was obligated to circulate among, he was strengthening his existing network, and rewarding their support by providing them with a space, and with 'the right people', in which to strengthen their own.

Utilising Instrumental Friendships

Connections are vital, not only in securing business opportunities, but in protecting business interests. Indeed, in both developed capitalist economies and developing economies, the elite and affluent face the prospect of encroachments by government regulators keen to supervise business transactions and to tax and redistribute part of the proceeds. In Pakistan, and other developing nations however, it is expected that at least some of the regulators involved in business will seek to extort businessmen and make themselves a quick profit (explored in detail in Chapter Six). Businesses, therefore, face the double burden of formal state regulation and informal coercion. Beyond the vagaries of rent-seeking bureaucrats; the major shifts in economic policy that follow most changes of government; and for some, disruptions to critical supply lines by acts of terrorism or political unrest; Pakistan's unstable political environment ensures that social connections are a critical means for elites to insulate themselves from external shocks.

Consequently, the personal relationships developed through repeated acts of socialising are a way of ensuring that elite individuals are able to insulate themselves from political insecurity, to repel both the legal and informal costs imposed by the state, and to remain competitive in an environment where the least connected individuals pay the highest prices in terms of delays and bribes from government officials. The possession of a sufficiently broad network of powerful friends minimises the possibility of severely disadvantageous shifts in regulation (or greater likelihood of achieving an exemption) and makes overly damaging demands from various parts of the state less likely. The result of this social reliance, and the need to reciprocate assistance from friends in circumventing state demands or repelling the threats of competitors, is that Pakistanis devote a great proportion of their own time and efforts to addressing the threats faced by those in their network.

The transactions and tangible favours that make up this generalised assistance are evident in the account Abid Afridi gave me of his relationship with a Police Superintendent. The assistance provided in this case illustrates the ambiguity between affect and instrumental relationships that often characterises elite relationships,

> I have a friend who is an SP [Superintendent of Police] and he is very clean and known for not taking bribes. But the other night he calls me up and says "Yaar [friend], your village has the best kebab in KP, could you please send some to me for my party?" And of course I do it. I give him little favours, little gifts like this that are so small that they do not even seem like bribes. But over a year of giving small gifts, I could easily have given one person 20,000 dollars' worth of gifts. Is that a bribe? It is a *favour* and of course he will have to return it to me. If I have a problem with the police, I call him, and he solves it for me. He would not take any money from me, but items and gifts, as long as they are not too big at one time, he will take.

Abid's relationship with the Superintendent was valuable to him, and it was something of which he was proud. Being seen together at a café increased his public standing. Further, having it known that he had an affective relationship with a senior member of the police force served as a degree of protection against those who might seek to extort him or interfere with the running of his business. It was also something with a specific problem-solving value, and a friendship that directly mitigated his vulnerability to demands from corrupt members of the police force. Having an instrumental friendship with someone in this position not only ensured Abid was personally protected from abuses of power by police lower in the ranks, it also ensured that he was able to draw on this relationship to provide favours to other friends being charged, investigated, or abused by the police.

As this friendship demonstrates, the ability of Abid to generate relationships involving mutual assistance with someone exercising power in a complementary sphere, in this case within the police, enabled him to use the relationship to extract specific, tangible favours. As a result, his personal power and privilege was routinely reinforced and consolidated in a highly transactional and individualistic manner, operating not primarily through organised, even if informal, networks, but through individual-level transactions. Yet the long-term nature of the reciprocal exchange had developed a genuinely affective component that rendered the relationship resistant to an exact exchange of goods or money for service provided. These micro-level interactions shored up elite power and configured it in specific ways that reflected not only the desire of elite individuals to pursue economic incentives, but also the desire of individuals to generate and reward affection, help and loyalty.

As a learned strategy to reduce vulnerability, Lyon (2004) argued that all Pakistanis assume shifting dominant or subordinate roles in response to the structural vulnerability of living in a society in which market, political and structural security does not exist (Lyon 2004). He argued that patron/client relationships in Pakistan are 'elastic nodes within human resource networks made up of both patrons and clients', with individuals serving variously in both roles depending on 'who is in contextual or situational need'. As is clear in the example above, the provider of assistance shifts depending on the circumstances and the relationship of parity is maintained.

Yet, in the Pakistani context, even accessing government departments designed to foster the effective running of business can be highly problematic without a personal introduction to facilitate the transaction and protect the interests of the businessmen involved. A former bureaucrat at the NAB, the government body that monitors, investigates and prosecutes corruption cases, described the challenges business people face from within departments that are meant to be on their side,

> Accessing people in power is one of the biggest problems in Pakistan. For instance, if someone wanted to contact one of us at the NAB, they would not be able to do it. We just cannot be contacted. Many business people pay a huge amount of money to get this access . . .
>
> I have a businessman friend, who is the sole importer of a particular item, and he had an import license cancelled. We were meant to be having lunch and he kept calling me and apologising for being late because he was sitting in a car outside while one of his staff people went inside to bribe a government official to have his import license reinstated. I asked him who he was paying, and once I knew which agency it was, I realised that the head of the agency was my walking partner. I told him to call his staff person back right away and to come and see me.
>
> That evening on our regular walk I explained the situation to my walking partner and asked him to just meet with my friend whose license had been cancelled, to review the merits of the case, and then to decide as he saw fit. So, there was a meeting between them, and it became apparent that a low-level staff in the department had cancelled my friend's license on a pure technicality just to extract money from him. Cancelled licenses of course cause huge losses to businessmen as their items spoil at the harbour or in storage while their shipments are delayed, so they are generally willing to pay a two-million-rupee bribe and take that from the profits. It is part of their cost of doing business. My walking partner promised to resolve it. When I told my other friend, he asked me what he could do to repay the favour, and I told him that my walking partner wouldn't take money. He was shocked that my friend in government had been willing to do a favour for him without him needing to pay him any money. I told him he could take us both out for a nice dinner instead. So that is what he did.

By taking the bureaucrat and the former NAB official out to dinner, the businessman not only reciprocated the favour they had each pro vided him, he also consolidated his relationship with the bureaucrat. The act of accepting a favour, and then repaying it in a social setting over a meal and relaxed conversation, allowed him to broaden his network of powerful friends, and enabled him to develop a direct, rather than mediated, relationship with a senior official in a position to assist him with his business in future.

Favours and gifts are a fundamental part of maintaining the relationships and networks needed for elite business in Pakistan. In opposition to bribes, which are financial payments for clearly-defined benefits, the ambiguity of the purpose of a gift is the very reason gifts are so useful. As Smart's (1993) research on business in China showed, gifts and bribes in business are different only in terms of the way the gift is given, not because of the type or value of the gift. He explained that for an item to be received as a gift,

> the relationship must be presented as primary and the exchanges, useful though they may be, treated as only secondary. If, instead, it becomes apparent that the relationship involves only material interest and is characterised by direct and immediate payment, the exchange is classified as one of bribery.

Consequently, in developing countries where weakly enforced regulations make mutual trust a requisite pre-condition for large-scale business transactions, business relationships are often conducted between individuals in relationships that involve a degree of personal friendship between those making a transaction (Osburg 2013, Smart 1993). In some circumstances, a veneer of friendship, when accompanied by gifts and favours, is used to legitimise what may otherwise be seen as an illegitimate, even unethical, transaction.

Favour giving, of course, is a part of most friendships. What differentiates favour giving in the instances described above is the scale and source of that favour – a private citizen giving their friend a favour shares their own resources (information, contacts, or goods), but a government servant, (e.g. a policeman or senior bureaucrat) receiving gifts from a private businessman is now indebted to provide the businessman with something of use to them. As a public servant on a government wage he is not in a position to provide goods of substantial value to a much wealthier friend, but what he does have is power and the ability to command other government employees to do his bidding, or to provide information not otherwise available to private citizens as in the case of Abid and his friend the police superintendent.

Favours between elites who engage in business often take the form of an opportunity that is not available to others – this may be the sharing of insider information, the awarding of a government contract, the offer to buy military owned-land, or a special price on a vital item required for manufacturing. Many of these opportunities are presented as private deals between individuals, even when they involve government or military interests. In circumstances where regulations are being thwarted, preferential contracts awarded, or cartelistic practices implemented, trust between business parties becomes even more critical to ensure government bodies such as the Federal Bureau of Revenue (FBR) or the National Accountability Bureau (NAB) are kept at bay. I return to these exchanges in Chapter Six.

Policing a Selective Moral Code

The presumed irreligiosity and excesses of the rich are regularly critiqued in the Pakistani popular media. Certain forms of distinction engaged in by many among the elite – particularly in terms of the consumption of alcohol, and the intermingling of unrelated men and women, are distinctly averse to the manners and religious principles of vast sections of the Pakistani population. Engaging in these behaviours comes to constitute a form of exceptionalism constructed by the elite to ensure their distinction (explored in Chapter Three), and to differentiate themselves from the religious piety valued and enacted by the lower and middle classes.

Yet, because these powerfully negative images can be so damaging to an individual's public reputation, the elite keep close watch of one another's behaviour, and usually adhere to a strict norm of maintaining secrecy within the class. The insulated nature of elite social forums ensures that the drinking of alcohol, interactions with women, drug use, or other perceived excesses are very rarely made public. Practices of self-policing ensures that the critiques of elite lifestyles that do make it into the popular media are vague, hyperbolic and usually based not on observation but on rumour. The individuals attending such occasions remain unnamed, and no action is taken by any government agency to curtail illegal alcohol consumption or drug use.

The self-policing that takes place within these forums includes primarily an etiquette against discussing potentially politically damaging behaviour outside of those attending, or in purposefully ensuring guests did not directly witness behaviours it may be damaging for them to have been privy to. At several events, for instance, the host had procured cocaine for those interested in partaking and arranged the white lines of powder in neat rows on the sparkling marble countertop of his personal en-suite, upstairs, away from the larger group convened in his sitting room. Quiet words were exchanged between guests known to enjoy the drug and one by one a select group disappeared briefly to the upstairs bedroom before re-joining the larger group. All were aware of the drug use, but those who did not wish to partake could both avoid directly witnessing the activity, and claim (or feign) ignorance should they later feel the need to. Though partaking in alcohol was much more ubiquitous, it was almost as carefully policed. On the rare occasions when photos were taken (for instance, during a birthday celebration I attended), without being instructed, the guests carefully cleared the bottles of Johnny

Walker and glasses of amber liquid from out of the camera's frame before any photographs were taken.

During eleven months of the year, the individuals who would not drink alcohol at the elite social events I attended were in stark minority. With the exception of an event I attended hosted by the Afridis in their village in KP, almost all of the events I attended with these business elites in the urban centres of Islamabad, Lahore and Karachi involved alcohol. This was notably not the case with the social events of middle-class, mid-scale industrialists where alcohol was usually not served. Among my elite informant group, however, even the younger generation of Afridis provided alcohol at their social events, though they themselves did not drink it. It was an expected social convention among most the elite. Because of the widely held connotation between drinking alcohol and a socially liberal and secular outlook, those Punjabis who did not drink often defensively proclaimed their socially liberal views.[2]

The friendly associations maintained between variously affiliated, and sometimes publicly antagonistic, members of the elite were another insider secret. For instance, when a young female guest at one of Kamil's regular gatherings used the camera on her mobile phone to photograph a prominent male journalist – widely known for his criticism of the current regime – in the lap of a government minister, she was swiftly and tersely reprimanded by another guest. The young woman was sternly instructed to delete her photographs, and informed that it would be highly problematic if the minister, or other guests, were seen to be frolicking with a member of the press.

* * *

Friendship in any context may be partly instrumental, regardless of affective ties. Yet, as has been demonstrated in this chapter, both inter- and intra-elite socialising in Pakistan is confined to a tightly guarded social space, whose membership is carefully policed. Within elite forums, the instrumental nature of these relationships is less about direct financial assistance, and more about access to a network of powerful individuals occupying complementary spheres of power that enable elite families to engage with the government in advantageous ways. The social medium in which these networks are fostered creates a hidden social world that cannot be easily accessed by those from outside the class. This exclusion is much more than social, it ensures that those outside the class are also prohibited from entering the forums where the nation's highest level of political and economic decisions are made.

Intra-elite social events enable Pakistan's elite to maintain economic and political dominance by creating a space of intimacy between elite individuals occupying complementary spheres of power and influence and belonging to separate ethnic communities riven with division and antagonism. A critical function of these events is to create temporary alliances between individuals who may be functionally useful to one another. By hosting events that people want to come to, that are known for having interesting and high-status guests, and quality alcohol, the business, political, bureaucratic and military elite generate trust; and through sharing recreation, develop relationships that transcend stratification along ethnic lines. in addition to fun and relaxation, intra-elite social events serve to both (1) unite individuals from separate institutional affiliations, and/or varied ethnic communities in support of shared strategic goals, and (2) to unify, consolidate and apportion the power and influence held by members of the *same* institutional, or ethnic and regional group emerging from the influence and assets they hold in their own region and community. Critically, in many cases, elites from across Pakistan's institutional spheres of influence, or ethnic communities draw their support from one another, regardless of the tensions inherent between the communities from which they originate.

Notes

Parts of this chapter were published previously as a journal article in *The Asia Pacific Journal of Anthropology* and are reproduced here with permission (see Armytage 2015).

1. Khan (2010) defines a ruling coalition 'as [comprised of the] factions that control political authority and state power in different societies'.
2. The term 'liberal' is often used pejoratively in Pakistan in reference to elites. Akbar Zaidi's (2008, 37) use of the term 'lifestyle liberals', for instance, refers to those among the elite who drink and socialise in mixed gender environments, but who may concurrently hold conservative or anti-democratic political outlooks. The converse is also true in that popular conceptions often equate religiosity, indicated by abstaining from alcohol, with political conservatism. As a result, those who both abstain and believe themselves to hold liberal political views are often challenged to state and defend them.

– Chapter 6 –

THE CULTURE OF EXEMPTIONS

The Pakistan Business Council will show you a hunky-dory picture of Pakistan, but Pakistan is not a hunky-dory place. Anything can happen here. So, you have to be a *mafioso* here. I have a black book where I list all the people who screw me, and then I get on and screw *them*. I have built a reputation so people know they cannot mess with me. If anyone messes with me, I will use the judiciary against them. You have to teach them a lesson once and for all. They know I will do something legally – or otherwise – to ensure they will not mess with me. I can take them to court. I can use stay orders. I can do *other* things. You need to be one step ahead of someone challenging you. If someone takes your rice bowl you go after them where it hurts them the most. You make them bleed. If someone comes and takes my customer, I will find a way to poach his most valued company. I will find a way.

—Mohsin, Businessman, Karachi

Laws are like cobwebs, which may catch small flies, but let wasps and hornets break through.

—Jonathan Swift, 1707

The global '1%' engages with the institutions of the state in very different ways from the middle and working classes, using the legal and regulatory infrastructure of the state to its fullest extent. As Mohsin's statement made evident, he viewed the courts as part of his competitive arsenal, and the law as a mechanism he could use to direct – even subvert – the governance structures relevant to his desire for market dominance, and to teach foolish rivals 'a lesson'. His statement above was not merely hyperbole and self-aggrandisement. Like elites across the world, his ability to punish competitors he believed to have stepped out of line through a coterie of lawyers and accountants[1] adept at navigating national, and international laws, was vast.

Discussions of the extra-legal activities routinely engaged in by the Pakistani elite were frequent throughout my fieldwork with businessmen, politicians and bureaucrats. Some of these activities were illegal, but most conformed to Nordstrom's (2007, 211) definition of the vast range of activities belonging to the *extra-legal*, including those which are 'illicit, and informal, *as well as* undeclared, unregistered, and unregulated, actions' and those that 'are *not technically illegal* in themselves, but [which] violate the letter of the law because they are not accountable to systems of declaration and taxation' [italics my own]. Like the global elite of which they are a part, the Pakistani elite direct the legal and regulatory structures that determine flows of wealth and opportunity within the country, while simultaneously operating outside of, and above, these structures, engaging in what I term a 'culture of exemptions'.

Internationally, elites engage a wide array of wealth accumulation strategies not available to the middle and working classes through the use of hedge funds, private equity houses and 'family offices', teams of professional lawyers, accountants and bankers who enable the rich to accumulate and transfer enormous wealth (Glucksberg and Burrows 2016). These professional services include income tax planning, financial planning, cash flow management, preparation of financial reports, philanthropic strategies, investment services (both foreign and domestic) and asset allocation (Rosplock and Hauser 2014). The assistance of this highly professional staff generates opportunities that are opaque to those below the elite classes – and which allow them to amass enormous profits, reduce taxation, transform tax avoidance into tax minimisation, circumvent investment limits through the ability to navigate complex international laws and regulations, and to exploit the gaps that emerge: the extra-legal, and the unregulated.

The marital, social and economic strategies analysed in the preceding chapters enabled elites to circumnavigate Pakistan's laws with a high degree of ease. They also reflect elite patterns of wealth accumulation and preservation not just in Pakistan, but globally. And in large part, so too does their engagement in extra-legal approaches to maximising wealth and minimising taxation. Manipulation or avoidance of the law through the protection provided by these networks was a ubiquitous and powerful component of the suite of strategies elite families used to secure their position within the elite class. For the most part, business elites in Pakistan referred to their engagement in illegal or extra-legal acts as minor misdemeanours undertaken in response to the actions of an unpredictable and immoral state. For

instance, one Karachi stockbroker told me in relation to his appropriation of the legal identity of his junior employees for illegal stock
trading, 'We all do it. You use the name of a driver or a peon. For
instance, my sister's maid made a million dollars and didn't even
know it'. For this stock trader, the trading of company shares under
the name of staff was foremost an act in which a great deal of profit
stood to be gained, second, an act in which no one stood to lose, and
only third, an act contrary to the laws of the State.

Foucault conceived of state power as 'a machinery that no one
owns' (Foucault 1980). It has its own operational momentum which
functions independently, even from the most powerful members of
society. But he also argued that power can be exercised 'only over free
subjects . . . who are faced with a field of possibilities in which several
ways of behaving, several reactions and diverse comportments, may
be realised' (Foucault 1982). Conceptualised this way, individuals are
both constrained by the state and its pervasive influence in processes
ranging from production to kinship and family, and yet remain free
to respond within these strictures in ways they perceive to be most
advantageous to their interests. This chapter examines the ways in
which elite individuals resist and subvert the constraints of state
power in the context of Pakistan's weakly enforced and easily manipulated government institutions, political instability, poorly regulated
economy and dangerous security situation.

The scholarship on Pakistan's business and political realm is
unanimous in noting its high rates of corruption (Islam 2004, Hull
2012, Burki 2015), and of more vaguely defined clientelism between
the state and private business (Khan 1999, Husain 2000, Khan 2010,
Ahmad 1981, Alavi 1972) implying much higher rates of corruption
and bribery than in countries with more developed economies and
more rigidly enforced regulatory systems. Pakistani court records
and the cases reported in the print media also indicate that failing
to comply with taxation laws is widespread among Pakistan's elite.
Among Pakistan's elite business circles, evasion of certain laws and
regulations, particularly those related to taxation, customs, production quotas and factory compliance (both legal and extra-legal)
are expected, and openly admitted. Though a number of Pakistani
businessmen and politicians are reputed not to engage in any form
of illegality (both a point of personal pride and a notable component
of their public reputation), most acknowledge the need to provide
gifts or bribes to ensure that approvals from the government are
granted or expedited, or to avoid taxation or export/import duties.
Many elites are aware that the opportunities they gain from evading

disadvantageous laws are not available to the middle and lower classes. Some even acknowledge that the cumulative effect of tax evasion or minimisation, cartelisation and bribery, both hinders the government's provision of basic public services and increases wage pressure on those in economically precarious positions through price increases. Despite these acknowledgements, I encountered very little condemnation within this small privileged class of the extra-legal advantages available to them, or self-reflexivity on the way that availing of these advantages strengthened and reinforced Pakistan's extreme social and economic inequality.

As noted in scholarship from other country contexts, the reasons for this widespread lack of condemnation reflect divergent structures of law and morality. Scholarship in contexts where weak states and regulatory bodies exist have noted that acts which are 'legal' and 'illegal' and those that are 'moral' and 'immoral' are often not synonymous (Baker and Milne 2015; Hull 2012; Gupta 2012; Gupta 1995; De Sardan 1999; Hasty 2005). Indeed, for most of Pakistan's elite actors they are sharply differentiated. Many elite businessmen described the appropriateness or inappropriateness of behaviour in business, as well as in their social and family lives, by whether or not it would be perceived by the public or by their elite peers as *'badnami'*, an act that is disgraceful, dishonourable, discrediting and entailing a loss of reputation; or as *'izzat'*, an act that is honourable. In shaping their moral discourses in these terms, business elites shift their perceptions on illegality, from potentially *badnami* behaviour, to that which could be understood as *izzat*. Engaging in extra-legality was not seen to be intrinsically immoral or personally problematic, as long as morally sound justification could be provided: the ends justified the means.

As such, the business elite circumscribed a number of laws governing business with both impunity and a sense that doing so was justified and necessary to ensure they remained competitive in the market place. Yet the context in which the Pakistani elite operate in their efforts to accumulate wealth and assets differs from their counterparts in many other national contexts in one key regard: they operate in extremely high political instability unparalleled in many other contexts. In the next section, I examine the prevalence of extra-legality within the Pakistani elite, and then the context and rationale for pervasive circumnavigation of the law: the immoral and capricious state. I then examine the Afridi family's engagement in extra-legal activities, before examining how elite businessmen utilise their cross-institutional social networks to engage in regulatory capture and amass enormous levels of profit through collusion with government.

The Immoral and Capricious State

Mohsin's comment at the start of this chapter is in many ways a familiar, though extreme, version of similar cases involving major businessmen in advanced economies across the world, where elites engage in similar processes to ensure the nation's laws and regulations are either not applied, or not enforced, in relation to their own activities. Yet the experience of the Pakistani elite differs from the global elite in one crucial regard which exacerbates both the degree of extra-legality engaged in, its ubiquity and the brazenness with which it is undertaken.

The Pakistani elite operate in a historical context of massive political and economic instability that has frequently demonstrated the state to be capricious, and for its laws and regulations to be applied in ways that are highly variable, and often personally vindictive (as explored in Chapter Three). Specifically, the betrayal they had experienced at the hands of certain individuals or government regimes was a key component of many elites' personal family narratives, and a key component of their rationale for everyday business decisions.

The majority of those I interviewed referenced one or more key moments in Pakistan's history (discussed in Chapter Two), and the dramatic shifts they engendered in the political and economic context which had come before. For a number of Pakistan's largest business families, many of these events undermined, temporarily or permanently, their position of economic and political dominance. These moments in the nation's history were familiar to even the youngest of those I encountered in business and they spoke strongly of the personal impact of these events on their lives. The turbulence engendered by these and other events, and the oscillations in policy they created, were used by both these business families, and the emerging business elite, as the primary explanation for their decision to engage in acts of extra-legality. This rationale had justified a 'culture of exemptions' which validated elite engagement in extra-legality and the advantages it conferred.

In Pakistan, the state is central to the 'strategies of accumulation and domination' (Martin 2015, 4) of the nation's powerful groups, and features centrally as a justification for elite exemptions. Martin's ethnography revealed the means through which Pakistani landlords reproduced their economic power despite various shifts in party politics and the implementation of policy disadvantageous to their interests through the support of powerful kinship factions in local elections, and through the patronage of various military regimes who required the support of the rural elite. While Martin's claim focused on the role of Pakistan's landlords, his analysis of elite–state power can be more broadly applied. Beyond the centrality of the state in generating opportunities to acquire and amass wealth and assets, most Pakistanis do not regard the Pakistani state as a moral actor (see Hull 2012). Many Pakistanis – of all class backgrounds – observe that the law functions primarily as a political tool, rather than a set of impartial guidelines and associated sanctions to protect the interests of individuals and communities. As a political tool, 'the law' becomes something that exists to be negotiated and manoeuvred. Individuals who are able to circumvent its penalties are often viewed as savvy and well connected by other elites, while those who cannot are regarded as politically inept and socially unconnected. Pakistan's business and political elite actively create the regulatory structure that administers the economic system that they dominate, just as they have actively sought – with a high degree of success – to exempt themselves from it.

Both the centrality of the state, and its immoral character, was frequently mentioned by my informants in discussing their attitudes towards their own extra-legality, and as a justification for circumventing certain laws and regulations. As one businessman told me,

> Here in Punjab you can only make money in partnership with the government. In Baluchistan and the Frontier province, it is all illegal activity that makes you money. We Pathans [Pakhtuns] in senior positions are all crooks. The goodies are brilliant.

The policy shifts engaged in by various regimes have contributed to the narrative of the unpredictable and immoral state, widely employed by the business elite, as evident in the experience of the Afridi family. The attempts of the Afridis to avoid regulation, taxation and restrictions on the production of their product had met with varying degrees of efficacy over the years of their operation. For the most part, they had successfully navigated regular state crises and the dramatic policy changes implemented by successive governments. In each regime, they had circumvented the laws opposed to their profit-making objectives. However, there was one very significant exception told to me by the brothers Abid and Kaleem Afridi and several of our mutual friends, supplemented by the online court proceedings for their case.

Abid and Kaleem's uncle, Roshan Afridi (also Shahzar's father), was a businessman and former politician. He remained influential in the affairs of his hometown of Fakra in Khyber Pakhtunkhwa, and was warmly regarded for his personal loyalty to his friends. He would deploy his substantial resources – both of funding and of loyal local supporters – to the aid of his personal network whenever they found themselves in a political or bureaucratic battle. As several of his old friends fondly told me, 'He keeps good relations with everyone'. Roshan Afridi was also something of a legend among elite businessmen and bureaucrats in Islamabad; renowned (and sometimes infamous) for his alleged distribution of illegal imports and undeclared exports, bribing of regulators and tax under-reporting on a massive scale. His notoriety was sharply illustrated by the comments of a bureaucrat originating from Fakra at the Ministry of Industry and Production, who once exclaimed, not knowing of my existing relationship with the Afridis, 'Given your research, you really should have met Roshan Afridi. He is a fraud and a smuggler!'

When General Pervez Musharraf assumed control of the government through a military coup d'état in 1999 – a major crisis point for many in business – he sought to appear decisive in tackling the nation's endemic corruption. One of his earliest initiatives was to establish the National Accountability Bureau Ordinance (NAB). Musharraf (2006, 150) stated that he had 'established the National Accountability Bureau to put the fear of God into the rich and powerful who had been looting the state'. The Ordinance provided his military government with broad powers to investigate and prosecute cases of corruption and financial mismanagement in business, politics and the bureaucracy (NAB 1999).

Beyond attempting to appear tough on corruption, Musharraf sought to remove the old political elite and create a new one with clear personal loyalties to himself and his regime (Cheema et al 2013). Several bureaucrats I spoke with confirmed that the government at that time had threatened many politicians with a NAB investigation unless they joined the current government. Indeed, many who rose to political prominence during this time did so as a result of their affiliation with the regime of General Pervez Musharraf and the political party he established, the 'Quaid-e-Azam' faction of the Pakistan Muslim League or PML-Q. Those with ties to the PML-Q fared well, and rivals were often harassed and sometimes even placed in jail. The Afridis already had close family ties with an opposition political party and were uninterested in joining Musharaff's alliance. Roshan Afridi was charged under the Ordinance 'for accumulating/acquiring immense wealth/assets, disproportionate to his known sources of income'.[2] It was alleged he had illegally smuggled goods, avoided export and import tax and massively underreported the total volume of goods his companies had produced. As a family business involving Roshan's brothers and nephews, the Afridis were charged with evading tax to the amount of US$ 10 million. Two weeks after NAB issued the charge, Musharraf ordered that the Afridi's factories be shut down overnight.

Like many business families, the family compound occupied the same grounds as several of the factory buildings, and government guards were placed around the perimeter of both the factories and the family home. The family lost all their sources of income in a matter of months. Most of the family's factory properties were sold to ensure the cash-flow needed to maintain a modest standard of living. The Afridis had employed 6,500 employees from the surrounding neighbourhoods, and the closure of their factories resulted in severe unemployment in the local area, and a massive loss in prestige and status for the Afridis as the thousands of families who had depended upon them found themselves without an employer or a welfare system to serve as a social safety net. To isolate the Afridis further, and highlight their loss of wealth and status, each visitor to their home, whether friend, relative, or business associate was interrogated by government guards and warned not to associate with the family.

Like many others in business known to have amassed income through extra-legal sources, Roshan Afridi had declared the family's assets in 1999 as part of the Foreign Exchange Bearer Certificate (FEBC) amnesty the Nawaz Sharif government had implemented in 1998 during his second term (State Bank 1998). The FEBC was a means to incentivise tax avoiders to declare their assets by changing Pakistani funds into US dollars or Pounds Sterling at the current currency rate, thus exempting all 'foreign funds' from wealth and income tax or the need to prove the source of the funds. Once on record, FEBC holders became exempt from legal proceedings related to the source of the funds with the rationale that future tax avoidance would be minimised once these individuals were on the government record.

The FEBC was rumoured to have been implemented by Nawaz Sharif as a tactic to ensure that the finances of both himself and his brother, Shahbaz, the Chief Minister of Punjab, could be 'whitened', enabling the Sharif family's own massive business fortune to avoid regulatory scrutiny. As it was also politically expedient for many politicians and businessmen who had amassed wealth through illegal means or sidestepped their obligation to pay tax, the FEBC also enabled the Sharif regime to appear tough on corruption while avoiding violent opposition from the elite classes who had acquired or enhanced their wealth through these means.

The Afridis believed that because Roshan had turned down Musharraf's personal request to join his government, Musharraf had ordered an investigation into his finances as personal retribution – overturning their formal protection under the FEBC scheme. Roshan Afridi failed to appear for his court hearings and was sentenced to 'rigorous imprisonment for three years in absentia' for tax evasion and corruption. He continued to evade arrest until 2004, when the Supreme Court acquitted him, along with his brothers, and nephews, Abid and Kaleem, due to inadequate evidence.

In 2014, however, ten years after the Khans' acquittal, during Nawaz Sharif's third government, Sharif ordered the NAB to establish a committee to re-examine corruption cases pending from 1999 until 2013 (Shah 2014). Although they had been acquitted, the Afridis' case was included in the list of pending cases. Abid, as the eldest son of the deceased head of family, took over management of the case that targeted himself, his brother Kaleem and two of his uncles. With customary frankness he matter-of-factly acknowledged both his family's engagement in illegal business practice and described the re-examination of their case as a politically motivated attack:

> Yes, of course our assets were acquired illegally, but the assets were made legal through the FEBC amnesty that was granted to business people to make black money, white. Many others did this and avoided charges. The amnesty made it legal. But they still went after us.

Both the use of the FEBC by the Sharif government and their decision to re-open corruption charges acquitted under a previous government, aptly demonstrate the uncertain political environment in which Pakistani business operates. That which was illegal can be made legal, and later pronounced illegal again. The calculations businessmen make to comply, or not, with certain laws are based on the presumption that (1) the law is likely to change within the mid-term horizon, (2) that legal rulings are easily subject to changes in government, and (3) that finances earned legally or illegally may be subject to confiscation with little warning. There is a widespread perception among the elite, drawn from experience, that rewards and punishments for compliance or non-compliance are likely to be implemented for only an intermediate period, no matter what their stated intended duration. Elites in more developed economic contexts do not face this precarity in the same way, and are less subject to the whims of whoever is in power.

During 2014, the period in which I conducted most of my fieldwork in Pakistan, Abid was often busy managing his family's reopened corruption case. As a guilty charge would have likely resulted in the re-confiscation of the family's assets, Abid had engaged all of his personal relationships to ensure the case did not result in a guilty verdict. After having not seen him for two weeks, I met him at the restaurant on the edge of the golf green of the Islamabad Club. I had been following his case closely and, knowing of my interest, he kept me informed of developments,

> I am sorry I haven't seen you. These last few weeks I have been busy polishing my contacts. I have delayed our case at the Supreme Court because my lawyer was not ready. Also, I need to make a few more meetings in relation to the hearing. I have a contact who is friends with the Chairman of NAB. I am looking to see if there is a way I can meet with him to discuss our case and see if I can make a deal with him.
>
> I have already made a deal with the Prosecutor who is our opposition. I am now paying his fee! One of my ex-girlfriends is now a junior judge and she works with the Chief Justice. The Prosecutor is one of her colleagues and they used to work together in the same law firm. We are not on very good terms, but I called her up and asked her to introduce me to the Chief Justice. She told me, 'Do not touch the judiciary' – she knows I would try to give them something – but then she put me in touch with the Prosecutor. She told me not to give him anything, but she knows me better than that. I gave him $20,000 to do badly on our case and not go after us properly.

Towards the end of my fieldwork in late 2014, the case against the Afridis was again dropped on account of insufficient evidence. Abid seemed assured the case would not re-emerge, though the cause for his confidence given past history was not clear to me. I could only conclude that this assurance enabled him to move on and focus on the next challenge.

For the Afridis, whether to act in accordance with the law, or to circumvent it, was a decision that had been made arbitrary by the unpredictability of the state system and associated shifts in policy that accompanied changes in government. Regulatory bodies tasked with overseeing the behaviour of businesses and with sanctioning non-compliance with the law could turn a blind eye under one government, actively collaborate in corrupt arrangements in another, or else exercise their authority to the fullest extent. Unlike the government systems of more stable democracies, where the bureaucracy ensures a significant degree of government continuity in all but a few

cases, in Pakistan the shift in leadership accompanying each change
in government often leads to laws and regulations implemented
under the previous government being reversed as was evident in
Musharraf's reversal of the FEBC.

The result of this history and the culture of exemptions it has
engendered was sharply evident in a conversation I later had with
Shahzar Afridi. I met Shahzar on the upper deck of a *Gloria Jeans* coffee
shop in the manicured neighbourhood of Lahore's Defence Housing
Authority (DHA). He seemed particularly upbeat and excited. His
posture was straighter than usual, and his boyish grin had the tinge
of smugness. As he lit up his cigarette, flicking the ash impatiently
on the ground as he talked, he launched into updating me on his
latest venture. At the age of twenty-four, his father had given him a
failing tafat production unit to manage and rebuild. Now, two years
later, his brand was doing well. He had expanded his staff and now
had a corporate office in a growing commercial area of the DHA. His
profits had soared.

As the newest and youngest member of his family to enter the
tafat industry, he often displayed a desire to prove his skill as a
businessman, a tough negotiator and as a savvy judge of character.
The previous day he had taken the bold move of convening a meeting
of the twelve largest nationally owned tafat manufacturers. Lured by
the promise of a significant increase in profit, they had all agreed to
come. Waving his cigarette as he talked, he explained his plan,

> We need to stop these price wars. I'm bringing everyone together so that we
> can expand the pie. It is in the MNCs [multi-national corporations] interest
> to have us all fighting among ourselves. Many of the tafat producers are
> members of our [extended] family, but the producers from outside our family
> are also coming. I am going to suggest that we form a new association and
> that we use the meeting to elect a President and a Vice President. Many in the
> group have already said they want me to be the President, but I don't know
> . . . It will cause a lot of work and attention for me and with all the illegal
> activities of these groups, and the tax evasion, and it could cause me a lot of
> problems.

After he had finished explaining his price setting strategy to me, I had,
rather insensitively, nodded and indicated that I had been paying
close attention by stating, 'Ahh, so you are establishing a cartel'. He
looked at me blankly, and then with some irritation. The association
of the word 'cartel', so often coupled in the popular media with
mafia-like organisations and violence, had momentarily thrown him.
Shahzar had conceptualised his efforts to bring together the tafat
manufacturers to set prices as a way to demonstrate his leadership

among his peers, and to instil an ethos of collaboration among his competitors to their mutual advantage. He felt my use of the word to be incongruous with his intentions. 'You're not listening', he said, with exasperation at my apparent denseness. 'I am proposing we *collaborate*. If we follow my strategy, everybody wins'.

Most of Shahzar's product was oriented towards the very lowest tier of the market – it was carefully priced to ensure even Pakistan's very poor could afford it, and it was sold in small as well as large quantities to facilitate its purchase by those on daily wages. Having personally travelled to many of the rural areas that were his largest consumer base, Shahzar knew his market well. He had observed the lifestyle of his buyers, and documented the fluctuations in their income and consumption patterns. His sales records demonstrated that patterns of consumption shifted noticeably by season and reduced significantly in accordance with other fluctuations on the market, for instance a rise in the price of petrol. By increasing the price of his product by even a few rupees per unit, the scale at which it was sold would have resulted in a significant increase in the profit margin of both Shahzar and his competitors. It would also have had a noticeably negative impact on the financial position of his very large and mostly very poor consumer base, increasing the pressure on their finances at a level carefully calculated to ensure they did not reduce the usual quantities purchased or seek out an alternative product.

Shahzar's perspective on the forming of a cartel was likely infused with a level of naiveté not possessed by his older and more experienced peers, but the personal ethics it portrays also highlights the chasm between engaging in acts of extra-legality (or in this case illegality), and individual and social perceptions of morally justifiable and normative behaviour. Shahzar knew that the agreement to set prices was not legal, but he felt morally justified in doing so because the benefits accrued from his plan would be shared with his competitors, individuals he had interacted with most of his life through his father and uncle's engagements in the industry. Shahzar saw himself to be extracting wealth from unknown, and therefore irrelevant, outsiders and then circulating it among both his elite peers and the dependents in his biraderi. Shahzar's obligations were first to his family, and then to ensuring the material well-being of the security guards stationed at his factory with whom he would often stop to drink tea and to hear valuable gossip on the state of his factories, and the family of his 'Man Friday'.[3] His responsibility was to the community with whom he interacted, embraced, conversed and shared food. He did not feel himself to be obliged to the un-named consumers he observed from the back seat of his air-conditioned vehicle. As with many of his peers, his moral obligations were confined to those with whom he shared physical proximity and the intimacy of the everyday.

As with much of the extra-legal activity engaged in by elite businessmen, Shahzar's circumvention of the law did not involve bribery, but instead the sharing of intangibles such as information and agreements to act in concert. This focus on intangibles reflects a similar distinction to that made between gifts and bribes across much of South Asia, and indeed beyond; for instance, in the practice of 'guanxi' in China (Kipnis 1997; Osburg 2013; Smart 1993) (discussed in Chapter Five). As Gupta (1995) noted, in relation to lower level bureaucrats in India, those without influential connections (*sifarish*) find it necessary to bribe, and those with influence make requests that it is not in the interest of lower status individuals to refuse.

Beyond the moral justification Shahzar engaged in whilst establishing a cartel wherein 'everyone' (who mattered) would win, Shahzar's attitude also reflected his own family's history of engagement with what they saw as an immoral and capricious State. In this, his attitudes built on two intertwined assumptions widely held by both elites and many in the middle and working classes, firstly that the State is immoral, and secondly that political instability can destroy wealth at any time.

The next part of the chapter examines an example of how elite businessmen utilise their cross-institutional social networks to engage in regulatory capture and amass enormous levels of profit through collusion with government.[4]

Regulatory Capture

We have a saying in Punjabi, '*Kutti chooran naal rull gaee*', which translates as 'the bitch [clandestinely] joined the thieves' and therefore did not bark when they came. Normally, it is quoted when regulators, NAB [National Accountability Bureau], or others, do not move against the corrupt politicians, or when the corrupt mafias co-opt politicians.

—Senior political journalist, Islamabad

A senior bureaucrat and I had been discussing recent media coverage of corruption charges against various government regulatory bodies. At the end of our formal interview he asked me to wait. He returned five minutes later with a freshly bound and printed copy of the Inquiry Report that the Securities and Exchange Commission of Pakistan (SECP) had provided to the Supreme Court judges presiding over the case of *Muhammad Ashraf Tiwana vs. Pakistan Etc.*[5] As he walked me to the elevator he asked me to put the folder in my bag before leaving the building:

> It's a public record, so I'm not doing anything wrong by giving this to you, but in reality, no one who didn't already know where it is would have been able to find it online or in the paper files. You would need to know the case number and to understand the logic of the filing system. Everything we have just been discussing is in there. Just don't tell anyone that you got it from me.

As I began poring over the enquiry report, I frequently stopped to track down references in the online media to the incidents the court documents referenced. Though the political motivations behind the creation of the document were outside of my knowledge, it remained an informative addition to the fragmented anecdotes of bureaucratic corruption and complicity with business provided by my elite informants. In following Gupta's (1995, 377) argument for the need to examine the 'multiply mediated' contexts through which the State comes to be constructed, I traced in this enquiry report and my other sources of information a trail interlinking bureaucratic activity, accusations of misconduct, reports of threats and references to requests for police protection. This data was drawn from case files, media reports and the anecdotes relayed to me by businessmen and bureaucrats. In following the paper trail of both the court and media coverage of *Muhammad Ashraf Tiwana vs. Pakistan Etc*, I discovered that the case was linked with a much larger case of mass-scale bureaucratic corruption and regulatory capture[6] involving the Karachi Stock Exchange (KSE). The magnitude of this corruption highlighted both the sense of impunity felt by many amongst the business elite that enabled widespread engagement in extra-legality, and the inability of Pakistan's legal and regulatory system to ensure impartial compliance among this powerfully networked group. It also illustrates the flexibility with which the law is applied, and the degree to which both the law and the regulatory bodies policing it can be manipulated.

The case began with the charge made by the petitioner, Muhammad Ashraf Tiwana, against the Chairman of the SECP, the regulatory body tasked with investigating and prosecuting instances of corruption in business. As an employee of the SECP, Tiwana charged that he was fired without reason from his position as Executive Director of Law at the SECP after refusing to drop his investigation of stock market manipulation against several firms. It was later determined that the Chairman of the SECP, Muhammad Ali, had remained a

Board Member with vested stock options on each of the firms under investigation for stock market manipulation (though conflicting news reports exist citing him having sold his shareholding in the company under investigation nine years earlier).[7] Tiwana's case was built on the argument that the SECP had become subject to 'regulatory capture', the process by which business interests assume control of the organisations that are mandated to curb their activities. In the trial against him, the Supreme Court ruled that the Chairman must vacate his position at the SECP due to a conflict of interest, but did not impose a prison sentence or financial penalty.

As the details of the case emerged during the trial, the level of influence of major business owners in the functioning of the bureaucratic agencies involved became starkly apparent. For instance, it emerged that the Chairman had been appointed following intense lobbying from a number of the KSE's largest businesses and shareholders. Several anonymous sources cited that the Chairman had been selected because his position on multiple company boards made it unlikely that he would conduct vigorous investigations into dubious stock market activities. Others alleged that he had been appointed on account of his personal friendship with the Minister of Finance (Dawn 2010).

Further, the trial revealed the Chairman had been appointed without the mandated Senate review, and that when the Senate panel insisted on a review process, there was widespread objection to the appointment of the current Chairman on account of his known conflicts of interest. As a senator noted in regard to this case, 'A brokerage house wants to fill vacant posts [in the regulatory sector]'. Similar concerns from political and legal commentators were also reported in the nation's English language newspapers (Darr 2012; Express Tribune 2012; Sattar 2012).

Beyond the initial circumvention of the Senate review process in the Chairman's appointment, and the Chairman's attempts to block investigation into the illegal activities of the companies on which he sat, evidence emerged implicating the former Chairman in an emerging regulatory scandal of much greater magnitude. In November 2011, the Chief of another regulatory body, the Oil and Gas Regulatory Authority (OGRA) was found to have manipulated official data by reallocating 'operating costs' to 'non-operating costs', significantly increasing the unit cost of gas to consumers and causing the loss of Rs 82 billion to the public exchequer. The OGRA Chief was also found to have taken massive kickbacks from the preferential award of OGRA contracts to private firms.

The 2013 case against the former Chairman of the SECP led to the NAB conducting further investigations, and revealed that the former SECP Chairman had collaborated with the OGRA Chief by tampering with the records of the nation's largest supplier of gas and pipelines and by deliberately impeding the investigation (Dilawar 2010). As the details of the OGRA case and the degree of conspiracy between the leaders of some of the nation's most powerful regulatory bodies continued to emerge, a number of mid-level staff of the NAB and SECP who were involved in investigating the OGRA scandal, received threats and harassment which resulted in them reporting a fear for their lives to the local police and to the media. The chief NAB investigation officer involved in uncovering the scandal reported that he was being followed, believed his mobile phone to be tapped and was so afraid for his safety that he was compelled to frequently change his accommodation. A staff member of the SECP involved in investigating SECP complicity in the OGRA scandal also reported severe harassment from senior SECP management (Rana 2011), while another officer investigating the scandal was reported to have died mysteriously (Tiwana Legal Counsel 2011, 37). Later, several witnesses who had earlier reported receiving threats, suddenly withdrew their statements without explanation. The case concluded when the NAB found insufficient evidence that the former SECP Chairman was complicit in the OGRA scam (Awaz TV 2013), and he resumed his work in the private sector. The SECP Chairman had found a way to use his networks, and his ability to manoeuvre the institutions of the State, to avoid penalty altogether.

As this case demonstrates, the Pakistani State and its regulatory institutions are often unable to serve as neutral arbiters of the nation's laws and regulations. The regulatory capture described in this case highlights the malleability of the State, and the unpredictability with which the regulation of the nation's largest and most profitable businesses is enforced. The most powerful, and best connected citizens are well placed to circumvent the laws they find to be disadvantageous to their profit gathering and personal aspirations, and middle-class regulators, like those threatened in the case above, find themselves unable to fulfil their mandate and fearing for their safety and that of their families. In contrast, less well-connected and powerful would-be competitors find the law impermeable, with minor infractions pursued and punished to the fullest reach of the law.

* * *

The extremity of Pakistan's history of political instability serves as a magnified example of a political and economic condition experienced in many economically advanced, and comparatively political stable democratic nations.

The historical instability with which the Pakistani State has emerged has enabled elites to disregard the state as a moral actor. In so doing, these individuals have reduced the ethical requirement to follow its edicts. For many within the elite, the decision to circumvent the regulatory structure of the State arises from their personal experiences of political instability, and of state institutions that rapidly implement and reverse policies critical to the success or failure of elite business. The rationale of an immoral State is also widely employed by the business elite to explain and justify their avoidance or disregard for the laws and regulations that impede their efforts to accumulate the greatest amount of profit. This is, in part, because they see the vulnerability of their position of economic dominance. It is also, however, largely a discursive tool to justify elite exceptionalism[8] under the law and a culture of exemptions.

The elite's rationale of the 'immoral State' provided ample justification for the placement of family members in the various senior branches of government – the bureaucracy, the military and within roles of political leadership – alongside their ownership of major family industries and corporations. Underlying these narratives of political instability and the challenges they can create, however, Pakistan's elite businessmen have also demonstrated an unrivalled capacity to insulate themselves from, and gain advantage through, the unpredictability of the political and economic environment in which they exist. The consequence of this environment is elite behaviour that it particularly risk-taking, and cut-throat. In employing these justificatory discourses for their dominance, the contemporary Pakistani elite are closer to their colonial predecessors – and their abuse of power on moral grounds – than they would like to acknowledge.

Notes

1. See for instance, the work of Glucksberg and Burrows (2016) on the role of family offices in amassing dynastic wealth in the UK, and Lopez et al (2013) on the role of family offices in contemporary wealth management both generally, and in Spain.

2. Section 18(g) and Section 24 of the National Accountability Bureau Ordinance, 1999.
3. Though originating from the faithful male aide in Robinson Crusoe, the term Man Friday was used by a number of my informants to refer respectfully to the individual they relied on to meet a wide variety of daily needs, often including housework, preparing meals, making deliveries, and serving as a driver. Its usage is a very particular throwback to the colonial era.
4. In seeking to illuminate the motivations, moral frameworks and intended objectives, as well as the actual outcomes, of the elite businessmen and senior bureaucrats engaged in this case, I examined legal archives, as well as coverage in the Pakistani print media. I also drew on the free-flowing circulation of rumours related to me by various informants in Lahore, Islamabad and Karachi.
5. As this case is on the public record, I have used the original names of the case, the individuals involved and referenced the actual media coverage of the event.
6. Stigler (1971) first coined the term 'regulatory capture' arguing that powerful industries appropriate regulations to protect and advance their own commercial interests, even when regulation is ostensibly implemented for the protection and benefit of the public.
7. See for instance Wahab 2013.
8. I use this term differently from Agamben (2005), who referred to a 'state of exemption', mainly in relation to instances of a suspension of the juridical order, for instance, martial law or emergency powers. Rather, I refer to the sense of many elites that they are exceptional, and therefore have a legitimate right to legal exemptions.

CONCLUSION

What Pakistan's Elite Reveals about Global Capitalism

᥾⁓

A year and a half after leaving Pakistan I was living in a small Italian city for a few months to draft this book. As I settled in at the local library for a day of writing, I got a call from a businessman and old friend, Imran,

> Rosita! What's up? I'm in Milan next week for business. I'm coming to visit you. Where are you again? Four hours south? Ok, I have nice car, no problem. Can you book me a good hotel? You know what I mean by *good*, right? Here are my credit card details. Gotta go, see you Tuesday!

As we sat at my local café at 9pm the first night, Imran in his fedora drinking Coke, I with an Americano, he showed me photos from his factory visit outside Milan, and talked about the partnership deal he was trying to make with an Italian conglomerate pioneering an advance in more efficient biomass fuelled power, a form of energy derived from processing waste from sugar cane, municipal solid waste, or landfill methane. Imran wanted to persuade the members of this Italian firm to partner with him, and to invest their resources in a power plant in Pakistan that he would co-own, and largely manage. Though energy production is big business universally, in Pakistan, where energy is constantly undersupplied and electricity shortages are crippling to both small business and major industry, the opportunities for profit generation are enormous. The photos showed Imran in a tailored suit and hard hat surveying a large industrial site surrounded by similarly dressed Italians. In most of the pictures he was gazing seriously out over landscapes of concrete ventilation towers, waste disposal units, generators, turbines, pressure vessels and a landscape of indistinguishable grey concrete buildings. In some he was listening attentively, while others caught him pointing or gesticulating mid-sentence, the other men leaning in, listening carefully. Several other photos showed Imran and the same men in front row seats at the Italian Grand Prix. In these photos the men had matching Grand Prix caps, big smiles, arms around shoulders and a table full of Italian beers and soft drinks laid out in front of them.

Imran's interest in partnering with a foreign firm in Pakistan enabled him to continue his local, and hugely successful, history of domestic investment. By bringing Italian investors to Pakistan, he was able to utilise his knowledge of Pakistani business practices and to utilise his extensive network in Pakistan, while benefiting from the foreign capital these investors were able to provide. As with his business in Pakistan, a significant component of Imran's work in Italy involved socialising, relationship building and establishing trust with his prospective partner investors. The major difference was that in Pakistan the informal elite male bonding experiences critical to the formation of business alliances occurred in private residences; in Italy, they took place in semi-public entertainment venues – racing tracks, bars and restaurants. Further, the exigencies of doing business internationally meant that Imran's Italian partners sought to fast-track a process of relationship building that Imran and his peers in Pakistan had built up over decades.

In Italy, Imran was perceived as a wealthy foreign investor seeking partnership opportunities which would bring new technology, and foreign investors, to Pakistan. His partner investors recognised the enormous opportunities Pakistan's large and growing consumer base guaranteed. They also recognised that the Pakistani market was volatile and defined by close networks of kinship, trust and loyalty (not unlike the business networks found in parts of Italy),[1] and that Imran's partnership as a local was critical to their ability to succeed in Pakistan's political and economic environment. Imran not only brought capital, he also brought access to the tightly knit business community in Pakistan, and offered himself as a guide and intermediary through both its regulatory structure, and the dense social and class network critical to successfully traversing it. As foreign businessmen interested in investing in Pakistan, they could not operate without Imran's assistance. And with their funds, Imran could considerably enlarge his domestic business interests.

But though Imran was interested in attracting Italian investment, and establishing a multi-national corporate partnership, this scheme was only one small component of his business portfolio and of the plans he had to expand it. His business plans lay firmly moored within Pakistan, the context with which he was most familiar, and where his extensive networks in government, business, the military and the local communities in which his factories were based were of value. He was not interested in investing his capital in Italy, but in luring foreign capital inwards, where his ability to successfully navigate the volatile context was most valued, and his ventures uniquely profitable. This centripetal focus – drawing both domestic and international resources inwards to the local – was a defining feature of the capitalist activity in which all of my informants engaged in Pakistan.

Is Elite Capitalism in Pakistan an Anomaly?

The purpose of this book has been to interrogate the everyday lived experiences of modern capitalism – and specifically the accumulation of wealth and political influence – among the most powerful members of a highly politically unstable nation. In examining the informal and social practices of the business elite of Pakistan, I have examined the relationships between power, social class and the informal processes used in major business in the context of globalised capital and increasingly international norms of doing business. By examining the lifeworlds of a group of powerful elites and the strategies they use to acquire and retain their power and affluence, I have also highlighted the enormous challenges non-elite individuals face in obtaining upward social mobility in Pakistan. The elite experience in Pakistan represents one model of how regional forms of capitalism, exchange and alliance-making continue to reassert their dominance despite the supposed hegemonic nature of global capital and the homogenising effects of global trade and business. And it has parallels in many other country contexts, including the global north.

Consequently the family stories and histories of social mobility of the Pakistani elite, challenges – or at least throws into question – a number of assumptions about the nature of global capitalism today.

Economic Growth Is Not Linear, and the Development of Western Style Institutions Are Not Inevitable

The rise of Pakistani wealth is part of a broader global shift in financial power from the West to the East. The financial dominance of Europe and North America which many in the West had seen as a natural reflection of the superiority of Western economic and governance institutions, is now increasingly challenged by the emergence of new financial elites in the fast expanding markets of Asia and the Middle East (Beaverstock et al 2013). The large-scale foreign investment Pakistan is now receiving, most notably from China in terms of major road and port infrastructure projects, but also from other nations, has again accelerated the opportunities for massive profit generation within the country. The economy is steadily growing at near to 5 per cent per year. Over the past five years governments have increased electricity supply to major industry, provided massive tax cuts to large companies, curbed terrorism through military operations in insurgent strongholds of the country and successfully lured major Chinese investment.

The growth that has emerged as a result promises significant improvements in the infrastructure available to millions of middle class Pakistanis, and is likely to significantly improve standards of living among the upper portion of the middle class who already find themselves with much higher levels of discretionary income. There is a widespread desire within Pakistan's middle classes for a better quality of life and access to the lifestyles and commodities they see as representing it. Shopping malls, foreign coffee and fast food franchises, cinemas and boutique clothing stores are proliferating in Pakistan's urban centres as a result (cf. Maqsood 2017). Yet increased consumerism and higher standards of living among this class does not appear to be generating a credible middle- and lower-class challenge to elite dominance, as other scholars have argued.[2]

The sustained economic growth and development that has reconfigured agricultural economies in other parts of South Asia into centres of finance, global trade and professional service staffed by a large and growing middle class, has not emerged in Pakistan – and does not look likely in the coming decades. Economic growth in Pakistan is not giving rise to a system of wealth accumulation defined by a Western-style model of meritocracy and impersonalised and efficient business structures.

Pakistani elites contribute to, benefit from and in a number of circumstances, help shape, processes of global capitalism. Yet, despite consistent economic growth over the past seventeen years, Pakistan's economic and governance institutions do not appear as Western style institutions 'in embryo' (Ferguson 2002). Patronage networks remain as strong as ever, but rapid economic growth, as well as the rise of corporations and major business conglomerates, has reconfigured these networks in new ways. Looking both at Pakistan,

and at other parts of the world, it is clear that despite the interna-
tionalisation of business in many realms, national networks and a
domestically-specific habitus of appropriate elite culture remains
dominant in many countries, despite their increasing integration
with global markets. The senior-most leadership of corporations
remain posts filled by domestic elites, and those roles are by and
large recruited from amongst domestic elite networks (Hartmann
and Leug 2017).

The cohesion of these elite groups, and the reliance of members
of the elite upon one another, has created an inward-looking political and economic focus. Pakistani elites interact with, and benefit
from, global forms of capitalism and commerce through export and
import trades, foreign investment and through partnering with
foreign firms, as Imran sought to do with Italian investors. These
international ties connect domestic elites to international economic
and political forums in myriad ways. However, the domestic economic environment they rule over and thrive within remains largely
insulated from the impersonal and immediate transactions usually
associated with global finance and capitalism. The source of their
economic and political power resides primarily in the localised zones
of their homes, natal villages and in the drawing rooms of the urban
elite across Lahore, Karachi and Islamabad. Rather than reflecting
an impartially regulated system of free market competition and a
mastery of the economic sphere; the transactions, alliances, friendships, conflicts and competition engaged in by members of the elite at
the individual and family level constitute *the* major conduit for flows
of domestic capital.

Consequently, major wealth continues to be concentrated in the
hands of a small group of families who dominate the nation's largest
political parties, major corporations and maintain close family ties
with the upper echelons of the military. In the process, patronage relationships are being reconstructed in new ways, providing avenues
for rapid upward mobility into a newly constructed elite class based
not upon family dynasties, but upon the ability of individuals from
varied class backgrounds to successfully cultivate personal networks with state officials. In turn, the resilience of these modes of
doing business reflects the inability of international forms of global
capital – represented primarily by multi-national corporations, or
international investors – to re-colonise local markets and extract the
nationally-generated wealth held by domestic elites. Those engaged
in business persistently reassert the crucial role of localised and personalised forms of doing business.

The resilience of local forms of business, networking and collaboration in business can be seen along a continuum of a rising rejection of Western influence, and of pride in regionalism. The rise of more provincial and ethnically based forms of elite distinction reflects both historically-rooted anti-colonial sentiments, and fierce resistance across all classes within Pakistan towards the neo-colonialism the interference of many Western nations is seen to represent. This backlash to Western involvement in the country stems from Western nations seen to be interfering in Pakistan through military funding, foreign aid and other forms of foreign policy pressure, and through foreign direct investment in business. Yet, non-Western states and private business partners seeking to collaborate with, influence and invest in the country, are viewed in very different and often vastly more favourable terms. This may be because these non-Western investors, for instance, the Chinese businessmen documented by Osburg (2013), conduct business in similarly personalised ways, investing in building networks of trust and reliance through repeated social interaction. By retaining and reinforcing more personalised and localised forms of doing business, domestic businessmen or owners reject Western models of capitalism as inadequate for responding to the challenges of massive-profit generation in the highly politically unstable and securitised national contexts in which they do business. In fact, elites in many parts of the world are increasingly turning away from, and no longer seeking to emulate, Western-style economic and political institutions. The new Russian elite, for instance, has shed the inferiority complex that had come to define their attitudes to the West in the post-Cold War era, and now display both a pervasive disillusionment with the West and an increasing sense of their own superiority in contrast (see Schimpfössl 2018).

This disillusionment with the West was also evident among certain members of the Pakistani elite. As explained to me by a businessman and politician from KP,

> Goras [white people] are unreliable. They are always working for their own satisfaction. They are selfish, all the Europeans – and the Australians too! I worked with the Europeans on a power project. It was a billion-dollar project for Malakand. We invited the EU. Now I know what they are *really* like, and I am more cautious.

Secondly, increased economic growth has also not entailed a new-found independence from the interference of the State, as Scott (1998) originally predicted in his landmark book, *Seeing Like a State*.

In the 1998 (7–8) edition, Scott significantly revised his thesis that the modernising developmental State exercised power by erasing local particularities through technical and seemingly a-political bureaucratic acts. His revised introduction argued, 'States with the pretensions and powers that I criticise here have for the most part vanished or have drastically curbed their ambitions'.[3] In Pakistan, the urban business elite exert a high level of influence over the State apparatus. This influence is critical to their ability to accumulate enormous quantities of wealth, and to retain their dominant status within Pakistani society. The importance of the State in serving as a primary provider of wealth, opportunity and valuable connections, has not simply diminished as countries become wealthier. Instead, the role of the State in providing connections and opportunities has oscillated under different governments and at different points in time. In Pakistan, for instance, it remains an extremely import-ant source of employment and family wealth-generation,[4] but the institutions critical for personal wealth accumulation shift back and forth, from the elected civilian government, to the de facto military regime, to the large corporations which are increasingly becoming major sources of employment for Pakistan's small but growing middle class.

The resilience of provincial and localised practices of major busi-ness and investment in Pakistan and other politically and economi-cally volatile parts of the world, illuminate that the concept of global capital and the homogenising of international business practices remains illusory. Further, the persistence of local networks and per-sonal practices in Pakistan, a place with close regional and interna-tional ties, indicates that personal networks may continue to shape the functioning of capitalist economies in other more developed and stable economies.

Rather than emulating the structural shifts taking place in other parts of urban Asia between national and global capital, I have shown that the Pakistani elite retain a hyper-provincialised, highly localised form of business and finance that contradicts widely assumptions that the world is transitioning towards an era of globalised and stan-dardised capitalism.

The Elite Class Is More Permeable than Before, but Rapid Upward Mobility Remains the Exception

It has been popular over the past few decades to ask if social class today is dead, and whether it holds any relevance in the contemporary context of seemingly self-made millionaires, and increasingly impersonalised and standardised commercial transactions. We see more and more 'self-made' success stories across the world. Scholars researching elites in the West are now arguing that there is a slowly growing trend away from inherited sources of wealth, and that 'the contemporary superrich are increasingly self-made multi-million and billionaires, who transcend typical class structures' (Spence 2016). But no success is entirely 'self-made'. Closer examination of the backgrounds of these people usually reveals a high degree of privileged access to the world's most prestigious educational institutions, and the social and professional networks these institutions provide. Inheriting wealth is now no longer the only way to enter the elite, but elites still inherit a great deal of privilege in terms of the networks to which they have access. Though many scholars have argued class is now irrelevant, both this work and others indicate that it is as relevant for determining the distribution of privilege and resources as it has ever been – no less in the Global North than in the economically developing economies of the Global South. Rather than disappearing, the criterion for belonging to a particular social class – both in terms of wealth, status and group identification – has in some instances significantly changed.

Social scientists in the UK, for instance, have developed a new categorisation of British class, dividing the population into seven categories accounting for factors including annual income, home ownership, occupation, breadth of social network and cultural tastes.[5]
Economically advanced countries like the UK are also among the worst countries for certain measures of social mobility, with parents' wealth strongly influencing the child's prospects of higher education and a good salary. Increasingly, British citizens are experiencing downward social mobility (Organisation for Economic Cooperation and Development 2010). These patterns of social change are also roughly similar in highly developed economies including the United States and Sweden.[6]

In Pakistan, social mobility is in general no greater. A study conducted by the Pakistan Institute of Development Economics (2012) found that there is a 72 per cent chance that that the son of a father who works in an elementary/basic occupation will hold a similar role. Of the families at the bottom of Pakistan's income categories, 44 per cent will experience no mobility at all, and the vast majority of the 56 per cent who do experience some upward economic mobility, will move only from the bottom 20 per cent to the next quintile. The real rags-to-riches stories happen for only 3 per cent of the population: where 3 out of 100 people will move from the bottom 20 per cent of the economic spectrum, to the top over the course of their lifetime.

In Pakistan, as in the 'developed economies' of the West, family dynasties continue to dominate elite educational institutions, major corporations and the senior ranks of business and politics. A few select instances of rapid upward mobility have emerged, not quite rags-to-riches stories, but more 'office worker to multi-millionaire mogul' stories. These cases have an almost mythical quality in Pakistan, and these 'self-made' millionaires are both harshly critiqued and strongly admired (as in the case of Malik Riaz discussed in Chapter Three). Despite the rumours that surround these cases, new sources of patronage – in Pakistan's case, the de facto military government – now provide a previously non-existent opportunity for upward social mobility. Individuals from middle and lower-middle class backgrounds who are able to successfully cultivate personal networks with state officials, now have a route – albeit limited and tightly constrained – for rapid upward mobility into a newly configured elite class.

The experience of the Pakistani elite throws into question assertions that the global elite is moving away from the trend of inherited sources of wealth, towards 'self-made' wealth and economic mobility (Beaverstock et al 2013, Spence 2016, 5). Undoubtedly, there are increased opportunities in certain Western contexts for individuals outside of traditional aristocracies to rapidly amass wealth and privilege. Yet the claims that these individuals are 'self-made' are usually found to be illusory, or at least inflated, upon closer inspection. Ho's (2009) ethnography of Wall Street bankers, for instance, noted both the opportunity to rapidly amass staggering fortunes within this group, whilst also highlighting the preferential hiring system that drew applicants from one of a very limited number of universities, whose alumni were themselves drawn predominantly from the nation's wealthiest and most privileged families.

Established Elites have actively sought to exclude prospective competitors in business and other fields from the informal social forums in which business and politics is largely conducted. The power of domestic elites is at least partly located in their ability to acquire and demonstrate distinction and other forms of symbolic capital acquired from, for instance, partaking in foreign education or securing an advantageous marriage. These forms of distinction serve to reinforce elite boundary making by reproducing appropriate forms of high and emerging culture, what Bourdieu (1984, 1998) termed 'distinction' and 'taste'. Possession of the correct taste – expressed in mannerisms, dress, style, preferences and language, reflect an important element of determining inclusion and exclusion within a specific social class, and of preserving their political and economic dominance through this boundary maintenance.

Historically, this intra-elite alliance-making has been limited to families possessing multi-generational elite histories. The status of these families has rested primarily on their colonial-era legacies and inheritance, and the particular forms of distinction associated with these histories. These forms of distinction have been used by the elite to police the boundaries of their power and privilege and to limit new entrants. These criterion of distinction and taste noted in the British class survey above, and in countless other studies of class, are very culturally and geographically specific. For instance, in the United States, Lamont (1992) demonstrated that the most salient marker of class membership for North Americans was socioeconomic position and power, whereas in France, elite class boundaries related less to power or wealth and were primarily assessed in terms of cultural erudition and refined tastes.

In Pakistan, in addition to excluding certain families, the elite class has had to engage in a process of strategic inclusion of the families who might seek to usurp their class dominance. As largely middle-class institutions like the military and the bureaucracy have continued to expand and consolidate their power through political rule, however, these institutions have provided patronage and opportunities for rapid upward social mobility for a new group of families, unaligned with previous regimes.

Until recently, what constitutes distinction has been determined by 'Established Elite' families who draw their claims for distinction from hereditary sources. Established Elites have based their claims for distinction largely upon family lineages intertwined with colonial power, and from symbolic capital derived from association with Western educational and cultural institutions.[7] The oldest and most prestigious of these families have served as gatekeepers of various elite institutions – private clubs, the school board of Aitchison's College, as hosts of the most exclusive parties and as arbiters of appropriate and inappropriate marriage. By gatekeeping these institutions, a small number of established families were able to ensure that those families not deemed suitable were denied entry to the social forums where decisions were made, and resources allocated – regardless of their level of wealth.

However, as Navay Raje elites have obtained influential roles in business, politics and the military, the Established Elite switched strategies. Being unable to fully exclude these Navay Raje elites from either economic networks or fee paying elite educational institutions, the Established Elite has sought to integrate select new members into the class through intense processes of socialisation in schools and in social clubs, designed to both develop, and test, the acquisition of a range of dispositions associated with the Established Elite. In absorbing these new class entrants, however reluctantly, the elite class has been able to curtail the broadening of privilege to a highly circumscribed group. In doing so, they have preserved the institutions through which their own power and privilege is acquired, circulated and protected. This method of alliance-making is the embodied form of the process Khan (2010) described as elites incorporating and absorbing other powerful factions as a means to subvert formal government institutions. As these patterns of elite inclusion have been implemented selectively, tensions between Established Elites and socially-excluded new elites have emerged as new entrants seek to access Pakistan's closely guarded elite social forums – and to access the opportunities for economic and political advancement membership in this social world provides.

As explored in earlier chapters, some Navay Raje elites have sought to acquire the dispositions of the Established Elite, and many have successfully done so. However, many others are embracing new forms of distinction from distinctly Pakistani sources: broad political and social alliances, provincial support-bases and ethnically-rooted markers of distinction. The result is a splintering not only of accepted forms of distinction, but a broadening of elite class gatekeepers to include those from among the Navay Raje. As Navay Raje families acquire greater wealth and social status, the policing of elite class boundaries is undertaking a major shift as Navay Raje elites impose new criterion for inclusion that are markedly different from those of earlier elite groups.

The process Pakistan's new rich are undergoing provides a template for elite class transformation – and the processes of accommodation and exclusion – occurring among the various subsets of the global elite. While, for instance, as Schimpfössl (2018) notes, the established elite of London continues to exclude most of the new money Russian oligarchs who have made their home in London over the past few decades, certain exceptions are being made. A few new rich Russians who have adequately demonstrated the sentiments of *noblesse oblige* – the sentiment that with privilege comes responsibility – through public philanthropy and engagement in the arts with sufficiently English restraint, are being incorporated into London's elite.

The Elite Is a Tightly Integrated and Domestically Interlinked Class

The concentration of wealth and political and economic influence in Pakistan reflects a broader global trend. The overlapping connections between elite families prominent in one institutional arena, whether that be business, politics, or the military, emerge to almost as great a degree in Australian[8] or Italian[9] society, for instance, as they do in Pakistan, continuing the long history of elite integration and cooperation first noted by Mills (1956) in his 1950s study of the elite of the United States.

Notwithstanding the intra-class fractures described above, the Pakistani elite have developed what may well be an unprecedented degree of ruling class integration not now found in any other part of South Asia, or the world more broadly. Formally, many of Pakistan's elite families are affiliated with various institutions whose objectives are unaligned, even opposed, to one another. For instance, the military is routinely accused of serving as a de facto government, and frequently curtails the activities of the elected civilian government. Many belong to rival political parties. And business families have at times openly critiqued various governments.

Over time, various threats to individual families, and to various elite factions, have contributed to an unprecedented degree of ruling class integration and collaboration between the business, political and bureaucratic classes. At times, this has involved allying the political and business elite with the military regime in power – a group separate from, and at times antagonistic to, the interests of the business and political elite. At all times, it has required a process of accommodation between the other factions of the elite and this powerful institution. Bearing in mind that elites possess both power and resources (Khan 2012), and 'are able to realise their will, even if others resist it' (Mills 1956, 10), Pakistan's military has emerged as another elite faction, which each of the other factions of the elite must accommodate and ally themselves with in order to ensure their own survival within the elite class.

Those among the elite who have retained their position have been able to foster intra-elite alliances with each of these factions through marriage, social practices and informal business dealings advantageous to each of the elite parties involved. Formally, the objectives of these various sub-groupings within the elite are often unaligned, with one branch of power constraining the influence, authority, or accumulation of capital of the others. At a personal level, however, the senior-most leaders of each branch operate in very mutually supportive ways. They are known to one another, usually attend the same high schools, universities and clubs, and frequently attend the same social events and parties. These individual relationships are managed through intra-elite social forums which provide a critical strategic function: they enable elites with different, sometimes conflicting, affiliations to overcome the distrust emerging from their ideological or other differences.

As a result of the linkages they have been able to establish with the political elite, the business elite have ensured their de facto leadership of economic policymaking: more than advising the government on economic policy, those who have achieved the greatest levels of success have developed intimate personal relationships with the political leadership dominant in each change of regime. In each of these relationships, they have negotiated and directed economic policymaking most advantageous to their interests. This collaboration has emerged as the most critical mechanism for ensuring the survival of the elite class as a group, and for protecting their ability to exercise power and access privileges.

Pakistan's urban business elite have sought to attain a balance between undermining competitors and seeking their collaboration. This balancing act requires a skilful negotiation between pursuing the broader interests of the elite as a class, and the individual interests of elite families seeking to gain advantages over their peers in accessing limited political and economic resources in specific competitions for contracts, business deals, or opportunities to demonstrate or increase social status. However, the urban business elite engage in collaboration much more than they engage in conflict. Elites support one another through sharing valuable information, safeguarding each other's indiscretions, facilitating the approval of legal exemptions, or ensuring the legal difficulties of allies are overlooked or mismanaged by regulatory bodies or authorities of the court. Intra-elite tensions based upon ethnicity, regionalism, political affiliation, or economic competition remain present and sometimes salient in elite interactions. However, among the members of the elite, these tensions are subordinated to the broader goal of maintaining the power and privilege of the class as a whole. As a result, the business and political class is highly cohesive, united in its need to defend itself from the groups seeking to undermine or usurp their position of power, by allying with whichever faction of the elite holds the requisite resources, influence, or authority to address the challenge of the day. Treading a delicate line between collaboration and securing each family's position within the elite, Pakistan's business elite oscillates between strategies of competition and collaboration to secure their economic and political advantage. Ultimately, however, capitalism in Pakistan is not marked by intense competition, but by intense alliance-making.

This integration does not extend, however, into a tightly integrated global elite as many other scholars have argued. As the example of the Russian oligarch noted above demonstrates, some elites do transcend the social barriers that defy their acceptance outside of domestic borders. But for each of these cases, a vast majority of foreign elites are excluded in the foreign urban centres where they make second or third homes. Elites living and working in other contexts still find themselves on the outer of the social worlds of their host countries, unable to command the status that derives from family history and connections in the host community, that they command in their own country. This exclusion reveals the image of a roving, homeless global elite to be a falsity: the global elite remains deeply mired in the political, economic and social base of their countries of origin (Hartmann 2017, Young 2017). As the experience of Imran, recounted as the beginning of this chapter, demonstrates, many elite Pakistanis seek investment opportunities outside of the unstable political and economic milieu of Pakistan, seeking to send their children to school in more prestigious (and presumably) safer schools in the UK or the US. While many among the Pakistani elite spoke of the desire to send their children to school in the West, away from the seemingly worsening security crisis of 2014, several noted that they could not possibly move elsewhere, despite often holding a second citizenship in a Western country – as life would be simply too dull, both in terms of the absence of the rich networks of which they were a part in Pakistan, and the near unrivalled turbulence of Pakistani politics.

Political or Economic Turmoil Often Creates New Opportunities for Economic Growth and Upward Social Mobility

Significant economic – and by extension social and political – structural change has been shown in contexts across the world to occur as a result of major events that disrupt the political and economic balance (Acemoglu and Robinson 2012). And often, these processes of instability and turmoil enhance, rather than undermine, the profit-generation tactics of the elite. In societies with extractive institutions in particular, those which 'are designed to extract incomes and wealth from one subset of society to benefit a different subset' (Acemoglu and Robinson 2012) political instability exacerbates the zero sum element of capturing the benefits of economic growth. The opportunities for rapid wealth accumulation and class restructuring are apparent across the world in contexts as diverse as Russia after the collapse of the Soviet Union,[10] and China during the Great Leap Forward of the late 1950s onwards.[11]

Other scholars have noted that 'periods of rapid institutional transformation frequently create zones of legal, ethical and practical ambiguity within which corrupt practices emerge and flourish' (Smart 1993, 9). Alongside corruption, these periods of rapid institutional transformation also provide powerful opportunities for innovation, rapid class mobility and large-scale profit accumulation that is not generally possible in periods of greater political calm and stability. Yet Pakistani capitalism also differs from most contexts in the Global North, insofar as it operates in a context of much higher political instability and physical insecurity. This instability both challenges and supports a starkly elite-dominated form of capitalism, as this book has demonstrated. The historical, social and political conditions that have been created, or entrenched, by various generations of first colonial, and then domestic elites, have created a structure in which the benefits of economic growth, and of political representation, are only narrowly distributed.

The growth Pakistan has achieved since its inception is the result of numerous set-backs, restarts and advancements, oscillating between the nationalisation of industry and partly redistributive social policies, a return to privatisation and the shifting economic policy of various civilian and military governments. For instance, as explored in Chapter Two, the almost complete absence of industrial manufacturing infrastructure within Pakistan at the time of partition, created both major economic upheaval and an opportunity to formulate a new economic elite from within the ranks of the largely middle-class trader community. Pakistan's stilted economic growth from its inception until the 1970s in large part reflected the investment in vital infrastructure the nation required to kick start its economic development, and to provide the goods required by its expanding population. It also reflects the Pakistan–India animosity that early on led to severe trade restrictions with India, its natural major trading partner, and for a period in the 1960s and 1970s, a complete ban on trade. Despite the national disadvantage, or rather, because of it, a number of families achieved rapid upward mobility at Partition to meet the manufacturing needs of the new state in the absence of existing industrial infrastructure. In the 1970s, opportunities to transition into the economic elite emerged again as many among the existing industrial elite lost their fortunes overnight and fled the country. And in the early 1980s, under Zia Ul Haq and the war in Afghanistan, a new group of military loyalists emerged from the ranks of the military to assume senior leadership in government, and with it government housing and pensions at a scale that facilitated entrance into the economic elite for the children and grandchildren that followed.

Generally, there have been exceptionally low rates of social mobility among the broader population. Yet for a small number of (often very prominent) families, the periodic bouts of extreme political and economic turbulence described above have provided opportunities for rapid and significant upward mobility. The political and economic structures that have developed as a result have perpetuated the power and privileges of the various factions of the elite class, and severely limited opportunities for upward social mobility for the rest of the population. Despite dramatic economic and political transformations within the country and the region, many of Pakistan's elite families have retained their class position over three, four and more generations. Though many elite families lost much, if not all, of their wealth in various political crises, they engaged social and family networks, and a range of associated informal strategies, to re-emerge from major economic losses and successfully rebuild their empires. These are not simple stories of the inter-generational transfer of wealth. At times, they reveal a very different process: certain political crises meant that for some families there was no wealth to transfer from father to sons. Instead of the transfer of wealth, these alternative stories reveal an inter-generational transfer of distinction, social status and of extended networks of powerful people who could be relied upon in times of trouble. They also reveal a parallel story of the growth of a new elite, adept at traversing crises and at forming networks with the leadership of newly powerful institutions – most notably, the military.

Many of Pakistan's elite businessmen have turned Pakistan's economic weakness, and the unwillingness of multinational corporations and other international firms to invest in the unstable Pakistani market, to their own advantage. The massive profits generated by a few key firms have depended heavily on the ability of local elites to navigate the inherently volatile political context of Pakistan and the impact of these economic and political upheavals on the Pakistani domestic manufacturing market. Kamil's work partnering with foreign investors in domestic Pakistani enterprises (discussed in Chapter Five) is one example of a member of the elite creating a niche for themselves as 'indentors', serving as the interlocutors between foreign firms and domestic players, and advising these actors on the politics, legalities and illegalities required to make investment in Pakistan work. Like Kamil, many among Pakistan's business and political elite actively benefited from the nation's crises. The intermittent political and economic upheavals that characterised their business and political dealings in Pakistan served both to legitimate their non-compliance with law and regulation, and as a strong disincentive for many among the class to advocate for, or demand, peace, stability, or conciliation between political and ideological factions.

Many of my other informants sold their products to foreign firms, ranging from selling textiles to major conglomerates like the American worldwide clothing retail company Gap Inc., to selling sugar-derived ethanol to alcohol manufacturers in Japan. The ability of these elites to access local producers; to manage their very cheap labour; to make informal payments to the right local leaders and government regulators; to extract significant profit by buying produce or manufacturing at local prices, and then sell these items to foreign firms at international market prices, enabled them to extract high profits. Most foreign firms, without deep personal linkages to local Pakistani systems of production, land cultivation and patronage, would be unable to operate in the Pakistani environment.

The inability of international investors to negotiate the local political scene both deters foreign revenue and insulates a locally-dominated domestic market from the interference of foreign investors. In his study of Bangladeshi elite factory owners, Gilbert (2018, 52) noted a similar phenomenon. Elite factory owners noted that their success in business was inversely related to the general ease of doing business in the country quantified by organisations like the World Bank Group, noting 'because it is so difficult, it gives us [Bangladeshi elites] a chance to thrive; if it was so easy, you [foreigners] would have come to exploit us . . .' Consequently, many among the Pakistani elite actively benefit from the crises that undermine the quality of life of middle- and working-class Pakistanis. Further, they face strong disincentives to advocate for, or demand, peaceful processes and economic and political stability.

Yet in addition to the opportunities created by instability, con-stantly shifting political and security conditions have also made elites – and their wealth and influence – vulnerable. The extensive personal networks and alliances most Pakistani elites cultivate with a broad array of individuals representing highly varied group interests is in large part a response to this political and economic volatility, and the inability of the state to secure a reliable and impartial environ-ment for economic competition.

A Culture of Exemptions

Globally, elites engage in efforts to feel and be perceived by others as morally worthy, and to justify their position within not just an economic hierarchy, but also a moral one (Piketty 2014). Elites seek to differentiate themselves as part of the 'good' rich, separate from what they and others categorise as the morally corrupt, exploitative, ostentatious and lazy rich.[12]

In weak states with easily manipulated regulatory bodies, moral-ity becomes a more slippery concept, where that which is 'legal' and 'illegal' and that which is 'moral' and 'immoral' are often not per-ceived by either the elite or the broader population as synonymous. There is a tacit pact established between members of the elite, which provides a high degree of impunity for illegality and extra-legality. This ability to manoeuvre around the laws and regulations of the State enables elites to constantly shore up and reconstitute their power in alignment with shifting political and economic conditions. The justification that these manoeuvres are necessary – particularly in the context of a predatory or extractive state – has led to a culture of exemptions which enables and justifies avoidance of the laws, regulations and democratic procedures to which all other strata in society are subject.

As noted in Chapter Six, my informants consistently attributed the inequality from which they benefited to the actions of others, disassociated in some way from themselves: businessmen often noted the corrupt activities of politicians; politicians often noted the unethical accumulation of wealth by businessmen; senior bureaucrats laid the blame on both; and all laid blame on the inefficiency and immorality of a vaguely defined 'State'. Elites enacted their ability to circumnavigate disadvantages laws and regulations by enlisting their allies to ensure court cases prosecuted by regulatory bodies were delayed by the failure of legal counsel to appear; by lobbying government peers to implement Statutory Regulatory Orders (SROs) with narrow application to a firm or monopoly industry; or by keeping double book systems that enabled them to misreport revenue and underpay tax.[13]

The belief that the elite engage in a high degree of illegality and corruption, and live licentious and immoral lifestyles, is both widely held and widely tolerated among the Pakistani population. Moral ideologies shape middle- and working-class perceptions of the business and political elite creating highly negative assessments. This double standard of law for those among the elite, and those in the middle and lower classes below them, sometimes raises resentment, but as I explored in Chapter Six, rarely results in serious penalties for elite offenders. As I have demonstrated, the efforts of some within the nation's regulatory bodies to curtail elite actions are often systematically undermined by the senior leadership of these same bodies.

Moral rationales also hold a significant role in the self-perceptions of many elites, but operate according to very different criterion. In fact, elite moral discourses occupy a central role in justifying their conduct[14] and the wilful avoidance of constraining laws and regulations to one another. Despite the presence of these moral rationales, issues of morality emerged as peripheral factors in shaping both elite attitudes and actions. Peer assessments of morality held a much less significant role in elite status and membership than did peer assessments of distinction and appropriate class dispositions.

Final Thoughts

The experiences of the wealthiest and most privileged members of Pakistani society provide powerful insights into the unequal processes of accumulation, and elite-dominated political structures that we now witness all over the world, including in economically advanced countries. As Pakistan's elite has become increasingly adept at managing the processes of regional trade and foreign investment, rather than dissolving the social ties and cultural practices engaged in by the nation's most powerful, these factors have remained central to determining the allocation of national wealth – along with those who are excluded from partaking in it. The case of Pakistan is a powerful prism through which to examine these broader global trends, as it serves as an exaggerated example of an increasingly elite-dominated, unequal global economy, whilst reflecting realities that go against widely held conventional wisdom.

Notes

1. A large anthropological scholarship in Italy and Spain exists on kinship and communal loyalty providing powerful parallels to similar forms of group affiliation in Pakistan. See, for instance, Yanagisako's (2002) research on the place of collectivity, filial loyalty and patriarchal authority in Italian capitalism; Schneider and Schneider's (2005) work on clientelism, familism, patriarchy and corruption in Italy; and Gilmore's (1986) study on male attitudes towards women, and women as symbols of honour in Andalusia.
2. See Zaidi (2017, 2008) and Akhtar (2008).
3. Scott (1998) further argued that the homogenising and standardising role of these states had been taken over by global corporations who functioned at an international level in the same way that the state had at a national one.
4. See Ali 2018.
5. See Savage et al 2013.
6. See Robson, 2016. 'How important is social class in Britain?', *BBC*: http://www.bbc.com/future/story/20160406-how-much-does-social-class-matter-in-britain-today.
7. A similar process is documented in Bhabha 1984 and Johnson 2013, among others.
8. See Gilding 2004.
9. See Pardo 2015.
10. See Schimpfössl 2018.
11. See Osburg 2013.
12. See, for example, Sherman's (2017) research on the New York elite, and Schimpfössl's (2018) research on Russian elites.
13. A culture of exemptions is further fostered by the ability of the elite to circumvent the deleterious effects of poor government service delivery and a serious law, order and safety problem through obtaining vital services on the costly private market – generators to cover power shortages, armed security guards to reduce risks to personal safety, and elite schooling to side-step abysmal standards of education provided by the public schooling system.
14. Though outside the scope of my research, assumptions about the morality of individual elites based upon their family background are likely to have influenced the legitimacy of certain business elites in my study, particularly those with rural landlord back-grounds, as they were found to do in Martin's (2015, 150) analysis. Martin found that prosperity has traditionally been associated with pious elders, and that consequently,

landlords with *pir* (hereditary saint) backgrounds were presumed by villagers to hold a higher moral status. As I briefly noted in Chapter Four, the significant numbers of religious scholars in earlier generations of Afridis is very likely to have facilitated their upward social mobility and success in trade and business by bestowing them with a high level of respect from the communities in which they did business.

REFERENCES

Abbink, J., and T. Salverda. 2012. *The Anthropology of Elites: Power, Culture, and the Complexities of Distinction*. New York: Palgrave Macmillan.

Acemoglu, D., and J. Robinson. 2012. *Why Nations Fail: The Origins of Power, Prosperity, and Poverty*. New York: Crown Business.

Agamben, G. 2005. *State of Exception*. Chicago: University of Chicago Press.

Ahmad, I. 1981. 'Pakistan: Class and State Formation'. *Race & Class* 22(3): 239–256.

Ahmed, A.S. 1997. *Jinnah, Pakistan and Islamic Identity: The Search for Saladin*. Milton Park, Abingdon: Routledge.

———. 2011 [1980]. *Pukhtun Economy and Society: Traditional Structure and Economic Development in a Tribal Society* Milton Park, Abingdon: Routledge.

———. 2011. *Millennium and Charisma among Pathans: A Critical Essay in Social Anthropology*. Milton Park, Abingdon: Routledge.

Ahmed, Z.S., and M.J. Stephan,. 2010. 'Fighting for The Rule of Law: Civil Resistance and the Lawyers' Movement in Pakistan'. *Democratization* 17(3): 492–513.

Ajit, D., H. Donker, and R. Saxena. 2012. 'Corporate Boards in India: Blocked by Caste?' *Economic & Political Weekly* 47(32): 39–43.

Akhtar, A.S. 2008. 'The Overdeveloping State: The Politics of Common Sense in Pakistan, 1971–2007', School of Oriental and African Studies (University of London). Unpublished PhD dissertation.

Alavi, H. 1971. 'The Crisis of Nationalities and the State in Pakistan'. *Journal of Contemporary Asia* 1(3): 42–66.

———. 1972. 'The State in Post-Colonial Societies: Pakistan and Bangladesh'. *New Left Review* 74(1): 59–81.

———. 1974. 'Rural Bases of Political Power in South Asia'. *Journal of Contemporary Asia* 4(4): 413–422.

———. 1976. 'Kinship in West Punjab Villages'. In T.N. Madan (ed.), *Muslim Communities of South Asia: Culture and Society*. New Delhi: Vikas Publishing House, pp. 1–27.

———. 1983. 'Class and State in Pakistan'. In H.N. Gardezi and J. Rashid (eds), *Pakistan: The Unstable State*. Lahore: Vanguard Books.

———. 1990. 'Authoritarianism and Legitimation of State Power in Pakistan'. In Subrata K. Mitra (ed.), *The Post-Colonial State in Asia: Dialectics of Politics and Culture*. New York: Harvester Wheatsheaf, pp. 19–71.

Aldrich, N.W. 1989. *Old Money: The Mythology of America's Upper Class*. New York: Allsworth Press.

Ali, S.A.M. 2018. *Staffing the State: The Politicisation of Bureaucratic Appointments in Pakistan*. School of Slavonic and Asian Studies (SOAS), University of London, Unpublished PhD dissertation.

Allison, A. 2009. *Nightwork: Sexuality, Pleasure, and Corporate Masculinity in a Tokyo Hostess Club*. Chicago: University of Chicago Press.

Altorki, S. 1982. 'The Anthropologist in the Field: A Case of "Indigenous Anthropology" from Saudi Arabia'. In H. Fahim (ed.), *Indigenous Anthropology in Non Western Countries*. Durham, NC: North Carolina Press, pp. 165–175.

Amjad, R. 1976. 'Industrial Concentration and Economic Power in Pakistan'. *Pakistan Economic and Social Review* 14(1/4): 211–261. doi:10.2307/25821361.

———. 1982. *Private Industrial Investment in Pakistan*. Cambridge: Cambridge University Press.

Amoranto, G., N. Chun, and A.B. Deolalikar. 2010. 'Who Are the Middle Class and What Values do They Hold? Evidence from the World Values Survey'.

Armytage, L. 2012. *Reforming Justice: A Journey to Fairness in Asia*. Cambridge: Cambridge University Press.

Armytage, R. 2015. 'The Social Lives of the Elite: Friendship and Power in Pakistan'. *The Asia Pacific Journal of Anthropology* 16(5): 448–463.

———. 2016. 'Alliance of State and Ruling Classes in Contemporary Pakistan'. *Economic & Political Weekly* 51(31), pp. 108–114.

———. 2019. 'An Evolving Class Structure? Pakistan's Elite and the Implications for Pakistan's Political Economy'. In Matthew McCartney and S. Akbar Zaidi (eds), *New Perspectives on Pakistan's Political Economy: State, Class and Social Change*. Cambridge: Cambridge University Press, pp. 153–175.

Ashraf, S. 2018. 'Honour, Purity and Transgression: Understanding Blasphemy Accusations and Consequent Violent Action in Punjab, Pakistan'. *Contemporary South Asia* 26(1): 51–68.

Awaz TV. 2013, 6 February. 'Officer Who Unearthed Rs82 Billion Ogra Scam Being Harassed'. *Awaz.Tv*.

Baker, R. 2005. *Capitalism's Achilles Heel: Dirty Money and How to Renew the Free-Market System*. New Jersey: John Wiley & Sons.

Baker, J., and S. Milne. 2015. 'Dirty Money States: Illicit Economies and the State in Southeast Asia'. *Critical Asian Studies* 47, 151–176.

Banerjee, M. 2000. *The Pathan Unarmed: Opposition and Memory in the North West Frontier*. Karachi: Oxford University Press.

Barhan, P.K. 1984. *Land, Labor, and Rural Poverty*. Oxford: Oxford University Press.

Barth, F. 1959. *Political Leadership among Swat Pathans (London School of Economics Monographs on Social Anthropology 19)*. London: Athlone.

Bear, L., K. Ho, A. Tsing, and S. Yanagisako. 2015. 'Gens: A Feminist Manifesto for the Study of Capitalism'. *Cultural Anthropology Online, Fieldsights – Theorizing the Contemporary*.

Beaverstock, J.V., S. Hall, and T. Wainwright. 2013. 'Servicing the Super-Rich: New Financial Elites and The Rise of The Private Wealth Management Retail Ecology'. *Regional Studies* 47(6): 834–849.

Beisel, N.K. 1998. *Imperiled Innocents: Anthony Comstock and Family Reproduction in Victorian America*. Princeton, NJ: Princeton University Press.

Bhabha, H. 1984. 'Of Mimicry and Man: The Ambivalence of Colonial Discourse'. *October* 28: 125–133.

Bourdieu, P. 1998. *The State Nobility: Elite Schools in the Field of Power*. Stanford, CA: Stanford University Press.

———. 2013 [1984]. *Distinction: A Social Critique of the Judgement of Taste*: Milton Park, Abingdon: Routledge.

Bourdieu, P., and L.J. Wacquant. 1992. *An Invitation to Reflexive Sociology*. Chicago: University of Chicago Press.

Bourgouin, F. 2013. 'Money Relations, Ideology, and the Formation of a Cosmopolitan Elite at the Frontier of Transnational Capitalism: An Ethnographic Study of African Finance Professionals in Johannesburg'. In J. Abbink, and T. Salverda, (eds). *The Anthropology of*

Elites: Power, Culture, and the Complexities of Distinction. New York: Palgrave Macmillan, pp. 227–247.

Blood, P. 1994. *Pakistan: A Country Study*. Retrieved 12 June 2014 from http://country studies.us/pakistan/.

Brandes, S. 1987. 'Sex Roles and Anthropological Research in Rural Andalusia'. *Women's Studies* 13(4): 357–372. doi:10.1080/00497878.1987.9978676.

———. 2008. 'The Things we Carry'. *Men and Masculinities* 11(2): 145–153.

Burki, S.J. 1988. 'Pakistan under Zia, 1977-1988'. *Asian Survey* 28(10): 1082–1100.

———. 2015. *To Understand Pakistan's Present, Study the Past*. Paper presented at the ICAS 9, Adelaide.

Candland, C. 2007. *Labor, Democratization and Development in India and Pakistan* (Vol. 2). Milton Park, Abingdon: Routledge.

Carrier, J.G., and D. Kalb. 2015. *Anthropologies of Class: Power, Practice, and Inequality*. Cambridge: Cambridge University Press.

Chakrabarty, D. 1991. 'Rethinking Working-Class History'. *Economic and Political Weekly* 26(17): 1117–1119.

———. 2009. *Provincializing Europe: Postcolonial Thought and Historical Difference*. Princeton, NJ: Princeton University Press.

Chatterjee, P. 2008. 'Democracy and Economic Transformation in India'. *Economic and Political Weekly*, 53–62.

Cheema, A., H. Javid, and M.F. Naseer. 2013. 'Dynastic Politics in Punjab: Facts, Myths and their Implications'. *Institute of Development and Economic Alternatives (IDEAS), Working Paper No. 01-03*.

Chibber, V. 2006. 'On the Decline of Class Analysis in South Asian Studies'. *Critical Asian Studies* 38(4): 357–387.

Chirol, S.V., and A.C.C. Lyall. 1910. *Indian Unrest*. London: Macmillan.

Comaroff, J., and J.L. Comaroff. 2015. *Theory from the South: Or, How Euro-America is Evolving toward Africa*. Milton Park, Abingdon: Routledge.

Conti, J. A., and M. O'Neil. 2007. 'Studying Power: Qualitative Methods and the Global Elite'. *Qualitative Research* 7(1): 63–82.

Craig, D., and D. Porter. 2006. *Development beyond Neoliberalism? Governance, Poverty Reduction, and Political Economy*. Milton Park, Abingdon: Routledge.

Credit Suisse. 2018. Global Wealth Report 2018.

Daily Pakistan. 2015, 28 July. 'Resisting Nepotism: Principal of Aitchison College Fired for Being Too Honest'. *Daily Pakistan*. Retrieved 26 August 2015 from http://en.daily pakistan.com.pk/pakistan/resisting-nepotism-principal-of-aitchison-college-to-be-removed-for-being-too-honest/.

Dawn. 2007, 17 October. 'The Economy under Musharaff'. *Dawn*. Retrieved 13 October 2015 from http://www.dawn.com/news/271347/the-economy-under-pervez-musharraf.

Dawn. 2014, 25 September. 'Aitchison BoG Accepts Principal's Resignation'. *Dawn, The*. Retrieved 11 November 2014 from http://www.dawn.com/news/1134175.

Darr, A. 2012. 'A Requiem for The SECP Law Division'. *Express Tribune*. Retrieved 17 November 2014 from http://tribune.com.pk/story/193437/a-requiem-for-the-secp-law-division/.

Das, V. 1973. 'The Structure of Marriage Preferences: An Account from Pakistani Fiction'. *Man* 8(1): 30–45.

de Lima, A.P. 2000. '"How Did I Become a Leader in My Family Firm?" Assets for Succession in Contemporary Lisbon Financial Elites'. In J.D. Pina-Cabral and A.P. de Lima (eds), *Elites: Choice Leadership and Succession*. Oxford: Berghahn Books, pp. 31–51.

De Lomnitz, L.A. 1987. *A Mexican Elite Family, 1820-1980: Kinship, Class, and Culture*. Princeton, NJ: Princeton University Press.

De Sardan, J. 1999. 'A Moral Economy of Corruption in Africa?' *The Journal of Modern African Studies* 37, 25–52.

Deshpande, A., and K. Nurse. 2012. *The Global Economic Crisis and the Developing World: Implications and Prospects for Recovery and Growth.* Paris: OECD Publishing.

Dilawar, I. 2010, 21 December. 'SECP Bows to KSE over Member Chairman'. *Pakistan Today*.

Durr-e-Nayab. 2011. 'Estimating the Middle Class in Pakistan'. *The Pakistan Development Review*, 1–28.

Elwood, S.A., and D.G. Martin. 2000. '"Placing" Interviews: Location and Scales of Power in Qualitative Research'. *The Professional Geographer* 52(4): 649–657.

Express Tribune. 2012, 24 February. 'Secretary Given 15 Days to Justify SECP Chief Appointment'. *Express Tribune* Retrieved 14 July 2014 from http://tribune.com.pk/story/341090/secretary-given-15-days-to-justify-secp-chief-appointment/.

———. 2014. 'Breaking Traditions: Aitchison College Abolishes "Quota" System'. Retrieved 27 July 2015 from http://tribune.com.pk/story/732317/breaking-traditions-aitchison-college-abolishes-quota-system/.

Ferguson, J. 2002. 'Global Disconnect: Abjection and the Aftermath of Modernism'. In Jonathan Xavier Inda, and Renata Rosaldo (eds), *The Anthropology of Globalization: A Reader.* Hoboken, NJ: Wiley–Blackwell, pp. 136–153.

Fine, G.A. 1993. 'Ten Lies of Ethnography: Moral Dilemmas of Field Research'. *Journal of Contemporary Ethnography* 22(3): 267–294.

Foucault, M. 1980. *Power/Knowledge: Selected Interviews and Other Writings, 1972–1977.* New York: Pantheon.

———. 1982. 'The Subject and Power'. *Critical Inquiry* 8(4): 777–795.

Freeland, C. 2012. *Plutocrats: The Rise of the New Global Super-Rich and the Fall of Everyone Else.* London: Penguin.

Freeman, C. 2014. *Entrepreneurial Selves: Neoliberal Respectability and the Making of a Caribbean Middle Class.* Durham, NC: Duke University Press.

Friedman, J. 2004. 'Globalization'. In David Nugent and Joan Vincent (eds), *A Companion to the Anthropology of Politics.* Hoboken, NJ: Wiley–Blackwell, pp. 179–197.

Geertz, C. 1973. *The Interpretation of Cultures: Selected Essays.* New York: Basic Books.

Gilbert, P.R. 2018. 'Class, Complicity, and Capitalist Ambition in Dhaka's Elite Enclaves'. *Focaal* 2018(81): 43–57.

Gilding, M. 2004. 'Entrepreneurs, Elites and the Ruling Class: The Changing Structure of Power and Wealth in Australian Society'. *Australian Journal of Political Science* 39(1): 127–143.

———. 2010. 'Motives of the Rich and Powerful in Doing Interviews with Social Scientists'. *International Sociology* 25(6): 755–777.

Gilmore, D.D. 1986. 'Mother-Son Intimacy and the Dual View of Woman in Andalusia: Analysis Through Oral Poetry'. *Ethos* 14(3): 227-251. doi:10.2307/640024.

Glucksberg, L., and R. Burrows. 2016. 'Family Offices and the Contemporary Infrastructures of Dynastic Wealth'. *Sociologica* 10(2): 1–23.

Goffman, E., and L.H. Lofland. 1989. 'On Fieldwork'. *Journal of Contemporary Ethnography* 18(2): 123.

Goldthorpe, J.H., and M. Jackson. 2007. 'Intergenerational Class Mobility in Contemporary Britain: Political Concerns and Empirical Findings'. *The British Journal of Sociology* 58: 525–546.

Graham, P. 2000. 'Hypercapitalism: A Political Economy of Informational Idealism'. *New Media & Society* 2(2): 131–156.

Green, L. 1994. 'Fear as a Way of Life'. *Cultural Anthropology* 9: 227–256.

Gupta, A. 1995. 'Blurred Boundaries: The Discourse of Corruption, The Culture of Politics, and the Imagined State'. *American Ethnologist* 22(2): 375–402.

———. 2012. *Red Tape: Bureaucracy, Structural Violence, and Poverty in India*. Durham, NC: Duke University Press.

Hannerz, U. 1967. 'Gossip, Networks and Culture in a Black American Ghetto'. *Ethnos* 32(1–4): 35–60.

Hart, K. 2001. 'Money in an Unequal World'. *Anthropological Theory* 1(3): 307–330.

Hartmann, M. 2017. 'The International Business Elite'. In O. Korsnes, J. Heilbron, J. Hjellbrekke, F. Bühlmann, and M. Savage (eds), *New Directions in Elite Studies*. Milton Park, Abingdon: Routledge.

Hartmann, M., and K. Lueg. 2017. 'Brexit: On the Declining Homogeneity of European Elites–and on the Importance of a Domestic Habitus in Times of Globalization'. *Culture, Practice and European Policy* 2(1): 28–34.

Harvey, W.S. 2010. 'Methodological Approaches for Interviewing Elite's. *Geography Compass* 4(3): 193–205.

Hasty, J. 2005. 'The Pleasures of Corruption: Desire and Discipline in Ghanaian Political Culture'. *Cultural Anthropology* 20, 271–301.

Haq, M.U. 1968. 'Industrial Concentration and Economic Power in Pakistan'. *Business Recorder (Karachi, Pakistan)*.

———. 1976. *The Poverty Curtain: Choices for The Third World*. New York: Columbia University Press.

Haqqani, H. 2005. *Pakistan: Between Military and Mosque*. Lahore: Vanguard Publishers.

Herod, A. 1999. 'Reflections on Interviewing Foreign Elites: Praxis, Positionality, Validity, and the Cult of the Insider'. *Geoforum* 30(4): 313–327.

Herzfeld, M. 2000. 'Uncanny Success: Some Closing Remarks'. In João de Pina Cabral and Antónia Pedroso de Lima (eds), *Elites: Choice, Leadership and Succession*. Lisbon: Etnográfica Press, pp. 227–236.

Ho, K. 2009. *Liquidated: An Ethnography of Wall Street*. Durham, NC: Duke University Press.

———. 2009. 'Disciplining Investment Bankers, Disciplining the Economy: Wall Street's Institutional Culture of Crisis and the Downsizing of "Corporate America"'. *American Anthropologist* 111(2): 177–189.

Hoang, K.K. 2015. *Dealing in Desire: Asian Ascendancy, Western Decline, and the Hidden Currencies of Global Sex Work*. Berkeley, CA: University of California Press.

Hull, M.S. 2012. *Government of Paper: The Materiality of Bureaucracy in Urban Pakistan*. Berkeley, CA: University of California Press.

Husain, I. 2000. *Pakistan: The Economy of an Elitist State*. Karachi: Oxford University Press.

Husain, K. 2015, 11 January. 'Pakistan and the IMF: The Ties that Bind'. *Dawn, The*. Retrieved 10 November 2015 from http://www.dawn.com/news/1155958.

Hussain, R., and A. Bittles. 1998. 'The Prevalence and Demographic Characteristics of Consanguineous Marriages in Pakistan'. *Journal of Biosocial Science* 30(2): 261–275.

Hussain, R. 1999. 'Community Perceptions of Reasons for Preference for Consanguineous Marriages in Pakistan'. *Journal of Biosocial Science* 31(04): 449–461.

Isaphani. 2013. ''Isaphani: About Us'. Retrieved 14 July 2014 from http://www.ispahanibd.com/about-us/.

Inda, J.X., and R. Rosaldo. (eds). 2001. *The Anthropology of Globalization: A Reader (Blackwell Readers in Anthropology)*. Hoboken, NJ: Wiley–Blackwell.

———. 2008. 'Tracking Global Flows'. In J.X. Inda and R. Rosaldo (eds), *The Anthropology of Globalization: A Reader*. Hoboken, NJ: Wiley–Blackwell, p. 2.

Indrawati, S.M. 2015, 4 August. 'What Will it Take to Realize Pakistan's Potential?' *The World Bank*.

i24news. 2014, 16 June. 'Taliban Warns Foreign Firms to Leave Pakistan'. *i24news*. Retrieved 14 July 2014 from http://www.i24news.tv/en/news/international/middle-east/34418-140616-taliban-warns-foreign-firms-to-leave-pakistan.

Islam, N. 2004. 'Sifarish, Sycophants, Power and Collectivism: Administrative Culture in Pakistan'. *International Review of Administrative Sciences* 70: 311–330.

Jabukowska, L. 2013. 'Land, Historicity, and Lifestyle: Capital and Its Conversions among the Gentry in Poland'. In J. Abbink, and T. Salverda (eds), *The Anthropology of Elites: Power, Culture, and the Complexities of Distinction*. New York: Palgrave Macmillan, pp. 45–69.

Jaffrelot, C. 2015. *The Pakistan Paradox: Instability and Resilience*. London: Hurst Publishers.

Jalal, A. 1985. *The Sole Spokesman: Jinnah, the Muslim League and The Demand for Pakistan* (Vol. 31). Lahore: Sang-e-Meel Publications.

———. 2011. 'The Past as Present'. In M. Lodhi (ed.), *Pakistan: Beyond the Crisis State*. London: Hurst & Company, pp. 7–20.

Jamasji-Hirjikaka, D., and Y. Qureshi. 2004. *The Merchant Knight: Adamjee Haji Dawood* (S.E.P. Services Ed.). Karachi: Adamjee Foundation.

Johnson, M. 2013. 'The Aesthetics of Diaspora in Colonial Fields of Power: Elite Nationalism, Art and the Love to Die For'. *Ethnos* 78(2): 175–199.

Kalb, D. 2015. 'Introduction: Class and the New Anthropological Holism'. In James G. Carrier, and Don Kalb (eds), *Anthropologies of Class: Power, Practice and Inequality*. Cambridge: Cambirdge University Press, pp. 1–27.

Kaur, R. 2006. 'The Last Journey: Exploring Social Class in the 1947 Partition Migration'. *Economic and Political Weekly* 41(22): 2221–2228.

Kaviraj, S. 1988. 'A Critique of the Passive Revolution'. *Economic and Political Weekly* 23(45–7): 2429–2444.

Keister, L. 2014. 'The One Percent'. *Annual Review of Sociology* 40: 347–367.

Khan, M. 1999. 'The Political Economy of Industrial Policy in Pakistan 1947–1971'. Working Paper. *Department of Economics, SOAS*.

———. 2010. 'Political Settlements and the Governance of Growth-Enhancing Institutions'. Working Paper. *SOAS* (July).

Khan, S.R. 2012. 'The Sociology of Elites'. *Annual Review of Sociology* 38: 361–377.

Kipnis, A.B. 1997. *Producing Guanxi: Sentiment, Self, and Subculture in a North China Village*. Durham, NC: Duke University Press.

Kochanek, S.A. 1983. *Interest Groups and Development: Business and Politics in Pakistan*. Karachi: Oxford University Press.

Kugelman, M. 2013. *Pakistan-India Trade: What Needs to Be Done? What Does it Matter?* Woodrow Wilson International Center for Scholars, Asia Program.

Lamont, M. 1992. *Money, Morals, and Manners: The Culture of the French and the American Upper-Middle Class*. Chicago: University of Chicago Press.

Lieven, A. 2011. *Pakistan: A Hard Country*. New York: Public Affairs.

Lindholm, C. 1982. *Generosity and Jealousy: The Swat Pukhtun of Northern Pakistan*, New York: Columbia University Press.

Looney, R. 2004. 'Failed Economic Take-offs and Terrorism in Pakistan: Conceptualizing a Proper Role for US Assistance'. *Asian Survey* 44(6): 771–793.

Lyon, S.M. 2004. *An Anthropological Analysis of Local Politics and Patronage in a Pakistani Village*. Lampeter: Edwin Mellen Press.

———. 2012. 'Networks and Kinship: Formal Models of Alliance, Descent, and Inheritance in a Pakistani Punjabi Village'. *Social Science Computer Review* 31(1). doi:0894439312453275.

Lyon, S.M., and M.A.Z. Mughal. 2016. 'Ties That Bind: Marital Networks and Politics in Punjab, Pakistan'. *Structure and Dynamics: eJournal of Anthropological and Related Sciences* 9(2). Retrieved from https://escholarship.org/uc/item/5378v2fx.

Maqsood, A. 2017. *The New Pakistani Middle Class*. Cambridge, MA: Harvard University Press.

Martin, N. 2015. *Politics, Landlords and Islam in Pakistan (Exploring the Political in South Asia)*. Milton Park, Abingdon: Routledge.

Mathur, N. 2016. *Paper Tiger: Law, Bureaucracy and the Developmental State in Himalayan India*. Delhi: Cambridge University Press.

Mateen, A. 2013, 13 February. 'Will the Real Malik Riaz Please Stand Up?-II'. *The Spokesman Pakistan*. Retrieved 14 July 2014 from http://thespokesman.pk/index.php/component/k2/item/1350-will-the-real-malik-riaz-please-stand-up.

Maurer, B. 2006. 'The Anthropology of Money'. *Annual Review Anthropology* 35: 15–36.

Mauss, M. 1966. *The Gift: Forms and Functions of Exchange in Archaic Societies*, trans. Cunnison. London: Cohen & West.

Mazzei, J., and E.E. O'Brien. 2009. 'You Got It, So When Do You Flaunt It? Building Rapport, Intersectionality, and the Strategic Deployment of Gender in the Field'. *Journal of Contemporary Ethnography* 38(3): 358–383.

Mears, A. 2011. *Pricing Beauty: The Making of a Fashion Model*. Berkeley, CA: University of California Press.

Mills, C.W. 1956. *The Power Elite*. New York: Oxford University Press.

Montaigne, M. 1991 [1580]. *On Friendship*, trans. M.A. Screech. New York: Penguin.

Musharraf, P. 2006. *In the Line of Fire: A Memoir*. New York: Simon and Schuster.

NAB 1999. National Accountability Ordinance. In National Accountability Bureau (ed.), *(XVIII of 1999)*.

Nader, L. 1972. 'Up the Anthropologist: Perspectives Gained from Studying Up'. In D. Hymes (ed.), *Reinventing Anthropology*. New York: Pantheon Books.

Nadvi, K. 1999. 'Shifting Ties: Social Networks in the Surgical Instrument Cluster of Sialkot, Pakistan'. *Development and Change* 30(1): 141–175.

Nasr, S.V.R. 2001. *Islamic Leviathan: Islam and the Making of State Power*. Oxford: Oxford University Press.

Naviwala, N. 2016. 'Pakistan's Education Crisis: The Real Story'. *Woodrow Wilson International Center for Scholars*.

Nelson, M.J. 2011. *In the Shadow of Shari'ah: Islam, Islamic Law, And Democracy in Pakistan*. New York: Columbia University Press.

Noman, O. 1989. 'Pakistan and General Zia: Era and Legacy'. *Third World Quarterly* 11(1): 28–54. doi:10.2307/3992219.

Nordstrom, C. 2007. *Global Outlaws: Crime, Money, and Power in the Contemporary World*. Berkeley: University of California Press.

Osburg, J. 2013. *Anxious Wealth: Money and Morality Among China's New Rich*: Palo Alto, CA: Stanford University Press.

Orwell, G. 1962 [1934]. *Burmese Days*. New York: Penguin.

The Punjab Essential Services (Maitenance) Act, 1958 W.P. Act XXXIV of 1958 Stat. (1958 25 April 1958).

Papanek, G.F. 1962. 'The Development of Wntrepreneurship'. *The American Economic Review* 52(2): 46–58.

———. 1964. 'Industrial Production and Investment in Pakistan'. *The Pakistan Development Review*, 4(3) 462–490.

———. 1967. *Pakistan's Development: Social Goals and Private Incentives*. Cambridge, MA: Harvard University Press.

———. 1970. 'The Location of Industry'. *The Pakistan Development Review*, 10(3), 291–309.

Papanek, H. 1971. 'Purdah in Pakistan: Seclusion and Modern Occupations for Women'. *Journal of Marriage and Family* 33(3): 517–530. doi:10.2307/349849.

———. 1972. 'Pakistan's Big Businessmen: Muslim Separatism, Entrepreneurship, and Partial Modernization'. *Economic Development and Cultural Change* 21(1): 1–32.

Pakulski, J., and M. Waters. 1996. *The Death of Class*. London: Sage.

Pardo, I. 2015. 'Italian Elite Groups at Work: A View from the Urban Grassroots'. *Diogenes*, 0392192117740026.

Paugam, S., B. Cousin, C. Giorgetti, and J. Naudet. 2016. 'How do the Rich See the Urban Poor? Investigating the Meaning of Inequality in Paris, Delhi And Sao Paulo'. In H. Silver (ed.), *Comparative Urban Studies*. Milton Park, Abingdon: Routledge.

Piketty, T. 2014. *Capital in the Twenty-first Century*. Cambridge, MA: Harvard University Press.

PIDC. 2014. 'Pakistan Industrial Development Corporation'. Retrieved 17 July 2015 from http://pidc.com.pk/pidc-profile/.

Pina-Cabral, J.D., and A.P. de Lima. 2000. *Elites: Choice, Leadership and Succession*. Oxford: Oxford University Press.

Polanyi, K. 1944. *The Great Transformation*. New York: Rinehart.

Prasad, E.S. 2009. 'Is the Chinese Growth Miracle Built to Last?' *China Economic Review* 20(1): 103–123.

Qureshi, S. 2015. 'Sharif's Turnover in 1981 was Rs 337 Million', *London Post*, October 10.

Rahman, S.U. 2006. *Who Owns Pakistan?* Islamabad: Aekia Communications.

Rahman, T. 2012. *The Class Structure of Pakistan*. Oxford: Oxford University Press.

Rana, S. 2011, 6 January. 'Senate Panel Objects to New SECP Chairman's Appointment'. *The Express Tribune*. Retrieved 4 July 2014 from http://tribune.com.pk/story/99680/senate-panel-objects-to-new-secp-chairmans-appointment/.

Reuters. 2016, 30 March. 'Malik Riaz on Bribes, Blackmail and Launching Media Empire'. *The Dawn*. Retrieved 4 July 2014 from http://www.dawn.com/news/1248654/malik-riaz-on-bribes-blackmail-and-launching-media-empire.

Rifkin, J. 2000. *The Age of Access: The New Culture of Hypercapitalism, Where All of Life is a Paid-For Experience*. Tarcher: New York.

Rivo López, E., N. Rodríguez López, and B. González Vázquez. 2013. 'The Family Office in Spain: An Exploratory Study'. *Management Research: The Journal of the Iberoamerican Academy of Management* 11(1): 35–57.

Robben, A., and C. Nordstrom. 1995. 'The Anthropology and Ethnography of Violence and Sociopolitical Conflict'. In A. Robben and C. Nordstrom (eds), *Fieldwork under Fire: Contemporary Studies of Violence and Survival*. Berkeley: University of California Press, pp. 1–21.

Rogers, J. 2010. 'Shadowing the Bar: Studying an English Professional Elite'. *Historical Reflections/Reflexions Historiques* 36(3): 39–57.

Rolls, M. 2008. 'Will "Devolution" Improve the Accountability and Responsiveness of Social Service Delivery in Balochistan, Pakistan? A Political Economy Perspective'. *Development Studies Institute Working Paper Series, London School of Economics and Political Science* (08–86).

Rosplock, K., and B.R. Hauser. 2014. 'The Family Office Landscape: Todays Trends and Five Predictions for the Family Office of Tomorrow'. *The Journal of Wealth Management* 17(3): 9–19.

Rothkopf, D. 2008. *Superclass: The Global Power Elite and The World They are Making*. New York: Farrar, Straus and Giroux.

Sanchez, A. 2010. 'Capitalism, Violence and the State: Crime, Corruption and Entrepreneurship in an Indian Company Town'. *Journal of Legal Anthropology* 2(1): 165–188.

———. 2016. *Criminal Capital: Violence,Corruption and Class in Industrial India*. Milton Park, Abingdon: Routledge.

Sanyal, K. 2014. *Rethinking Capitalist Development: Primitive Accumulation, Governmentality and Post-Colonial Capitalism*. Milton Park, Abingdon: Routledge.

Sattar, B. 2012, 25 June. 'SECP Has Now Become a Captured Agency'. *The News* Retrieved from http://www.thenews.com.pk/Todays-News-2-54439-SECP-has-now-become-a-captured-agency.

Savage, M., F. Devine, N. Cunningham, M. Taylor, Y. Li, et al. 2013. 'A New Model of Social Class? Findings from the BBC's Great British Class Survey Experiment'. *Sociology* 47(2): 219–250.

Savage, M. 2014. 'Piketty's Challenge for Sociology'. *The British Journal of Sociology*, 65(4): 591–606.

Schimpfössl, E. 2018. *Rich Russians: From Oligarchs to Bourgeoisie*. Oxford: Oxford University Press.

Schneider, J., and P. Schneider. 2005. 'Mafia, Antimafia, and the Plural Cultures of Sicily'. *Current Anthropology* 46(4): 501–520. doi:10.1086/431529.

Scott, J.C. 1998. *Seeing like a State: How Certain Schemes to Improve the Human Condition Have Failed*. New Haven, CT: Yale University Press.

Shah, S.A. 2014. 'NAB Has Recovered Rs 260bn during Last 15 Years, Says Chairman'. *Dawn, The*.

Shaheed, Z.A. 1979. 'Union Leaders, Worker Organization and Strikes: Karachi 1969–72'. *Development and Change* 10(2): 181–204.

Shaikh, F. 2009. *Making Sense of Pakistan*. New York: Columbia University Press.

Shenon, P. 1991, 5 August, 2001. 'B.C.C.I.'s Best Customer Is Also Its Worst Customer'. *New York Times*. Retrieved 17 August 2014 from http://www.nytimes.com/1991/08/06/business/bcci-s-best-customer-is-also-its-worst-customer.html.

Sherman, Rachel. 2017.*Uneasy Street: The Anxieties of Affluence*. Princeton, NJ: Princeton University Press.

Shore, C. 2002. 'Introduction: Towards an Anthropology of Elites'. In C. Shore and S. Nugent (eds), *Elite Cultures: Anthropological Perspectives*, London: Routledge, pp. 1–21.

Siddiqa, A. 2007. *Military, Inc. Inside Pakistan's Military Economy*. London: Pluto Press.

———. 2013, 5 June. 'Pakistan beyond Liberal and Conservative'. *Kafila*. Retrieved 27 August 2015 from http://kafila.org/2013/06/05/pakistan-beyond-liberal-and-conservative-ayesha-siddiqa/.

Sinha, M. 2001. 'Britishness, Clubbability, and the Colonial Public Sphere: The Genealogy of an Imperial Institution in Colonial India'. *The Journal of British Studies* 40(4): 489–521.

Sklair, L. 2016. 'The Transnational Capitalist Class, Social Movements, and Alternatives to Capitalist Globalization'. *International Critical Thought* 6(3): 329–341.

Smart, A. 1993. 'Gifts, Bribes, and Guanxi: A Reconsideration of Bourdieu's Social Capital'. *Cultural Anthropology* 8(3): 388–408. doi:10.1525/can.1993.8.3.02a00060.

Smart, A., and C.L. Hsu. 2007. 'Corruption or Social Capital? Tact and the Performance of Guanxi in Market Socialist China'. In G. Anders and M. Nuijten (eds), *Corruption and the Secret of Law: A Legal Anthropological Perspective*. Milton Park, Abingdon: Routledge, pp. 167–190.

Smith, I.S. 2013. 'Management Consultants at Work with Clients: Maintenance and Contestation of Elite Status'. In J. Abbink and T. Salverda (eds), *The Anthropology of Elites: Power, Culture, and the Complexities of Distinction*. New York: Palgrave Macmillan, pp. 207–226.

Spence, E. 2016. 'Eye-spy Wealth: Cultural Capital and "Knowing Luxury" in the Identification of and Engagement with the Superrich'. *Annals of Leisure Research* 19(3): 314–328.

Staff Writer. 2010. 'Muhammad Ali Appointed SECP Chief'. *The Dawn*. Retrieved 17 August 2014 from http://www.dawn.com/news/593364/muhammad-ali-appointed-secp-chief.

Staff Writer. 2012, 13 June. 'A True Rags to Riches Story'. *Pakistan Today*. Retrieved 17 August 2015 from http://www.pakistantoday.com.pk/2012/06/13/national/a-true-rags-to-riches-story/.

Staff Writer. 2013, 24 September. 'Profile: Nawaz Sharif'. *BBC News*. Retrieved 2 June 2014 from http://www.bbc.com/news/world-asia-22167511.

Staff Writer. 2014. 'Malik Riaz Feels the Pain of Overs', *The Pakistan Observer*. Retrieved 17 August 2015 from http://pakobserver.net/detailnews.asp?id=245557.

Staniland, P., A. Naseemullah, and A. Butt. 2018. 'Pakistan's Military Elite'. *Journal of Strategic Studies*: 1–30. doi: 10.1080/01402390.2018.1497487.

Pakistan, S.B. 1998. Issuance of Three Years Foreign Currency Bearer Certificate Denominated in U.S. Dollar, and Pound Sterling. In State Bank, P. (ed.), *F.E. Circular No. 04*. Islamabad: State Bank Pakistan. Retrieved 29 June 2015 from: http://www.sbp.org.pk/epd/1998/c4.htm.

Stigler, J. 1971. 'The Theory of Economic Regulation'. *The Bell Journal of Economics and Management Science*: 3–21.

Stiglitz, J.E. 2002. *Globalization and its Discontents*. New York: Norton.

Strickland, M. 2010. 'Aid and Affect in the Friendships of Young Chinese Men'. *Journal of the Royal Anthropological Institute* 16: 102–118.

Swift, J. 1975 [1707]. *A Tritical Essay upon the Faculties of the Mind. Miscellanies in Prose and Verse*. London: John Morphew, pp. 247–259.

Thompson, E.P. 2002. *The Making of the English Working Class*. London: Penguin Books.

Touraine, A. 1988. *Return of the Actor Social Theory in Postindustrial Society*. Minneapolis: University of Minnesota Press.

Muhammad Ashraf Tiwana vs. Pakistan Etc., Supreme Court of Pakistan. 2013.

Wolf, E.R. 2001. *Pathways of Power: Building an Anthropology of the Modern World*. Berkeley, CA: University of California Press.

Wacquant, L.J. 1998. 'Foreword'. In P. Bourdieu (ed.), *The State Nobility: Elite Schools in the Field of Power*. Palo Alto, CA: Stanford University Press, pp. ix–xxii.

———. 2004. *Body and Soul*. Oxford: Oxford University Press.

Wahab, A. 2013. 'Removal of Securities and Exchange Commission Chairman'. *The Express Tribune*. Retrieved 14 July 2014 from https://tribune.com.pk/story/541647/removal-of-securities-and-exchange-commission-chairman/.

Warren, C.A., and J.K. Hackney. 2011. 'Gender and Fieldwork Relationships'. In C.A. Warren and J.K. Hackney (eds), *Gender Issues in Ethnography*. London: Sage Publications, Inc.

Weber, M. 1946. 'Class, Status, Party'. In *From Max Weber: Essays in Sociology*. New York: Oxford University Press, pp. 180–195.

———. 1978. *Economy and Society: An Outline of Interpretive Sociology*. Berkeley, CA: University of California Press.

Weber, M., and S. Andreski. 2013. *Max Weber on Capitalism, Bureaucracy and Religion* (Vol. 4). Milton Park, Abingdon: Routledge.

Weiss, A.M. 1991. *Culture, Class and Development in Pakistan: The Emergence of an Industrial Bourgeoisie in Punjab*. Lahore: Vanguard Books.

Wilder, A. 1999. *The Pakistani Voter: Electoral Politics and Voting Behaviour in the Punjab*. Oxford: Oxford University Press.

Wilson, A. 2013. 'Intimacy: A Useful Category of Transnational Analysis'. In G. Pratt and V. Rosner (eds), *The Global and the Intimate: Feminism in our Time*. New York: Columbia University Press.

Wolf, E.R. 1966. 'Kinship, Friendship, and Patron–Client Relations in Complex Societies'. *The Social Anthropology of Complex Societies*, 1–22.

Yanagisako, S.J. 2002. *Producing Culture and Capital: Family Firms in Italy*. Princeton, NJ: Princeton University Press.

Young, C. 2017. *The Myth of Millionaire Tax Flight: How Place Still Matters for the Rich*. Stanford: Stanford University Press.

Zaidi, S.A. 2007. 'Musharraf and His Collaborators'. *Economic and Political Weekly*, 42(45/46): 8.

———. 2008. 'An Emerging Civil Society?' *Journal of Democracy* 19(4): 38-40. doi:10.1353/jod.0.0042.

———. 2014. 'Rethinking Pakistan's Political Economy: Class, State, Power and Transition'. *Economic & Political Weekly* 49(5): 47–57.

———. 2017, 28 February. 'In Pakistan, it's Middle Class Rising'. *The Hindu*. Retrieved 19 September 2018 from http://www.thehindu.com/opinion/lead/in-pakistan-its-middle-class-rising/article17378526.ece.

Zaman, F., and N.S. Ali. 2016, 18 April. 'Bahria Town Karachi: Greed Unlimited'. *The Dawn*. Retrieved 7 March 2017 from http://www.dawn.com/news/1252809/bahria-town-karachi-greed-unlimited.

INDEX

Focaal
Journal of Global and Historical Anthropology

Managing and Lead Editor
Luisa Steur, *University of Amsterdam*

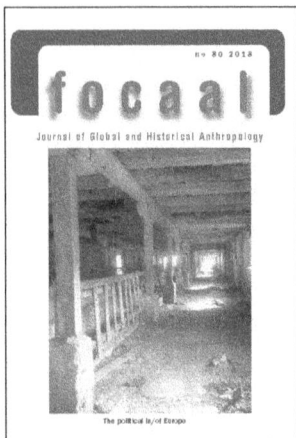

Nr 80 2018

focaal

Journal of Global and Historical Anthropology

The political in/of Europe

Aims & Scope

Focaal is a peer-reviewed journal advocating an approach that rests in the simultaneity of ethnography, processsual analysis, local insights, and global vision. It is at the heart of debates on the ongoing conjunction of anthropology and history, as well as the incorporation of local research settings in the wider spatial networks of coercion, imagination, and exchange that are often glossed as "globalization" or "empire."

Seeking contributions on all world regions, *Focaal* is unique among anthropology journals for consistently rejecting the old separations between "at home" and "abroad," "center" and "periphery." The journal therefore strives for the resurrection of an "anthropology at large" that can accommodate issues of the global south, postsocialism, mobility, metropolitan experience, capitalist power, and popular resistance into integrated perspectives.

Recent Articles

- Safe Milk and Risky Quinoa: The Lottery and Precarity of Farming in Peru
  Astrid B. Stensrud
- The Promise of Education and its Paradox in Rural Flores, East Indonesia
  Thijs Schut
- Elite Ethnography in an Insecure Place: The Methodological Implications of "Studying Up" in Pakistan
  Rosita Armytage
- Contending with School Reform: Neoliberal Restructuring, Racial Politics, and Resistance in Post-Katrina New Orleans
  Mathilde Lind Gustavussen

berghahnjournals.com/focaal

ISSN 0920-1297 (Print) • ISSN 1558-5263 (Online)
Volume 2020, 3 issues p.a.

berghahn

journals
NEW YORK · OXFORD

www.ingramcontent.com/pod-product-compliance
Lightning Source LLC
Chambersburg PA
CBHW070928030426
42336CB00014BA/2576